पुरातत्त्व
PURĀTATTVA

Bulletin of the Indian Archaeological Society

No. 12 1980-81

Editor
K. N. Dikshit

D.K. Printworld (P) Ltd.
New Delhi

Cataloging in Publication Data — DK

[Courtesy : D.K. Agencies (P) Ltd. <docinfo@dkagencies.com>]

Purātattva : bulletin of the Indian Archaeological
Society, no. 12, 1980-81 / editor, K.N. Dikshit
p. cm.
Includes bibliographical references.
ISBN 8124602883

1. Archaeology — India — Periodicals. 2. India
— Antiquities — Periodicals. 3. India — Civilization
— Periodicals. I. Dikshit, K.N. II. Indian
Archaeological Society.

First Published in 1983
First Reprinted in 2005
ISBN 81-246-0288-3
Price for volume 12 (1980-81): Rs. 800 US $ 40

Reprint authorised by
Indian Archaeological Society
New Delhi - 110 016

The Editors are not responsible for the opinions expressed by the Contributors.

Purātattva is published annually.

Manuscripts (whether in the form of articles or notes or book reviews) offered for publication should be sent to the Editor, Purātattva, Indian Archaeological Society, B-17, Qutab Institutional Area, New Delhi - 110 016.

Published and printed by:
D.K. Printworld (P) Ltd.
'*Srikunj*,' F-52, Bali Nagar
New Delhi – 110015
Phone : (011) 2545 3975, 2546 6019 Fax : (011) 2546 5926
E-mail : dkprintworld@vsnl.net
www. dkprintworld.com

CONTENTS

EDITORIAL

In October 1982 the Indian Archaeological Society and the Indian Society for Prehistoric and Quaternary Studies held an International Seminar on the premises of the National Museum, New Delhi to honour our distinguished archaeologist, Professor B.B. Lal. This was attended by a large number of Indian and many foreign archaeologists, the more noteworthy amongst the latter being Dr. V.A. Ranov from USSR; Dr. Gregory L. Possehl, Prof. K.A.R. Kennedy and Dr. Richar Davis from USA. There were delegates from France also.

All these scholars paid very rich tributes to the everlasting contribution of Professor Lal to Indian archaeology. Shri Jagmohan, Lt. Governor of Delhi, adding his own tributes, honoured Professor Lal in the traditional Indian style, by presenting him a woolen shawl.

At the Seminar twenty one key-papers on Indian Archaeology were presented by eminent scholars; these are being published in a separate volume, dedicated to Professor Lal. In the present issue we have published the other papers of the open session presented at the Seminar. Also included herein are the addresses given by Prof. Lal himself and those by Mrs. D. Mitra and Shri K.V. Soundrarajan, who presided over the deliberations respectively of the Indian Archaeological Society and Indian Society for Prehistoric and Quaternary Studies.

* * * * * *

Debates on academic issues is a normal feature all the world over. Scholars would recall the controversy that went on regarding the site of Jericho amongst Dr. Kathelene Kenyon, Sir Mortimer Wheeler and Prof. R.J. Braidwood through the medium of the *Antiquity* in 1956 and 1957 (Volumes 30 and 31). In the *Puratattva* also we encourage such debates, the idea being a search for the truth. Thus in our numbers 8, 10 and 11, we published a debate on the identification of Ayodhya, between Shri M.C. Joshi and Prof. B.B. Lal. We hope to publish the next instalment of the debate in the next issue of the *Puratattva.*

Kausambi is another important site which requires an academic debate. Readers would recall that in *Puratattva* No. 11, we published three papers commenting respectively on the antiquity of the defences, the so-called Kushan arches, and the supposed Harappan and Chalcolithic affinities of the pottery from his famous site. We drew the attention of the excavator of Kausambi, Prof. G.R. Sharma, to these articles and requested him to send to us his counter-comments for publication on what these scholars had stated in their papers. Unfortunately, however, instead of giving an academic reply, Prof. Sharma chose to blame the editor and the most senior, respected internationally renowned authors. We reiterate that the columns of *Puratattva* will remain open for an academic rejoinder from Prof. Sharma as a part of the general policy of our Bulletin.

* * * * * *

It was largely due to the financial grant from the Archaeological Survey of India that this publication could be brought out. Shri S.G.Rao of the Society and Smt. Seema Mukerjee and Shri R.K. Lamba of Filmahal Enterprise took the responsibility for publishing this volume in time.

K.N.D.

Recent Archaeological Activities in India

DR. (SMT.) D. MITRA
Director General Archaeological Survey of India
New Delhi

My Presidential address* is not going to be an erudite discourse, nor do I have anything like some startling findings of a systematic research to announce. What I can do is to place before you for your consideration a few reflections on recent archaeological activities, particularly in the fields of excavation and prehistoric investigation.

You will all agree that in recent years there is a spurt in archaeological excavations. Yet, there is hardly any appreciable dialogue amongst the excavators. Perhaps, a good many of these excavators are carrying out their arduous tasks in virtual isolation. I do not know how far such Societies and Congresses provide forums for any effective dialogue amongst historians, prehistorians and archaeologists who are pursuing in many cases more or less common problems. Reading a paper on a discovery or presenting a gist of the results of some investigation here or in a symposium is not what I envisage as dialogue. To me it is an intimate knowledge of each other's problems, methodology, aims and objectives and findings; it is the sharing of each other's experience at close quarters, even in the field. It is not at all a difficult proposition once the excavators establish communion amongst themselves.

According to my understanding, archaeology as a discipline is being used by many of the excavators in recent years as an end itself and not as a means to reconstruct, restructure or supplement the history of man in this part of the globe at a given situation. For reconstructing and examining the history of man before the use of writing, archaeology is the only source available with us. The results of archaeological researches must get blended and incorporated in the themes of history —history of social, economic, cultural and technological development. To what extent our archaeological findings have shaped or reshaped Indian history is a question to be answered satisfactorily. One or two historians have tried to make use of archaeological data, but the general trend is to avoid archaeological correlation even with the known facts of history or not at all using it in bridging hiatus that exists in the accounts of Indian history and culture. Let us take the role of archaeologists in this task of making India's history a worthwhile account. Here we are not sure whether all the excavations carried out in different parts of the country have the goal of achieving specific results. Let us try to have a close look at the overall performance of the various excavation teams which carried out archaeological excavations in the 1970s.

On a rough estimate I find more than seven scores of sites have been excavated during the period from 1970-71 to 1978-79. Surprisingly, the majority of the sites belong to the historical period. Here I must make it clear as to what I mean by historical

* Presidential Address, Indian Archaeological Society XLV Annual Congress, 1982.

period, though I am quite aware that such division like history, protohistory and prehistory is rather arbitrary. I will revert to this point later. Suffice it here to say that we generally take the beginning of the so-called historical period from about 600 B.C. Most of the megalithic sites will undoubtedly fall within this period. And if these are added to the list of historical sites, the number of sites other than historical can be counted on fingers. In Bihar 13 sites were excavated during the peroid in question and out of these 11 belong to the historical times. Sites anterior to say 600 B.C. have mostly been excavated in Haryana, Jammu & Kashmir, Punjab, Rajasthan and Maharashtra; out of 32 sites from this region about 16 or so belong to what is generally termed as protohistoric period. To cite yet another instance, no less than 24 sites have been excavated in Andhra Pradesh and amongst them 4 are monasteries, 4 temples, 10 megalithic sites, 3 historical sites belonging to the Satavahana or post-Satavahana times, 1 medieval and the remaining 2 yielding neolithic/chalcolithic vestiges. Thus, the vast majority of the sites excavated during the period have yielded remains of the historical times. But what is the net result of these discoveries?

There was a time when we were busy working out the cultural sequences and relative chronology, and quite understandingly, the emphasis was on "vertical digging", to use an oft-repeated expression. The earlier practice of the pre-Wheelerian epoch was to expose the entire layout of the structural remains of a particular area. Whatever might have been said about their stratigraphical inadequacies, these excavations offered glimpses of the nature of settlement and the life pattern, including the cultural legacy of an extinct community. As soon as an acceptable chronological framework of cultural sequences was available, some of the archaeologists realized that time had come to unravel the life and living of the community whose settlement had been laid bare. The excavations at some sites like Kalibangan, Lothal and Inamgaon are the tangible expression of this new thinking. Indeed, in recent years a number of sites have been excavated in, what is commonly called, horizontal digging method, but these though aimed at bringing to light structural remains of a site, are mostly partial excavations. It is high time that excavations are planned in such a way as to lay bare the whole settlement and the cultural vestiges so that facts collected from archaeological sources could be assessed against the perspective of other historical material. It should be our endeavour to select single-culture sites of different periods for such large-scale excavations so that our aims and objectives are achieved without any risk of damage to the overlying vestiges.

A heartening change in the approach is the conscious application of the scientific methods of other disciplines in solving or attempting to solve archaeological problems and filling in lacunae in reconstructed history of a particular society at a given time and place. As a result of employment of various techniques of physical and natural sciences, we are in a position to postulate the pattern of gradual unfoldment of the story of cultural development in relation to various ecological factors. Even now there are scholars who are talking of "New Archaeology" with its methodology of morphological, ecological, anthropological and geographical paradigms in Indian context, though these concepts in some form or the other are to be seen in the writings of several earlier archaeologist. However, is this wind of change felt at every level of the researches?

I have talked about the excavations of a large number of historical sites. However, we cannot help realizing that the contribution of these digs in supplementing our history is rather insignificant. A total number of 21 megalithic sites has been exposed in southern States of Andhra Pradesh (10), Tamil Nadu (6) and Karnataka (5) during the 1970s; but do we have a comprehensive idea of their common or disparate traits? Is there any attempt to snythesize the evidence disclosed in differnt sites in other States? So much material came to light, but there is no appreciable attempt to sift the data or to reconstruct a coherent picture. Perhaps many of our archaeologists still think that their jobs ends with listing the sites and exposing some structures and their associated artefacts.

I agree that the collection of facts is an important task in the field of archaeological research;

in fact, this very idea is a legacy of the historians who flourished in the nineteenth century. These thinkers, particularly those belonging to the positivist school, claimed history as a scientific discipline, and hence universal. This attitude to a great extent led to the advent of the cult of facts; and facts were taken to be sacrosanct. The historians following this concept thought that the primary duty of a historian was to ascertain facts much more than anything else. However, the other contemporary school, though not as dominant as the school believing in the objective presentation of events, "conceived their task to be that of interpreting past ages and of explaining their significance to contemporary readers even at the risk of substituting fiction for fact". (Madge, 1963 : 109).

Our accumulated facts have not been examined, analysed or synthesized either in an objective manner or in accordance with a particular interpretation of history. To say that it is the task of the historians alone to make use of the data thus unveiled is to avoid a bounden duty. An archaeologist has every right to piece together the data to recreate the picture of bygone days. Since the days of Sir Mortimer an excavation report in some cases has sections dealing with the results of the excavation wherein the available data have been compared with the earlier findings with a view to deriving certain generalized conclusions. For instance, Sir Mortimer propounded the theory of the Arvan invasion in his report on the excavation at Harappa, while Lal advanced the theory of the contemporaneity of the Painted Grey Ware phase with Mahabharata period in his Hastinapura report. Now that we are dealnig with the historical periods in many sites there is a greater need to assess the material evidence of a period in the light of the known facts of hsitory. We have to see how the new archaeological findings fit in with the known events and trends, cultural and social milieu and economic condition of a time. Without being a slave of facts, we are to interpret the facts in an orderly fashion, so that a pattern emerges out of several amorphous heaps and collections.

It is a well-known fact that the positivist trends of historical study gave rise to minute specialization—the logical outcome of the collection and authentication of an ever-growing mass of evidence or facts. The historians soon turned themselves into archaeologists, epigraphists, palaeographists, art-historians, numismatists and so on. Vincent Smith's sojourn into archaeological excavations comes under such compulsions. Soon the historians, besides being a historian, mastered one or more branches of specialized research; D. R. Bhandarkar anad R. D. Banerji were not only epigraphists, art historians or field archaeologists but also historians; N.G. Majumdar or Hirananda Sastri made their marks both as field archaeologists and epigraphists.

I had to perforce use the term "field archaeology", as in the wider connotation of archaeology are included disciplines like epigraphy, numismatics, architectural studies, historical geography etc. Vincent Smith in 1908 takes archaeology as one of the four sources of history and according to him it may be subdivided into monumental, epigraphic and numismatic (Smith, 1908:8).

Marshall brought within the scope of Archaeological Survey archaeological excavations, study of art and architecture, epigraphy, etc. Many of the archaeologists between Marshall and Wheeler came generally from the disciplines of classical studies and history; and important amongst them are Daya Ram Sahni, K.N. Dikshit, R.D. Banerji, N.G. Majumdar, D.R. Bhandarkar, Hirananda Sastri, T.N. Ramachandran, A. Ghosh, Krishna Deva and a host of other luminaries. These scholars participated in archaeological excavations and at the same time were experts variously in the fields of epigraphy, art history, and other areas. So archaeology had then a wider connotation than what is now popularly conceived of. After the arrival of Wheeler, the emphasis was laid on stratigraphy and the sequence of pottery, which was no doubt found a necessity in our vast culturally-rich country with many unexplored sites havnig the potentiality of supplying the missing links in the cultural sequence. Wheeler though himself belonged originally to the classical discipline, did not put much emphasis on the classical studies in India or on the knowledge of the original sources like epigraphy, numismatics- and the like. In subsequent times the same attitude continued to a large extent. Archaeology began to depend more and more on other sciences, including the exact ones. All this created a situation for field archaeology to emerge almost as a distinctive discipline. It is no distortion of facts to say that in recent years the term archaeology has almost become coterminous with field archaeology, the principal task of which is to carry out archaeological excavations and explorations and to present their findings, taking the help of scientists and scholars of different branches. But to what extent is archaeology, as it is now thought to be, of help in reconstructing the history of man?

On these very premises and at the same time the sessions of the Indian Archaeological Society and Indian Society for Prehistoric and Quaternary Studies are being held. The very existence of two Societies is likely to suggest some demarcation in the spheres of respective studies. In other words, here we have an impression of dealing with two different disciplines—archaeology and prehistory. By implication one is inclined to believe that history is somewhat different from these subjects. At the same time, none will deny that all these disciplines are meant to write or rewrite a true history of man. Let us for the sake of convenience, postulate the existence of three disciplines: "prehistory", "archaeology" and "history" and proceed further in our deliberation.

As we are aware, the nineteenth century witnessed one definitive trend when geologists, including the palaeontologists, began to unfurl the earlier part of human history. Historians, too, recognized that history does not start from an event like, say Alexander's invasion of India or the conquest of England by the Romans. It starts from the coming of man, his first act as a social animal. Thus. history when pushed back falls in the realm of prehistory and there is practically no dividing line between the two. As the earlier part of human history is also connected with the physical evolution of man, anthropologists came into the field leading to the preparation of the first chapter of the culture-history. Bruce Foote remains for us the classical example of the first category. while Heine-Geldern and Hutton of the second.

Anyway, having begun from two different sources, two areas of human history—prehistory on the one hand and history on the other—began developing along independent lines. This mutual aloofness was so pronounced that the respective initiates came from separate disciplines; it was the historians, generally with classical background or from ancient history, who came to the fore in the field of the archaeology of the protohistoric or historical times, while prehistoric researches fell in the domain of geologists and later of anthropologists. However, these are cases where the former too make their presence felt in the field of prehistory, and the names that come to me instantly are Sankalia, Lal and Soundara Rajan. At the same time, it has to be acceeded that with the further development it was found that whatever discipline one might have come from, the ramification of technology has become too overbearing to allow them to keep contacts with the subjects they had originally thought of specializing in.

From the beginning of the third decade of this century the knowledge had dawned on historians that one can either be a technician or a historian but hardly both. Having freed themselves from the burden of collecting facts, historians now could choose from among facts collected by archaeologists and others in order to build edifices —each one after his own liking, each school after its own philosophy. Thus, historians's job is to add flesh to the disarticulated skeleton dug by archaeologists whose main concern, as the idea is now gradually gaining ground, is to collect and describe facts. It is up to you to judge how far this division is logical and fruitful. I do not know in what way an archaeologist is less competent to handle his own material and to interpret the evidence with a view to giving a shape, a clear picture of an event, a society or a material culture of a community than a professional historian. In his own limited sphere he should be the master both of his facts and ideas.

True, specialization on periods or some division of time of space has to be there; for, that alone makes it possible to handle the ever-growing demands for the analysis of the ever-increasing accumulation of facts. Furthermore, expertise can be developed in a very wide field. This specialization is there also in the domain of historical study; for that matter, it is present in any field of scientific research. What I want to say is that let there be two different roles of an archaeologist—as a hisorian of a particular area or a period and a technician. In the latter role, this being the generally accepted role, his primary occupation is to record meticulously the evidence and to prepare multi-dimensional catalogues to present the facts or data. All these facts are now documented for the use by historians who are the primary clients of archaeology. These days some of our historians write under the inspiration of a certain ideology or philosophy of history and such history is bound to have a tenor of subjectivity: facts are arranged in a set pattern to suit the need of an interpretation of history. Perhaps the assessment of an archaeologist may prove to be more objective than that of a historian, should the former take upon himself the role of the latter and develop expertise in original sources like epigraphy, numismatics and ancient literature. In fact, an archaeologist should have the proper knowledge and understanding of these sources, without which he will not be able to develop a correct perspective for the assessment of his excavated evidence.

Admittedly, there should be a constant dialogue amongst historians, archaeologists and prehistorians of diverse fields, for they must from time to time put their facts and ideas, methodology and techniques for mutual scrutiny and inspection. I have shown earlier that the vast majority of our excavations deal with historical period, but no proper planning is evinced in many cases. This area of study is out of bounds for prehistorians; and it is not considered to come within the purview of another class of scholars called protohistorians. Will it be then the task of our archaeologists to accept the challenge and combine in themselves the roles of both the archaeologists and historians? Or have we to create another discipline called "historical archaeology"? The fallacy in our approach is obvious: we cannot divide archaeology into protohistory and history; the periods when combined into one become a continous history of man from the time he acquired the knowledge of writing. The term "prehistory" has acquired a sense by virtue of its constant use; otherwise it makes no sense (as there is no such thing as a vacuum before the starting of what is called history. This term is meant to be preliterate history—the time-span before the advent of writing. I am glad to note that a few young scholars are quite aware of this paradoxical situation when we find their preference for the term "palaeohistory" instead of "prehistory".

I am quite conscious of the fact that whatever may be my personal reaction to the vague division of human history into prehistory, protohistory and history, these terms have come to stay. What I want to say at this stage is that let us be conscious of the inherent fallacy of this vague periodization and the ephemeral lines of demarcation. Let us also be cautious in not mixing the time-scale with the culture variability; they may coincide or not. If two sets of people are coexisting, it is possible that their cultural levels are very much different in the evolutionary scale, since no history can be completed without a reference to the variation in culural levels wihin a geographical unit. But they can never be said to have belonged to two different periods of history, for the very framework of history is time; and time has one dimension. Archaeologists must, therefore, reconcile with the concept of contemporary tribalism and cultural disparity in any period of history in a given spatial unit. Thus, primitive factors and uneven growth of cultures need not necessarily be taken to be yardsticks for any temporal sequence or in framing our scheme of periodization.

Periodization is the very essence of archaeology, as much at it is of history of geology. Significant events like the discovery of agriculture, or the coming of cities, the use of iron or discovery of steam-power, by any reckoning, are the milestones of history. They equally represent landmarks in archaeology. As in geology, historian also use different milestones of different proportions to demarcate their epoch, age or period even though in a highly generalized or even inexact way. Prehistorians using geological pattern also classify their finds accordingly. Coming to the historical period we use linear scale of years and give certain names which immediately conjure up a picture of graduated time-scale. When we say pre-Vedic, Vedic or post-Vedic we assume a time-sequence. Even periodization on the basis of religion like Hindu and Islamic or dynasty like Nanda, Maurya, Satavahana, etc. have the same significance. The other common form of periodization is to divide history into ancient, medieval and modern and this is clearly a linear scale of years where we fix rather arbitrarily the events that mark the beginning of periods. In archaeology the sequence of pottery and artefacts offers a time-scale which is also linear. But in geology the form of life is used as the scale. A particular form of life at different places may, however, be of different age in years, and application of time-scale in such situations is fraught with considerable difficulty.

The prehistoric stage, as is well known, practically covers the major part of human history and is divided primarily into three major parts—Palaeolithic, Mesolithic and Neolithic. The oldest, i.e. Palaeolithic, falls into the geological period of Pleistocene and its sub-division—Lower, Middle and Upper—being in Europe at specific points of Pleistocene, the end of which coincides with the end of the Palaeolithic stage. Thus the term Palaeolithic age or a sub-division thereof denotes its cultural phase and a fixed time-table for it. When the work started in other continents it was realized that the culture-chronology of the Palaeolithic age was not a universal feature; as a matter of fact, it was typically European.

This perception of the innate contradiction in the use of European terms in Africa and elsewhere resulted in convening the First Pan-Africa Congress on Prehistory in 1951 and terms Palaeolithic and Mesolithic were discarded and in their places came a new threefold division—Early Stone Age, Middle Stone Age and Late Stone Age. The Early Stone Age, corresponds, by and large, to the lower Palaeolithic, though this correspondence is confined generally to typological similarity. That is why the term Lower Palaeolithic was permitted to be used as an alternative to Early Stone Age. On the contrary, the Middle Stone Age had nothing in common with either the Middle Palaeolithic or Upper Palaeolithic of Europe. It occupies a position as the successor to the Early Stone Age. However, in broad typology the Late Stone Age corresponds to Mesolithic. It is clear that in adopting this change in nomenclature, the African scientists accepted the fact that their culture-pattern is different in the periods following the Early Stone Age. Moreover, the cultural dating was divested from exact chronology as used in the European context. It is significant that the adoption of this parallel system of nomenclature in 1951 came on the heels of the international Geological Congress in 1948 wherein the exact Pleistocene boundaries were fixed.

Coming to India, we find that the realization about the internal contradiction as to the non-correspondence of cultures and chronology took the concrete shape in 1961. The First Internal Conference on Asian Archaeology held in New Delhi appointed a committee to consider this issue of the use of new terminology in Indian prehistory. It was decided by the committee and duly endorsed by the Conference that the older terms Palaeolithic with its sub-divisions and Mesolithic be dropped, and, until a suitable terminology is evolved, the Indan Stone Age may be divided into Earl,y, Middle and Late followed by Neolithic. Thus, the African pattern was copied and European system of classification discarded. Among the arguments advanced to decide upon the unsuitability of the European terms, the principal reason was the difficulty to put an industry in any definite group even on the basis of typology, apart from difficulty in age-fixation. Thus De Terra's proto-neolithic was Sankalia's proto-microlithic; Burkitt's Series II and III were not Sankalia's Series II and III. It was, therefore, argued that with the adoption of the new terminology the prehistoric studies could be freed from prefixes and that some amount of order can be brought about in the use of terms. However, in recent years it is seen that the ardent advocates for this change have reverted to the original and the prefixes 'proto' and 'epi' have made their appearance. Being myself a novice in this field I am confronted with the problem of cooosing between the two sets of terminology—Palaeolithic, Mescolithic, etc. on the one hand and Early, Middle and Late Stone Ages on the other. But why this reversion to the old terms of European origin and having definite connotation? Am I to believe that the Pleistocene study has been brought to the same level as in Europe and that like Europe every point can be clearly demarcated? I am told at last Indian Upper Palaeolithic has been defined and isolated and that its date along with its typological correspondence established. I hope due care has been taken by the prehistorians in correlating its date with the geological scale. One has to bear it in mind that the geographical unit may not correspond to those of the other areas. Before giving an all-India currency to a term we have to be careful as to its applicability. Furthermore, I am told that the handaxe industry of the Narmada, according to Badam, belongs to Late Pleistocene. Will that industry be called Lower or Uppr Palaeolithic? In my humble opinion, time is ripe for the experts to examine th evidences closely and to reassess dispassionately the suitability or otherwise of the use of a particular set of terms in our prehistoric studies. I also feel that a committee of experts should also make an in-depth examination of the paintings of the rock-shelters of Bhimbetka along with those who claim these as prehistoric.

REFERENCES

Madge, John, 1963, The Tools of Social Science; London.

Smith, V.A., 1908 Early History of India, Oxford.

Eco-Functional Frame of Early Man—Some Factors

K. V. SOUNDARARAJAN
Additional Director General
Archaeological Survey of India.

I

The story of man, unravelled in India, similar though it is with those of many other countries, in its cultural direction is nevertheless so full of interesting such characteristic disparities symptomatic of the evolution of Indian nationhood in the remoter past.* It calls for a proper organisation of the frame work of programmes designed not simply to reveal the empirics of the palaeo-environment climate and natural resources, but to identify which of these and in what manner the ancient man in India was preserving in. Archaeology owes it almost entirely to the natural sciences towards the adaptation of methodology to discipline for factual appreciation of evolutionary data. But when archaeological teams of interdisciplinary character have to function, the purpose, one presupposes, is not merely to digress into the scientific exposition of the physical environment, but to implicate early man in it meaningfully—without which it would be devoid of cultural emphasis. This caution is all the more necessary in India, because we have no norms for the primary spade work in scientific cross-fertilization of expertise for archaeological research, though we do adopt often the apparel and posture of science in presenting the traditional anatomy of cultural research.

Our ancient seers tried to place themselves always as inseparable specks in the physical environment of which they were always conscious. We shall be only continuing that exercise if the environment is always interlinked with human endeavours. It is by creating viable approaches to the manner in which man interacted with the cosmos, its physical, formal as well as metaphysical dimensions that the ancients created the cherised and invaluable legacy of ours called Indian culture. Of all sub-human primates, it was given only to the hominoid species to evolve their brain capacity to break the shackles of mere anatomical or biological evolution and to discover the multifaceted spectrum of the phenomenal world and to react to it fruitfully for onward progress. Archaeology would certainly do well to give priority to the full understanding of the material remains of man. across the centuries. But archaeology, without sociological bias and ethnological inferences or mooas will be dry-as-dust and will leave the archaeologist more as the undertaker or grave digger than the recreator of the past inheritance.

II

We are at a stage of research in archaeology where the increasing dependence on both natural sciences and exact sciences are keenly felt for quantifying and refining the chronology as well as the patterns of functional diversification of human communities. This helps to explain reationally the implications of the pattern of occurrence of antiquities, deposits, landscapes and structural

* Presidential Address, Indian Society for Prehistoric and Qurternary Studies, IXth Annual Congress, 1982.

erections and layout in the habitation sites. The decades that had gone by since archaeology loomed large as an essential avenue of endeavour had given us some important instruments like the stratigraphic and typological assessment of remains left by man and in the stages leading to urbanism, of the pottery craft created by him. However two significant approaches that had overtaken the field of archaeology elsewhere, since then, are what are termed, rather conventionally, as 'New archaeology' and 'Analytical archaeology'. The former was initiated by such works as 'Method and theory in American archaeology' by Willey and Phillip (1958) and 'New perspectives in archaeology' of L.R. Binford (1968). The latter—'Analytical Archaeology'—was profoundly spear-headed by David Clarke in Britain, in his works Analytical Archaeology (1970), Models in Archaeology (1972) and Spatial Archaeology (1977). The general principles that underscored these two are somewhat different from one another, in as much as the former was emphasizing mainly the *mode* of recognition of 'types' and the theories of archaeological methods that can help in identifying these types and is thus essentially methodological. The latter, however, was concerned deeply with the very dynamics of cultural process and culture change, and how archaeological data could be effectively grafted into the perception of the process. It inevitably underscored the need for formulations of 'generalization' or what is sometimes called the 'goodness of fit test' of the principles and regularities of time-pattern and system pattern. Thus, both these new developmets deal with system-analysis and systems-metaphor on the processes that stimulate patterns of material cultures. In essential terms, this is necessary for all socio-cultural studies, be it archaeology or art, and sociological and ethnological analogies help give the theoritical pattern. This was so profound that in Europe, specialists in Prehistory like Bordes started integrating these principles in the study of the variegation of tool types in relation to stratigraphic, ecological and climatic contexts, and initiated new quantified lines of enquiry into it. Gordon Childe already opened the vistas of reconstruction of past in his stimulating scientific study 'Piecing together the past'. Sir Mortimer Wheeler dauntlessly and effectively attempted the same for field archaeology all the time in his summations and declared that dead archaeology is the driest dust that blows. He, however, believed in the jud.cious use of science in the cause of archaeology and felt that archaeology must be seasoned with humanity

In the ultimate analysis, this study of the scheme of the social functions of the archaeological remains, within the hypothetical limitations of their contexts in Prehistoric, protohistoric and even early historic (or tribal) situations would eventually redeem archaeology from merely a documentational and single-point development of typology of the culture-differentiate and give us the motivations for culture change (or digression or stagnation, as the case may be). Physical environment and geography was long considered as effective factors in causing changes in man's behavioural pattern in given groups. But Analytical Archaeology and New Archaeology only radicalise and quantify the approach. The crux of the matter was touched by David Clarke when he said: 'the message that the author wished to communicate was mainly one of stimulus.......since the theory of archaeology nowhere exists in an integrated, sophisticated or comprehensive form' (Clarke 1970).

III

I propose to deal with the general theoritical frame work under which, as revealed by his cultural and technical output across the Stone Ages and the eventual Chalcolithic revolution, man laboured under, mainly with a view to emphasizing how archaeology may grow with modern scientific disciplines in the reconstruction of the story of early Man. Its articulation has already been made by several renowned scholars, as discussed earlier.

The reconstuction of pre-literate societies, in the prehistoric and Protohistoric periods has been one of the important preoccupations of archaeologists and after nearly a century of discoveries, identifications of culture-differentiae and documentation of the basic distributive and diffusionary patterns of these ancient societies and human communities in the Eurasian continental stretch, the stage had reached when the facile summations of the cultural developments in each of the major stages of man's as a gregarious animal, have to be radically tested and refined. The analysis was certainly made more imperative by the advancement of science, and the postulation of the chrono-cultural spectrum of this bio-physical universe, of which the human species is but a viable organism, albeit the most significant and dominant one. Environmental studies have also loomed large, in the perception that without placing man in his eco-functional framework, it would be unavailing to make isolated assessments of his handiworks in the onward progress of his socio-cultural, socio-economic and socio-religious propensities, even granted that human societies had never been capble of a uniform lineal progress, but only *conditional* responses to the *extant* stimuli.

Archaeology, no more is overmuch or exclusively obsessed with mere typology or taxonomy —notwithstanding the firm empirical need for the statistical scheme of ancient cultural handiworks, portable and stationary, elegant and functional, preferred and casual. It is the viable analysis of the motivations for his primary urges to react in a concerted pattern to the potentialities available to him for overcoming the pressures and benefits of his physical, organic, climatic, or biopsheric environment that has now been conceived as holding the key to understanding his biological mental, intellectual and manual moods and his own creativity. It is proposed to touch upon the component factors of this eco-function of early Man briefly in his Old and New Stone Age contexts and examine the critical acumen such a study bestows upon the whole gamut of archaeological data, relevant to a better interpretation of these data.

In the Old Stone Age context, approx mately from 300,000* year B.P. to c. 40,000 B.P. (which latter could be called the start of the upper Palaeolithic and the Mesolithic stages), the occurrence of a tool should have had four dimensions, namely, its relationship to (a) the habitat, (b) the work floor, (c) the quarry zone for food collection by hunting and (d) the raw material source and its procurement. At that stage, all these four were not only interrelated but also were falling within a reasonable close ambit. Of course, during the stages of development of this vast time-span, this ambit of activity was progressively expanding, but simultaneously, it was also variegating and becoming broken into aspects of analogous zones of activity was resulting in multiplication of sub-zones. The habitant is the most well identified and almost unitary focus where, over long period of time, because of their proven physical and climatic advantages, a continuous use had been pursued. The physical advantage was satisfied by its closed feature, as in a cave shelter or on the brim of an overhanging rock or a mere natural high level depression. The reflexes of man were almost those of an animal then.

The work floor was roughly strewn with loose stones or boulders in order to provide hard seating, utilization potential for lighting fires, and expediency for self-protection against attacks by predatory wild beasts straying in. The stones also provided the anvil for tool fabrication. It followed the natural depressions of the original floor and much of these boulders had been caused by natural rock falls from the ceiling in the more distant past, and were cleared only at a few places for any cosy sleeping ground or avoidance of draft of wind for lighting fires. The cultural deposits which accumulated on this boulder-strewn floor were rather thin (except for occasionally seen bone dupms of left-overs of food) over long periods allowing the cave to be utilized for several successive generations if not centuries. As only rearely there was water erosion or soli-fluction within the cave premises, this was even more helped.

The empirical scope of the activities of early man, will be categorizable into several parameters in each stage of his development. For instance, under Old Stone Age, it would involve the tool, its type functional tool advancement, preferred habitational location, nature of the collective groups involved in the activity, the food resources, the link between the group strength and the re-

* This upper limit is hardly amenable to fixing, except by datable evidence like fossils and often tends to give a picture that is uniform everywhere. That it need not be so has already been pointed out by African evidence where the Acheulian culture is seen continuing up to the Gamblian pluvial in certain areas. In India, one of the primary tasks of the prehistorian is to fix the time scale for the inception of early Stone Age, because if it is shown for instance that the Hand axe cultures could even extend to the end of the Pleistocene, the time-concept of further developments in flake and blade have also to be suitably revised.

sources. Under the tool category, we have already seen that it would be relatable to the habitat, work floor, quarry zone and raw material. Under tool types it was relatable to techniques, proportions, utilization ration, variations in similar type, response to food source, response to distribution of group function, and changes in ecology (stratigraphic or shift of location). Under tool advancement, it will be relatable to resource management, shifts in food habits, growth of the group and its bearing on production itself variously of tools, of food resources (both direct and controlled) and the matter of tool attrition due to change in food habits. Under habitational location, it will be relatable to change due to increased group strength, climatic, resource depletion, and other deterrent factors like cataclysmic events. Under collective groups, it would be relatable to tool manufacture, food consumption, spare-resource-ration etc. Under resource category itself, it would be relatable to natural and perennial food, natural and seasonal food, erratic and distant food and entirely foreign food resource. Under resources category, further, in relation to the group, it would involve also shift in tool output by diminution of types, diminution of number, appreciation and substitution. The techniques, the types, the locational span, the food resource ration in relation to each of the spots, in a changing climato-ecological spectrum, will also be interrelated.

The focal shelter aspect will again be relatable variously (i) to similar centres of open type, (ii) dissimilar centres of open type, (iii) shifted centre of changed type and (iv) shifted centre with reduced or increased tools and degeneration, and disarray of the community itself. The tool use itself will be primarily relatable to freshness, retouch, wear-and-tear, the nature of the object tackled such as wood, animal bone, animal skin and organic materials. It is highly tempting to suggest that in a prolific site like Bhimbetka in Madhya Pradesh, these theoritical specifics of the eco-frame could be tested by a carefully arranged interdisciplinary team, so that the norms of a cave habitat and its distinctions from the open air stations and fluviatile Stratigraphy for India could be eventually well established. Three such sites one from the lower south Acheulian belt including the Kurnool caves, another in Bhimbetka and a third on the sub-Himalayan Siwaliks, one wishes, could be desirable National Programme where the scientist could integrate his expertise with the Stone Age archaeologist.

The quarry zone for food was a potent factor of the zone of movement of the Stone Age hunters and, though not too circumscribed, was yet confined to the natural geomorpological tract, mostly of adjacent valleys only. While the cave shelter could not always be ideally located, its access, after hunt, which would have involved the dragging of the hunted animal carcase to the cave habitant should have been reasonably convenient. We know that from the II glacial, Peking man had been using fire, although it is in Tabun cave in the III inter glacial, in Acheulian stage, we see the firm use of fire and Vestonice Kiln of the Upper Palaeolithic Europe is the deliberate invention of it. No true cave habitat was known before Late Acheulian even in Africa. Matapan cave belongs to the last interglacial. Riss-Wurm interglacial saw the fragmentation of the Acheulian traditions in Europe (corresponding to the Kanjeran inter-glacial of Africa) and Sangaon-Fauresmith cultures emerged in the Gamblian (Wurm). Flesh was mostly consumed by European, Palestinian Homo and the Asian Pithecanthropus. But the African, in the early stages, as seen in Zinjanthropus of Olduvai Gorge ate mostly lizards, frogs, birds, rats, and mice, while the Acheulian of Kanya ate zebra, pork and baboon. Only in the Middle Palaeolithic, ostrich eggs are seen consumed in great quantities, although this is seemingly continued over a long stretch of time, as is found even at Patne site on the Tapi valley in India, in levels taken to be upper Palaeolithic (?) stratigraphically.

There are, apart from this, open stations where the tools of early man had been picked up in large numbers, both from what can be considered as regular 'factory sites' and from river banks. These open air stations are more in India, especially in the Old Stone Age activity zones. These are often influenced by the provenance of heavy raw material concentrations, as for instance, in the Alicoor hills of the quartzites of Cuddapah Series on the Korttalayar in Tamil Nadu. Similarly the calcarious rocks of chert etc. In the Inter-Trappean beds in the Maharashtra had formed copious raw materials for the Middle Stone Age. Open air sites are in plenty on the Narmada, where Stone Age occurrences have been confined to the middle stretch of the river and are not generally found either on the upper most or the lower most reaches. These are contingent upon the appropriate hunting conditions and the eco-physical balance and floral and faunal potential of the central zone for the predatory animals as well as man, such as jungle growth, wide lake formations in the river itself and availability of the prey. Fossil evidence shows that several animal species of Elephas and Bos had been existing in the Narmada and Godavari areas in the period between late mid-pleistocene stage to the end of Pleistocene stimulating tool culture development.

These open air stations therefore show that a typical ecology is perhaps more conductive, demography-wise to the proliferation of men and thus in relation to men, animals of predatory nature could have been comparatively much less; and what more the decimation of men (or in other words the mortality rate) from time to time might also be higher. Further, with larger number of men, more tools were fabricated and thus the total quantity of tools in early Stone Age in the tropical and sub-equatorial regions of India, and Africa are very much more comparable than those of Temperate Europe. But, by the plethora of tools, one may not necessarily conclude that the activity of men was more with reference to the animals but only that men themselves were more and they multiplied tools for individual usage, which is more in open air station, while *collective and coordinated usage* is stimulated by a cave habitat, for the hunting groups.

The Middle Stone Age and 'Upper Palaeolithic' stages of man are, in a way, highly specialised diversificaions of his activity, by a confident and imaginative application of skills in chipped and retouched tool outfit, useful for a variety of situations he had to face, in the comparatively more peaceful and sedentary pursuit of daily life. It can be held that this life style was still of an uncertain degree in food storage, was fraught with difficulties of changes quicker of climate in the late and post-Pleistocene certainly far from the truely organized life style. Perhaps definable natural family groups could have emerged in the next major stage of man's progress, namely the Mesolithic and Neolithic phases. Elements of life which are not directly concerning mere collection of food for survival have entered the picture and deliberate exploitation of the environment in order to identify continuing sources of sustenance was also being perceived. The water source which did not loom large for exploitation in the lower Palaeolithic and was often a formidable obstacle to movement of groups, was slowly becoming a friendly and familiar feature, helpful in providing him with much of the nourishment through fish and shell food that was seemingly perennial, and means of transport, mostly from the post (glacial/ Pluvial times also. Perhaps preparing crude rafts which can enable him to move across the water for hunting and fishing also ensued in the Mesolithic. The decrease in the sizes of the tools, the effective specialised edges and points which have been fabricated as part of the tool-repertory, would also show that he had certainly diversified his functional diurnal activity and was having secondary usages like perforators and skin scrapers and spoke-shaves, which would clearly reflect on the specific varied nature of the avocations of these communities. It is thus the *avocational increment-factor* that in middle Stone Age and Late Stone Age tool outfit, lighter game fauna and general climatic environment which help in visualizing the strides made by the human groups, innovating from every new situation for a new turn of events and in that process allowing their faculties to develop and grow thereby producing imperceptibly subtle anatomical and skeletal changes.

IV

When we reach the food-framing community stage, we see the whole set of parameters drastically changing and a more viable analytical frame of the humanistic as well as technological content of the activity-cycle emerging. The line of thinking and examination of the data as well as what to look for, in a field study, itself changes. The resource and eco-system change, resulted in the advent of 'subsistence framing'. The problems raised by the above from a chrono-cultural view point, which leave a hiatus between Early Stone Age economy and the Neolithic economy, are in terms of demographic, faunal, floral and climatic balance, of the natural wild food grain resources which had casually attracted him and changed the pattern of distribution of *work-input* for *food output* and in direct proportion to changed distribution of work itself, increased strength of the communities consumption rate, controlled exploration within each zone, closer adaptation to the eco-system, local expansion of work and production through ancillary activities like pottery and dwellings and problems connected with storage of food space for the domesticated animals, etc.

The transition from mixed tool assemblages of the old stone into pointedly specialized categories of farm tool fabrication, as related to soil, hydrology and organic fertility, is indeed a first phase in *settlement pattern.* At new factor is also the new distribution pattern of work among the population of men, women, and children. It has also a relationship between his own metabolism and the edible food grains and leafy food around him, different from flesh of animals and fish which was the chief food till then. It has been suggested that the need to digest high protein food must have driven man in search of edible leafy vegettables and grains that help in this process and create a healthy body and vocational development—the necessary—the necessary pre-requisite to mental development.

V

This Neolithic—agricultural occupation which was a pervasive subcontinental sustratum had been suddenly impacted upon by the refinement, urbanisation and functional versatility of human ingenuity in a civilizational context, and the process received its greatest culmination, later, in the early Iron Age. The Chalcolithic urban cultures were thus centralised apex zones, motivated out of a basal spectrum of affluent agricultural output which indeed indirectly triggered an input of secondary craft and technology and consumerism (in the mildest sense of the term) and thus, it is not as if the births of civilazations were instant miracles, but only the explosions, out of a critical point of pastoral surplus and food affluence, leading to the utilization of that affluence to new dimensions of skills and efflorescence of the inventive faculties of man. If so, the very base of agriculture in that process was itself widened also into a rural bloom of life-style, from a mere pastoral monotony of farm activity. As the farm activity itself was a product of soil, rainfall, climate and tool improvement besides transportation including cattle traction and coordination with secondary uses of cattle drawn vehicles, it led to expansion of the distribution of the surplus to everwidening areas of need. This should have surely resulted in a rural bourgeois economy, national acquistion of the ownership of land and trends of sedentary life, caused by increased man-power and controlled management in natural family groups, besides giving fillip to the ancillary lores like, astronomy, building science, hydrology harnessing of water resources and diversification of animal husbandary which were directly related to his work.

Prehistoric land use itself is divisible into three characteristic patterns regarding (a) kinds of use (b) frequency of the different kinds of use and (c) the spatial distribution of use in a specified area of study. The first involves types and varieties of activities in the cultural assemblage content, with reference to assemblage area. A wide range of activities may be suggested and may indicate whether the use of the area is all the year round or only specific or occasional. For instance, a high percentage of waste flakes in a cluster and the overall limited size of the site of tool assemblages may suggest relatively limited activity, while the inherent and consistence technology therein may suggest the intensity of usage.

VI

Inferring of the general characteristics of the activities in the area of study, the variety of activity, rhythmatic recurrence of activity are all factors which need a proper methodology for indentification Settlement patterns could be defined from these for that stage of Prehistoric or protohistoric activity and empirical behavioural reconstruction may also be hypothesised, if rigorous sampling strategy, intensive recording of data recovery methods and detailed quantification by the assemblage analysis are carried out. Such statistical methods are yet new in archaeological methodology and their potential indicates the need for increased application of such techniques, and will lead to proper ethno-taxonymic models, out of the enormous stone or pottery assembale seen in Prehistoric and Protohistoric archaeology, through acceptable culster-analysis and its interpretation. Scientific methods have to be employed in this, if we have to make archaeological analysis meaningful.

Archaeological sampling package (ASP) is already becoming popular in west, which is a composite computerized programme designed towards, generalized random sampling as well as stratified random sampling. These can provide precise horizontal assessment in a settlement, side by side with establishing a formal grid system in an excavation. Such aids deserve more or more to be utilized both as an inter-disciplinary coordination and interaction between the archaeologists and the scientists. The latter in India are waiting to be adequately exploited by the archaeologists who are still conventional and slow in their motivation for result-inter-pretation techniques. A natural perception of the patterns of social behaviour in archaeological situation can thus be made only on a strictly objective and quantified basis.

Development of methodology is moving at such a pace that such a course is now strongly urged on the archaeologists. The tardier he is, the less justice he is doing to his calling and to the culture classification, identification and eventual preservation. May we hope that this terminal part of the current century which is on the brink of an explosion of science, as an aid to human resources, will find the archaeologists not wanting in coordinating their endavour with the potentialities of scientific investigations and will present the total culture of man, in a given area, in a country as rich as ours, with fitness, clarity and acceptable norms?

REFERENCES

Binford L.R. and S.R. Binford—1968—New Prespectives in Archaeology, Chicago.

Bordes F. 1968—Old Stone Age (London and New York).

Chang K.C. 1967: Rethinking Archaeology (New York).

Childe V.G. 1956: Piecing together the past (New York).

Clark D.L. 1970 & 1979—Analytical Archaeology (Reprint) (London)

————1972—Models in Archaeology (London).

————1977—Spatial Archaeology (London).

Clarke J.D. 1965—The Later Pleistocene Cultures of Africa, in Science 1950 (pp. 333-47).

————1970—The Prehistory of Africa, London and New York.

Collins D. *et al.* 1973— Background to Archaeology (London and New York).

Hawkes, Jaquetta,: Pre history—(London and New York)

Issac Glynn, 1981 : 'Analytical archaeology' Antiquity L.V. pp. 200—205.

Jon E. Kalb, Elizabeth B. Oswald, Sleshi Tebedge, Assifa Mebrak, Emmanual Tole & Dennis Peak (Ist July 1982), Geology and Stratigraphy of Neogene Deposits, Middle Awash Valley, Ethiopia, Nature, Vol. 298, pp. 17—29.

Mahapatra G.C. 1981—Research Bulletin (Arts) Acheulian discoveries on the Sivalik frontal range current Anthropology Vol. 22 No. 4.

H.D. Sankalia 1974—The Prehistory and Protohistory of India and Pakistan, Poona.

Wainwrigth 1964—Pleistocene deposits of Lower Narmada river—Baroda.

Archaeology in India Since Independence : Some Random Thougths

B.B. LAL
Indian Institute of Advanced Study
Simla

When at midnight between August 14 and 15, 1947, power was transferred by the British to India, with the same stroke, unfortunately, the ancient sites of Harappa and Mohenjo-daro, reflecting the acme of civilization on this subcontinent were taken away from us, there remaining hardly any site worthy of the name of the Indus Civilization on this side of the border. Indian archaeologists*, however, took up the challenge, and by now we have discovered hundreds of sites ascribable to this civilization. And it is not merely the number that matters. Certain altogether new dimensions have been added to our knowledge of this civilization: for example, the existence of a dockyard at Lothal in Gujarat, or that of ploughed agricultural field which even antedates the Harappan remains, at Kalibangan in Rajasthan. Additional light has been thrown on the rituals as well as burial practices of the Indus people.

In fact there is no period of man's story on this subcontinent to which substantial additions have not been made since Independence. As in the case of the Indus Civilization, in the case of the Stone Age Sohan Culture too, all the sites had gone to Pakistan. By now, however, nearly a hundred sites of this culture have been discovered along the Himalayan foothills in Jammu and Kashmir, Himachal Pradesh, Panjab and Haryana. It was once thought that there was a hiatus between the Early Stone Age and the Late Stone Age in India, but this gap too has been bridged, thanks to the work of our colleagues in central and south India. The microlithic industries were regarded by certain writers to be very late, but excavations have proved beyond any shadow of doubt that some of the microlithic industries in India are as old as their counterparts anywhere in the world. A great deal has been done to explore prehistoric paintings and we have now in India the cave-paintings of Bhimbetka which stand up to the reputation of Lascaux and Altamira in Europe.

To come to what is commonly called the proto-historic period. The Copper Hoards, which in the pre-1947 days were hanging in the air, have since been assigned to their proper chronological horizon, viz. in the second millennium B.C. The vast gap between the end of the Indus Civilization and the beginning of the historical period is almost on the point of being bridged. It is to this period in northern India that the Copper Hoard Culture, the Ahar Culture and the Painted Grey Ware Cul-

* It is not proposed to mention here the names of individuals who have made the discoveries, the primary focus being on the salient acihevements and not on those who achieved them. Likewise, it is obvious that in this rapid review many an achievement may not find mention. Nor is it a region-wise survey, It is an overall perspective of what has been achieved, there also being a mention of some lacunae which deserve to be filled in.

I would be failing in my duty if I did not mention that in this task of unravelling India's past, many foreign scholars have also made noteworthy contribution even after Independence. For obvicus reasons, it is not possible to mention them individually.

tures belong: practically nothing was known about the latter two prior to Independence. Likewise, central India and central and northern Deccan are no longer *terra incognita.* Here one finds the Malwa and Jorwe Cultures flourish.ng in the second millennium B.C. In fact, the horizontal excavations carried out at Inamgaon throw very welcome light on the settlement-pattern of the Jorwe Culture.

In south India too vast strides have been taken. Prior to Independence it was thought that the Neolithic Culture did not go earlier than *c.* 1000 B.C. and that the Megalithic Culture may be only as old as *c.* 300 B.C. Extensive work in the region has shown that these dates are highly conservative. It is now known that when the Harappans were occupying the Indus Valley and the adjacent areas, it was the neolithic folks who were living in south India. The megalith-builders too are likely to have emerged on the scene as early as the first quarter of the first millennium B.C., and not in the last quarter as had been envisaged earlier.

Prior to Independence the *Mahabharata* and the *Ramayana* were thought to be scare-crows from the strictly archaeological point of view. Even many historians regarded them as figments of the imagination. On the other hand, there were and still are those who regard these epics as true to the very letter and have no hesitation in stressing that Rama lived a lakh of years ago and did travel in an aeroplane *(pushpaka-vimana)* back to Ayodhya after his conquest of Lanka. However, extensive work at Hastinapura, Mathura, etc., associated with the Mahabharata story, and at Ayodhya, Sringaverapura, Bharadvaja Asrama, etc. associated with the Ramayana story, has shown that the truth lies in between the two extremes. These epics do have a historical basis, though poetic imagination and subsequent interpolations have resulted in the presentation of the basic simple stories in an highly exaggerated form.

A very heartening development of recent years is the increasing application of science to archaeology. In certain cases we were groping in the dark regarding the dating of the archaeological remains. Scientists at the Physical Research Laboratory, Ahmedabad, and Birbal Sahni Research Institute, Lucknow, have come out in a big way to help us. The former has given a very large number of dates, based on the Carbon-14 method, which have helped in fixing most of the known archaeological cultures in their respective chronological niches. This laboratory, as also to some extent the Bhaba Atomic Research Centre, are actively pursuing another method of dating the past, viz. that of thermoluminescence. And the application of scientific methods is not confined to dating only. Environmental studies are on the march and the international workshop on the Late Cenozoic Palaeoclimatic Changes in Kashmir and Central Asia, just concluded at the PRL, Ahmedabad, shows the big strides this branch of learning has taken in recent years in the country.

While delivering my Presidential Address to the Indian Archaeological Society in 1975 at Chandigarh, I had stressed the need to go in for under-sea archaeology, for thus alone could we expect to recover the evidence of ships, which may have by chance sunk in our coastal waters during ancient times. We have evidence of the Roman trade, and indeed even of the Harappan trade with Western Asia, and it is not unlikely that one day we may come across the remains of actual ships that carried cargo to and from the western regions. It is gratifying to note that a beginning, howsoever small, has since been made in this direction.

But what I said some twenty years ago in the Epilogue to my little book *Indian Archaeology Since Independence* holds good even today.

What has been done is but a part
   Of what remains, things all apart.
Let not a praise then make us burst,
   Complacency the spade nor rust.

Indeed, a self-search would reveal that there still are many lacunae in our overall approach to archaeology and its associated problems.

The first thing that strikes me is the great dissipation of energy in excavating sites without any specific problem in mind. Sometimes excavations are undertaken just because funds are available and there is an ancient site in the neighbourhood. This tendency should be curbed and only those sites should be excavated which help in answering specific questions of national or regional importance.

Such a curtailment of activities will help us in canalizing funds in a more fruitful direction. And here I would like to stress the need for horizontal excavation of some selected sites whereby light may be thrown on the total way of living of the people in a given region during a given period. Inamgaon is a good example of this kind of work. But how much do we know, for instance, of the details of the Painted Grey Ware Culture which played a vital role in providing the foundation to the early historical culture of northern India? We do not yet know the various stages through which the villages of the Ganga plains grew into small towns and thence into the cities which were in existence around the middle of the first millennium B.C. I know it is very difficult to find a single-period site, particularly in the Ganga plains where tendency has been to keep on living at the same place through the centuries, thus producing a terrific mound, sometimes over 15-20 metres in height. But conscious efforts through exploration might reveal some short-lived sites which may be easily amenable to horizontal excavation. If this is not possible, I will plead even for the removal of the upper strata, of course after their careful recording has been done, so that adequate area becomes available for digging in the lower levels. At present what happens is that whereas in the upper levels a very large area may have been taken up for excavation, by the time one goes down to the lower levels only a slit here and a slit there remains available, because the overlying structures completely block the way.

I have always felt that archaeology should not be treated as an end in itself. It is one of the many tools that help in reconstructing the history of mankind. While for the period prior to the written records it is perhaps the main tool, even for the period for which there exist literary texts it is no less important, for it provides material evidence for what is mentioned in the texts. Thus, a correlation ought to be attempted between the literary data and the archaeological evidence. In my own humble way, I made an attempt to correlate the data provided by the later Vedic texts on the one hand and the Painted Grey Ware Culture on the other and it gives me satisfaction to note that many historians in India as well as abroad have concurred with me to a considerable degree. However, I believe very much more has to be done in this direction, and I can tell you that even for the historical period the attempts can be fully rewarding. As an example, I may be permitted to refer to a problem on which I have just now been working.

If one casts a glance over the excavation-reports of early historical sites, say, for example, Sisupalgarh in eastern India or Arikamedu near Pondicherry in south India, or Hastinapura in the north, one finds a variance in the brick-sizes even *within* what may be called one "group" as distinct from another. At Sringaverapura, in one and the same structure, viz. the tank, the length, breadth and thickness of the bricks vary respectively from 41.5 to 44.0 cm., 27.0 to 28.5 cm., and 5.5 to 7.0 cm. I was completely flabbergasted by this variation. However, the mystery was solved only by reference to ancient texts which indicate that bricks are to be manufactured by using *angulas* (thickness of the fingers), *vitasti* (span), *hasta* (fore arm) and *pada* (foot) as the units of measurement. The millions of bricks used in the Sringaverapura tank were evidently not supplied by one individual; there must have been a dozen or so suppliers. And since the thickness of the fingers and the size of the span and forearm vary from person to person, though within a limited range, the length, breadth and thickness of the bricks also varied accordingly. This is just one case-study which stresses the need that the archaeological evidence ought to be studied in the light of the literary data, to make the former more intelligible and meaningful.

I now come to another important point. There used to be a time when an average Indian archaeologist could not only excavate but also handle his coins and inscriptions. But now, unfortunately, that tribe is fast disappearing, for more credit is being given to the study of pottery and stone tools. While no doubt these items do have their importance, it was high time that a fresh fillip was given to the study of coins and inscriptions, nay, even to the study of the classical languages. For, if things are allowed to go their present way, the archaeologist may find himself reduced to a mere excavation-technician.

While we have no doubt taken long strides in

briding many a gap in our knowledge of India's past, an aspect which has sadly been neglected all these years is the study of the archaeology of countries with which we have had connections in the past. While Nepal may have received some kind of attention from our archaeologists, precious little has been done in respect of other countries. If a straight question is put, 'Do we have in India *even a single* archaeologist who has any expertise of ancient Chinese civilization, or of ancient Egyptian civilization?', the answer will be an outright 'No'. More or less the same would be the answer if I refer to the archaeology of ancient Rome or Greece, and nearer home, of Iran, Iraq and Central Asia. South-east Asia has been catered for no better, although it is well known that in many a way the countries in this region had been greatly influenced by Indian civilization. And mind you this is the sorry state of affairs even after thirty-five years of our Independence. Should we not feel ashamed of it I know that there are more urgent developmental schemes of the country that take away our funds. But, indeed, not much funds would be needed—perhaps an yearly expenditure of about 50 lakhs would do—for starting a centre which could fill up this great lacuna. And I am confident that the gain to knowledge and more so to India's prestige would be many times more than the petty expenditure involved. Will the highest authorities in the country care to listen to this voice which has become hoarse by crying for over a decade now for the establishing of such a centre?

I may be permitted now to have little digression from archaeological research to the preservaton of our archaeological heritage. First of all, I would like to congratulate the Director General of the Archaeological Survey of India and her colleagues on the excellent work they have been doing in regard to the conservation of monuments. In recent months even those monuments in Delhi which were not under the direct charge of the Survey have received adequate attention, and one feels proud about it. But there is a sore point too, and, I am sure, the Director General will not mind my mentioning it. This is no personal comment on her, for I too should share the blame, having been myself the D.G. Archaeology once.

This is something which requires much more serious attention than what has been given to it hitherto: I refer to the conservation of excavated remains. Year in and year out we have been excavating ancient sites but how many of them have we successfully conserved for posterity? More often than not, it is a pitiable sight—and I am sure most of you present here will agree with me— to see an excavated trench just two to three years after the excavations are over. Even very important sites of international importance have suffered badly over the years. For example, while a visitor to Lothal in Gujarat may find some solace by seeing a few of the excavated structures preserved in some sort of way, a visitor to Kalibangan in Rajasthan will, I am told on good authority, get shocked at the utterly dilapidated condition of the ancient remains. Around 1970 one could walk proudly through the grid-patterned streets of this township of the Indus Civilization. The agricultural field, going back to the pre-Indus days, was the only one of its kind in the world. It was excavated with the utmost care with soft brushes to bring out the furrows. But today, it appears nothing is left of it. We are currently excavating a tank at Sringaverapura near Allahabad, wnich is more than 200 metres in length. With the canal which brought water from the Ganga, the silting chambers, inlet and interconnecting channels and terraced side-walls showing evidence of what are technically known as 'horizental and vertical warnings', it again is a unique examples in the world. Our hydraulic engineers have every reason to be proud of the fact that their forbears some two thousand years ago could produce such a remarkable complex. However, it yet remains to be seen whether or not we are able to conserve this magnificent monument. I say this because the problem is manifold: it involves in equal measures not only the will to do the job, but also funds as well technical expertise.. The tank is pretty deep and thus the sub-soil water rises within it up to about a metre in height. The retaining walls, though made of well fired bricks, are affected by saltpetre. During the rainy season, water pours down into it not only from the top but also from the sides. Maybe we will have to erect a suitable shed over it—a step considered unconventional in India, but quite normal elsewhere. As an example, I can cite the enormously long and wide shed which the Japanese have built over an entire prehistoric site. Can't we do the same in our case? Some fifteen years ago there was an archaeological conference in Afghanistan and we the delegates were given an audience by the then highest dignitary of the land. I can well recall the advice that was given to us: "Do not make naked a damsel if you cannot provide her with clothes to cover herself up again!"

I am afraid I have taken too much of your precious time and would now like to conclude by saying that were we in India to visualize a deity presiding over Archaeology, she should be a eight-handed one *(ashta-bhuji),* holding in her hands respectively: (i) a spade, signifying skill in excavation; (ii) a book stressing the need to correlate the literary data with the archaeological evidence; (iii) an *ekatara* (a stringed musical instrument), suggesting the utilization of folklore and tradition in understanding the past; (iv) an inscribed slab, emphasizing that the diminishing interest in the decipherment of inscriptions and coins has to be revived; (v) a glass-tube, pointing out that more and more of scientific aids and new techniques have to be applied to archaeological research; (vi) a travel-bag, indicating that study of the archaeology of countries with which we had relations in the past ought not to be neglected; (vii) a trowel, reminding us that the excavated remains deserve as much attention in respect of conservation as do the standing monuments, and finally (viii) a pen, for not unoften reports on excavation fall into heavy arrears —a charge of which, in one case, along with my colleagues I too plead guilty, whatever may have been the bottle-necks.

Upper Palaeolithic Cultures of the Mid-Son Valley

J.N. PAL
University of Allahabad

The existence of Upper Palaeolithic culture, has now been accepted beyond doubt in the Indian sub-continent. Not only a large number of surface sites of this culture but also its occurrence in definite geological horizon and its primary occupational sites have been located in different parts of the sub-continent (Murty 1968: 83-101; 1970: 106-128; 1974: 196-230; Paddayya 1970: 165-170, Sali 1974; Allchin and Gaudie 1971:248-265; Reddy 1970: 227-234; Ghosh 1970: 1-68, Misra *et al.* 1977; Misra 1982; Sharma 1973). In the middle reaches of the Son valley in the districts of Sidhi (Madhya Pradesh) and Mirzapur (Uttar Pradesh) also primary and secondary sites of this culture have been located. In the following pages an attempt has been made to bring together the salient features of the Upper Palaeolithic cultures of the middle Son valley.

Nisar Ahmad while exploring the Son valley in 1961-62 had found a few blade tools of Upper Palaeolithic affinity along with Middle Palaeolithic artefacts at Baburi and Jogdaha in Sidhi district (Nisar Ahmad 1966). On the basis of this find Sankalia (1974) proposed that when this area is properly explored 'it will not be difficult to separate the Upper Palaeolithic blade industry from other assemblages'. In 1968-69 R.K. Varma and B.B. Misra located some Upper Palaeolithic sites near Jogdaha bridge on the Son (*IAR* 68-69). Attracted by fresh looking tools of these sites Sharma and his colleagues of Allahabad University started extensive exploration in the Son valley, located a large number of Upper Palaeolithic sites along with other Palaeolithic sites and collected a large number of artefacts and animal fossils (*IAR*/1975-76; 77-78; 80-81). In this archaeological expedition D.C. Dassarma and S. Biswas of Geological Survey of India also participated for two field sessions to study the geological formation of the Son valley (*IAR*/74-75; 75-76).

Between Bichhi in the east and Chorahat in the west, Kaimur in the north and Gopad river in the south about 3000 sq km area of Sidhi district (*IAR* 74-75) was explored. To confirm the nature of the geological formation of the Son and its tributaries studied in Sidhi district, a systematic exploration was made in 1977-78 of the Son valley and its tributaries Kanhar, Ghaghar, Rihand and Bijul in Mirzapur district (Uttar Pradesh). Between village Newari near U.P. and M.P. border in the west and the Son-Kanhar confluence in the east, village Kurhul in the north and Obra in the south, about 800 sq. km area was explored in Mirzapur (*IAR* 77-78).

In January 1979 while seeing the rich collection of fresh Palaeolithic artefacts and vertebrate fossils of the Son valley, in Allahabad University Museum, Desmond Clark expressed his desire to work in the Son valley. In 1980 and 1982 further exploration and excavations of selected Palaeolithic sites were carried in the Son valley by G.R. Sharma and his colleagues in collaboration with J. Desmond Clark and his team from Berkeley. M.A.J. Williams of Macquire University, Australia along with Keith Royce (1982) and M.F. Clarke (n.d) studied in detail the Quaternary geology of the middle Son valley. Quaternary history of the middle Son valley can be summarised as below (Williams and Royce, 1982, Williams and Clarke, nd):—

Geological formation	Description	Lithic Industry	Age
Sihawal formation gravels	Bed rock erosion, pedimentation of lime stone, shales cherts and sand-stones, deposition of debris flow rubble and alluvial fan gravels and clayey gravels	Lower palaeolithic, cores, flakes, handaxes and cleavers of quartzose, sand stone and quartzite on and in these gravels	Early to Middle Pleistocene
Sihawal formation-silt	Deposition of fine sandy clay during and after accumulation of Sihawal gravels.		Middle Pleistocene
Patpara formation	Erosion followed by deposition of Patpara format on gravely clays and fluviatile sands. Syndepositional and/or post depositional reddening of clays and sand	Upper Acheulian to Middle Palaeolithic artefacts	Middle to Upper Pleistocene
Baghor formation	Erosion followed by Baghor formation, channel sands, overbank clays and yellow brown loam	Middle to Upper Palaeolithic	Upper Pleistocene
Khetauhi formation	Several intervals of episodic down cutting, lateral planation and inset terrace formation	Upper Palaeolithic, Mesolithic and Neolithic	Pleistocene to Holocene

Among these formations the Baghor formation having relevance to the Upper palaeolithic culture is of great interest both stratigraphically and archaeologically. Near the main river there are two distinct divisions of this formation:— Baghor formation-Coarse member and Baghor formation-fine member. The coarse lower member consists of cross-bedded and planar bedded sands and gravels. The coarse member is capped by horizontally bedded silts and clays. But away from the river both the members merge laterally into massively bedded aeolian clays. Rolled and abraded Middle Palaeolithic artefacts, fresh Upper Palaeolithic artefacts and abundant fossil vertibrate fauna have been obtained *in situ* in the coarse member of Baghor formation. The fossils are comparatively well-preserved and include bos, buffalo, hippo, deer, antilope, elephant, crocodile, tortoise, etc.

Unabraded fresh Upper Palaeolithic artefacts have been found from both the members of Baghor formation (nearly 20 m thick deposit) and also in the Khetaunhi formation *in situ*. This indicates a long time-span for the Upper Palaeolithic industry in the region undergoing many morphological and technological changes.

So far 123 sites of Upper Palaeolithic culture have been located in the mid-Son valley in Mirzapur and Sidhi districts. These sites are situated on the bank of river Son, on the medial ridge running parallel to the north bank of the Son and on southern slope of the Kaimur. A large number of cores, flakes and blades, along with tools in different stages of manufacture have been found from most of the sites. Evidently these are the surface factory sites. A study of the technique and morphology of the artefacts of Upper Palaeolithic industry of this region has revealed at least three distinct stages of Upper Palaeolithic cultures of the area (Varma and Pal, nd).

The first stage is charcterised by thick blades with triangular cross-section, sometimes containing patches of cortex on dorsal surface. Majority of the blades are removed from simple cores (flake cores) as is eviden by irregular flake-scars on dorsal surface. Only 8% fluted cores are encountered in this stage. Bold retouching has been done on the working edges of the tools. The main tool types include retouched blades, burins, various types of scrapers (end scraper, side scraper, round scraper, notch scraper), knives, denticulates, borers and a few points.

In the second stage majority of the blades are removed from fluted cores. 54% fluted cores have been used in this stage. The blades have become slenderer and smaller in comparison to the first stage. Number of blades with trapezoidal cross-section is increased considerably. Tool types of this stage are retouched blades, backed blades, truncated blades, burins, scrapers (end scraper, nocth scraper, nose scraper, found scraper and thumb nail scraper) and points.

In the third stage all the blades are removed from fluted cores. The blades have become smaller with appreciably thin trapezoidal cross-section. Fine regular retouching is the main feature of the tools of this stage. The tools in this stage include retouched blades, backed blades, truncated blades, burins, borers, scrapers, points and lunates.

Recent excavations at Rampur, Baghor III and Baghor I (Fig.1) in Sidhi district, Madhya Pradesh by a combined team of prehistorians from University of Allahabad ,India and University of California, Berkeley have extended our knowledge of Upper Palaeolithic culture in several respects. Excavation at Rampur and Baghor III was confined to a very restricted area whereas Baghor I was extensively excavated.

Rampur (Lat. 24°33′30″N., Long. 82°12′30″E.) is situated on the northern bank of the Son. In 1980 artefacts of the Upper Palaeolithic culture were collected from 1 x 1 m area. The analysis of the artefacts suggested that Rampur industry compares well with that of Baghor in typology, technique and use of raw material (Misra, et al. 1982). These artefacts were scattered on the present exposed surface, apparently lying on the rock-surface. With a view to ascertaining total thickness of artefact-bearing horizon, a small square of 1 x 1 m was laid out almost in the centre of the site. From this small excavation it was established that the artefacts were not on the rock-surface but were found in a 30 cm thick deposit of red brown sandy clay loam, concentration being near the top.

The site of Baghor III is situated approximately, 3 km north of Merhauli village and approximately 2 km south of the Kaimur, half way between Baghor I and Baghor II. Blade/bladelets were found scattered in a grey clay deposit at Baghor III. In 1980 for ascertaining the stratigraphic horizon of these artefacts a trial trench of 3 sq. m was laid out which had yielded 68 artefacts—2 shaped tools, 3 modified pieces and 63 waste (Clark and Richard 1982). In 1982 with a view to ascertaining the nature and character of small blade industry a 5 sq. m trench was laid out. The deposit was divisible into three layers—humus, yellow sandy loam and greyish clay. 10

cm thick artefact horizon was in the greyish clay 0.75-0.85 cm below surface. The blade industry recovered from this excavation ,on the basis of stratigraphy, technique and morophology of the tools has been assigned to the late Upper Palaeolithic phase. Baghor III offered the earliest stratigraphic evidence for small blade industry in the middle Son valley, Madhya Pradesh. The artefacts are fashioned mainly on greyish chert. The assemblage consists of fluted cores, flakes, blades, debitage and finished tools. The finished tools include retouched bladelets, backed bladelets, truncated bladelets, lunates, triangles, trapezes, borers and scrapers.

The Upper Palaeolithic site of Baghor I (Lat. 24°35′2″N., Long. 82°18′54″E.) is situated at a distance of about 4 km north-east of *Merhauli* village in Gopad-Banas sub-division of the Sidhi district, Madhya Pradesh. The site was first excavated in 1980 by a combined team of archaeologists from University of Allahabad and University of California, Berkeley, under the joint direction of G.R. Sharma and J. Desmond Clark (Kenoyer, *et al.* 1982). The site was exposed for further excavation by the same team in 1982.

The site is about 1 km south of the Kaimur and 5 km north of the Son on the bank of a small nala emanating from the Kaimur. The area of the site though now a cultivated field was identified on the basis of scatter of fresh artefacts. As there seemed a thick soil cover over the artefact bearing horizon the site was selected for excavation.

In 1980 with a view to excavating the site horizontally 100 grids of 1 x 1 m were laid out in an area of 10 x 10 m in the north western sector of the settlement, the orientation of grids being 17° east of the north. To study the stratigraphic relation with geological formations a test trench (2 m x 1 m) was dug veritically in the east of main excavated area.

The exposed area showed a heavy concentration of artefacts towards south and east, therefore, in 1982 the excavation was extended in both these directions. While in the southern direction 130 and in the eastern direction 20 more squares were added thus expoisng the artefact-bearing area in its entirety. But to mark definately the limits of the occupation area two eastern squares (I and J) were extended towards north covering an area of 24 squares metres. Similarly 2 more squares in the south and 6 squares in the west were further exposed. Thus 284 squares meter area of the total occupation area (660 sq. m) was exposed.

The stratigraphy of the site is as under:—Layer 1 with an average thickness of 35 cm is a sandy clay loam of orange colour whose upper portion is disturbed by ploughing. Layer 2 with an average thickness of 20 cm is a greyish brown clay. Layer 3 composed of dark clay loam varies from 7 to 10 cm in thickness. This layer is the artefact-bearing horizon, the overlying layers being devoid of any *in situ* artefact. A close study of the stratigraphy of the index trench by Williams, Royce and Clarke indicates that the artefact-bearing horizon is a part of Baghor formation ascribable to the Upper Pleistocene period.

The exposed occupation surface showed some interesting features. In the heavily concentrated artefact area huge number of nodules, cores, flakes, blades and debitage were accumulated along with finished and semi-finished tools. Mostly on the periphery, hammer stones and anvils have been found along with chert nodules, cores, flakes and blades. Evidently these were the actual tool-manufacturing spots. In the whole area of occupation there were spread of sand stone rubbles. Some of the flat stones were marked with rubbed surface, possibly due to their use as lower grinding stones.

Main raw material for manufacturing the artefacts is chert, although pieces of chalcedony and agate are also found. One interesting thing is that the nodules are heat-treated before manufacturing is started. This is evident by the occurrence of heat spalled nodules, cores, flakes, blades, and even finished tools. The nearest rich source for the raw material is the river bed of the Son. Experiment of heat treatment of chert nodules, collected from Son, surprisingly showed that original cortex colour (yellowish) turned into reddish colour resembling very much the artefacts obtained from excavation at Baghor I.

The artefacts recovered from excavation are divided into three main groups: a. unmodified waste, b. modified waste and tools (Fig. 2). A detailed analysis of the artefacts is still in progress. and the final report, when published will furnish a complete quantitative analysis of the composition of an Indian Final Upper Palaeolithic assemblage. However, the frequency of the arte-

Fig. 1

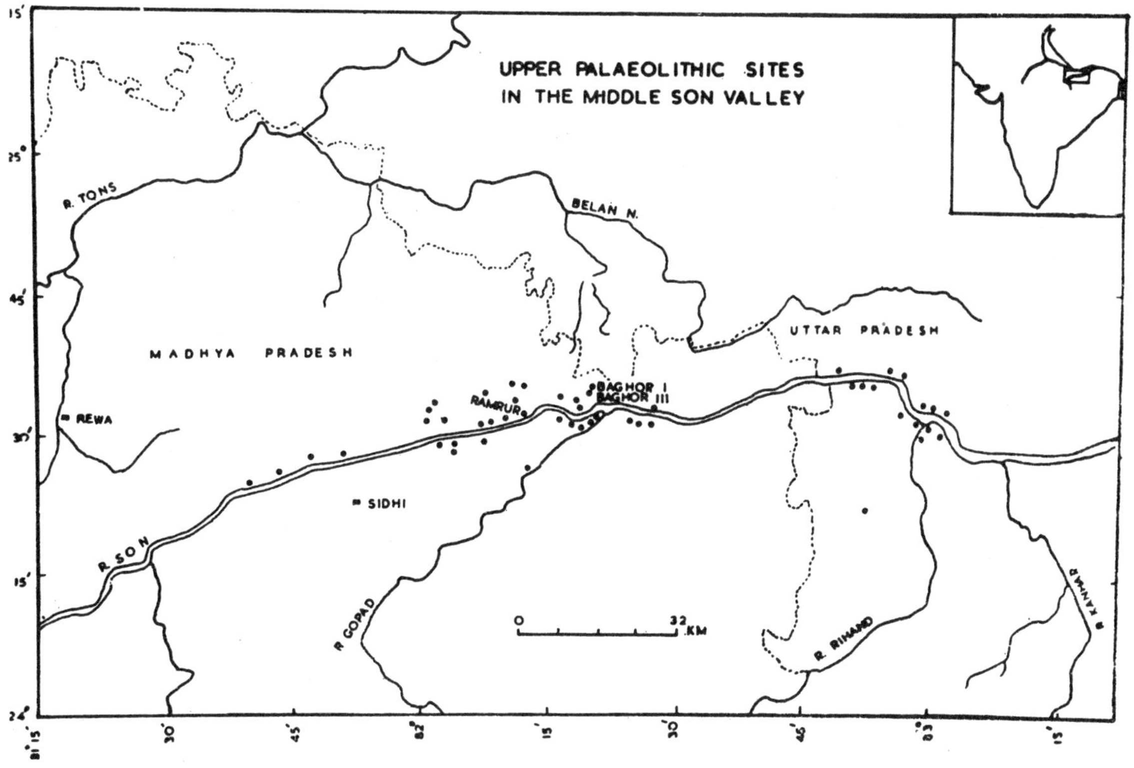

fact types for the time being, can be guessed, on the basis of the yield of two grids—1-9 and 1-10 (2 x 1 m). The unmodified waste (98.85), includes flakes with cortex (70/2), flakes without cortex (78), flake fragments with cortex (1672/57), flake fragments without cortex (2460/60), blades with cortex (23), blades wihout cortex (447), blade fragments wtih cortex (51), blade fragments without cortex (177/13), core rejuvinating flakes with cortex (II), core rejuvinating flakes without cortex (17/1), core trimming flakes with cortex (47/1), core trimming flakes without cortex (25/2), chunks with/without cortex (107), poor quality chert/siltstone pieces (144), heat spalled pieces (246), single platform core (5) and double platform core (1).

The modified waste (0.18%) consists of modified/edge damaged blades (9) and hammerstone (1). But from other squares modified flakes/flake fragments, modified chunks, choppers, bored stone, lower grinding stones, etc. also have been found.

The finished tools (0.97%) include straight backed blades/blade fragments (19), scalene triangles (3), partly backed blades (2), straight backed and truncated blades (11), convex backed and truncated blades (4), partly backed and truncated blades (2), truncated blade (1) backed and

Fig. 2
Tools from Baghor I

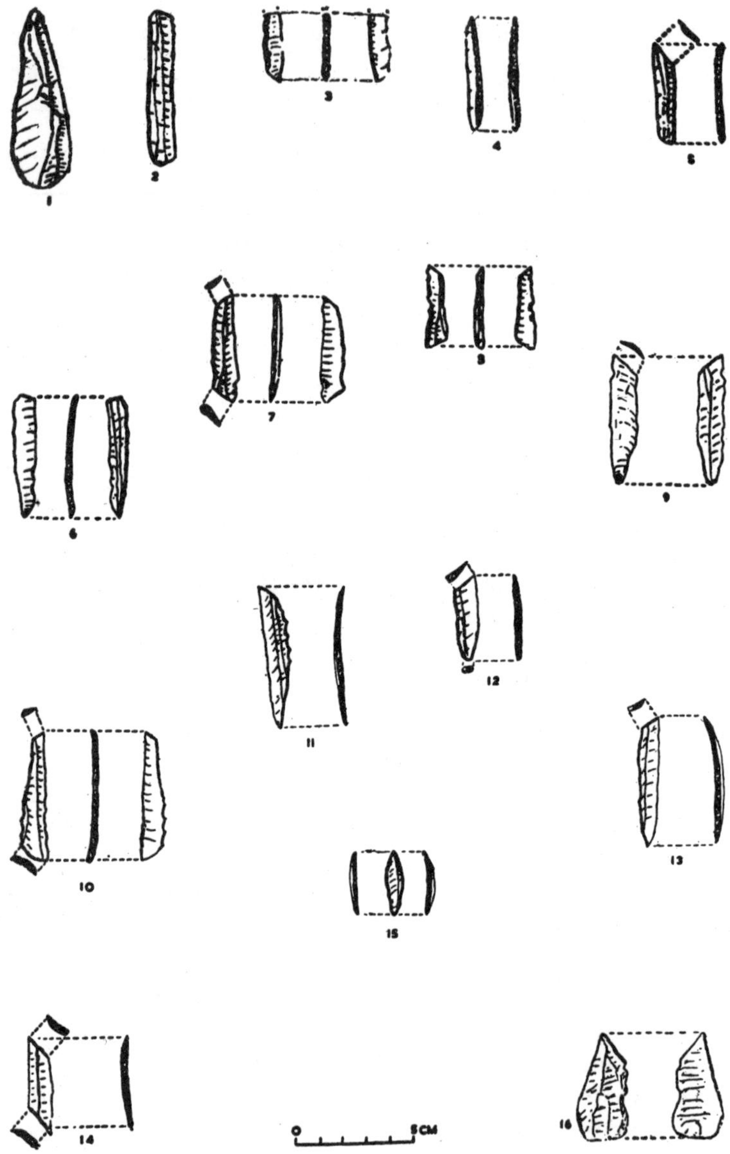

denticulated blades (2), blade with ouchtata retouch (2), blade with normal retouch (1), blade with inverse retouch (1), flake fragment with normal retouch (1), side scraper (1), transverse scraper cum bec (1). The tools recovered from other squares are convex backed blades, double backed blades, half backed and half denticulated blades, denticulated blades, denticulated blades with distal truncation double truncation, trapeze, parallelogram, drill, percoir, end scraper, convex side scraper, round and double side scraper, etc.

The excavation has revealed interesting evidence of conjoining the blades/flakes with respective cores. There are many finished tools which are so similar that, they demonstrately show that these were removed from one and the same core by similar technique using equal force of percussion.

One of the most important finds of the 1982 excavation was the discovery of a probable shrine of mother goddess at the fag-end of excavation. In squares I-9 and I-10 (2 x 1 m), as in other squares, tool manufacturing waste-flakes, flake fragments, blades, blade fragments, cores, nodules, etc. with some shaped tools and sandstone rubbles were exposed. After lifting the exposed artefacts we began removing the underlying debitage and encountered numerous pieces of sand stone rubble interspersed with numerous artefacts, which were left *in situ* for plotting. After lifting the chert artefacts we discovered that sandstone rubble formed roughly a circular platform about 85 cm in diameter. In the centre of this platform was fragment of a natural, ferruginous laminated stone, the colour of which ranges from light yellowish red to dark reddish brown. Additional fragments of the same stone were found lying next to the first fragment and two pieces were found on the periphery of the platform while one fragment was 90 cm to the south of the centre of the platform. So far ten fragments have been found and they all join together to form a triangular shaped natural stone — 15 cm high, 6.5 cm wide and about 6.5 cm thick.

As seven fragments of the central part of this stone were found in the centre of the platform, it can be said that the complete stone was placed, originally, in this central) position. Being very weak in physical structure due to lamination the stone got cracked, broke apart and thus scattering on the platform.

It is interesting to note that the present tribal inhabitants of the area, specially the Kols and Baigas worship this type of colourful natural stones with concentric laminations as the mother-goddess. The central position of the stone on the platform, its striking similarity to the sones worshipped at Kerai-ki-devi and in the shrine below a Neem tree in Merhauli village and other such shrines in the area and the immediate and spontanious recognition of its significance by the local inhabitants all indicate that there is very strong probability that this structure and the triangular stone represent a shrine of the mother goddess.

In the absence of radiocarbon dates and other datable material, the chronology of the Upper Palaeolithic culture of the mid Son valley is not fixed. But in the Belan valley, north of the Son valley some radiocarbon dates are available from the Upper Palaeolithic horizon. Cemented Gravel III of the Belam has yielded two 14C dates reading 23840±430 B.C (PRL 86) and 17765± 340 B.C. Cemented gravel IV, of the Belan which is associated with Late Upper Palaeolithic implements has provided four 14C dates B.C. (PRL 602) 3395 + 110 B.C.aETAOINTAOT reading 12190 ± 410 B.C. (PRD 603), and 8080±115 B.C. (SUA). On the basis of these dates a time bracket ranging from 30,000 B.C. to 10,000 B.C. may be proposed for the Upper Palaeolithic cultures of the Belan valley. Almost the same time bracket may be suggested for the Upper Palaeolithic culture of the mid Son valley.

REFERENCES

Allchin, B and Gaudie, A. 1971, Dunes, Aridity and Early Man in Gujarat, Western India *Man*, Vol. 6, pp. 248—265.

Clark, J.D. and Richard, P. 1982, in *Palaeoenvironment and Prehistory of the Middle Son Valley*, (eds) Sharma G.R. and Clark, J.D., Allahabad.

Ghosh, A.K. 1970, The Palaeolithic Cultures of Singhbhum, *Transactions of the American Philosophic Society*, new series, Vol. 60, Part I; pp. 1—63.

Kenoyer, J.M., Misra, V.D., Mandal, D. and Pal. J.N., 1982, Preliminary Report on Excavation at the Late Upper Palaeolithic site of Boghor I, *Palaeo Environment and Prehistory of the Middle Son Valley*, (eds) Sharma, G.R. and Clark, J. Desmond, Allahabad.

Misra, V.N., Mathpal. Y. and Nagar, M. 1977 *Bhimbetka, Prehistoric Man and his Art in Central India*, Pune.

Misra, V.D. 1977, *Some Aspects of Indian Archaeology*; Allahabad.

Misra, V.D., *et al.* 1982 Rampura—a late Upper Palaeolithic Surface site, in *Paleoenvironments and Prehistory of the Middle Son Valley,* (eds). Sharma, G.R. and Clark, J.D., Allahabad.

Murty, M.L.K. 1968, Blade and Burin Industry near Renigunta on the Southern Coast of India, *Proceedings of the Prehistoric Society,* Vol 28, pp. 83—101.

1970, Blade and Burin and Late Stone Age Industries around Renigunta, Chittor district, Indian Antiquary, Vol. 4, No. 1—4, pp. 106—128.

1974, A Late Pleistocene cave site in southern India, *Proceedings of the American Philosophical Society,* Vol. 118, no. 2, pp. 196—230.

Nisar Ahmad, 1966, The Stone Age Cultures of the Upper Son Valley, unpublished Ph.D. Thesis Poona, pp. 127-28, pl LVI, fig 34; quoted by Sankalia, H.D. in *Prehsitory and Protohistory of India and Pakistan.*

Paddayyan, K. 1970, The Blade Tool Industry of the Shorapur Doab, Peninsular India *Indian Antiquary,* (n.s.) Vol. 4 nos. 1—4, pp. 165—190.

Reddy, K.T. 1970, Vemula Industry in Cudapa Basin, *Indian Antiquary,* Vol. 4, (Nos. 1—4, pp. 227—234).

Sali, S.A. 1974, Upper Palaeolithic Research since Independence, *Bulletin of the Deccan College Research Institute,* Vol. 34, no. 1—4.

Sankalia, H.D. 1974, *Prehistory and Protohistory of India and Pakistan,* Pune.

Sharma, G.R. 1973, Stone Age in the Vindhyas and the Ganga valley, *Radio-carbon and Indian Archaeology,* (eds). Agrawal. D.P. and Ghosh, A., Bombay.

Varma, R.K. and Pal, J.N. nd. The Upper Palaeolithic Cultures of the Vindhyan reg.on, Paper read in the annual conference of IAS and ISPQS at Allahabad in 1980.

William, M. and Clarke, M.F. nd, Quaternary Stratigraphy and Prhistoric Environments in the Belan and Son valley.

William, M. and Keith, R. 1982, Alluvial History of the middle Son valley, North Central India, *Palaeo-environments and Prehistory in the middle Son valley, Madhya Pradesh, North Central India,* (eds). Sharma, G.R. and Clark, J. Desmond, Allahabad.

Animal Bones From Gufkral-Evidence of Human and Non-Human Activities

BY A.K. SHARMA,
Archaeological Survey of India.

Excavations were conducted at Gufkral (J.&K.) Lat. 35°54′N, Long. 75° 60′ E, by the Prehistory Branch of Archaeological Survey of India in 1981 and 1982. The excavations have brought to light five periods of occupation—

Period IA— Aceramic Neolithic
Period IB— Early Neolithic
Period IC— Late Neolithic
Period II— Menhir Period
Period III— Historical Period

It has been clearly established that at Gufkral right from Aceramic Neolithic Period to Historical Period man has been substituting his diet by hunting and gathering of food alongwith cultivation of some cereals, like wheat, barley, pea, rice etc. In the beginning hunting-gathering diet dominated over cultivation. This was the result of easy availability of game animals, particularly the preferred game, like wild cattle, wild sheep and goat, Himalayan Ibex, red deer etc. Detailed analysis has revealed that during Aceramic Neolithic Period 'the kill' consisted of animals of all age and sex indicating that the assemblage belonged to purely hunted animals. But subsequently i.e. from Period IB onwards, animals butchered are mostly young ones with predominance of male, an evidence of herding.

During the Neolithic Period due to the climatic conditions and high latitude and altitude of the area, when cultivation of cereal grains had just started and probably there was not sufficient open field for extensive cultivation, hunting naturally became an important element in their diet. Moreover, in this part of the country supply of available plant food was neither regular throughout the year nor reliable. The process got reversed after enough land was available for cultivation and herding and stock raising became a regular and reliable source of food. As compared to hunting, in plant food expliotation and stock raising low risk was involved. In fact during mature and late Neolithic Periods the emphasis shifted from mostly dependence upon wild mammals to domesticated mammals and plants.

During hunting, slaughtering and consumption, man leaves various marks on the animal bones. Similarly after the dismembering of the parts of the kill and after meals, the refuse left by man is subsequently scavenged by scavengers like dogs and at times wolves. Fragments of bones recovered from the garbage of settlements mostly contain the modifications brought about by human and non-human agencies. In case of scavengers teeth are the implements that have created modifications on the scavenging material. In this short paper an attempt has been made to identify such modifications and their probable cause on the animal bones recovered from two seasons of excavations at Gufkral. Bones from all the five periods examined have revealed some very interesting details.

Human activity:—

During human activity the following modifications in bones are likely to occur:—

I. Butchering marks (cutting and breakage)

II. Skinning marks.

III. Marks produced during dismembering of parts (chopping).

IV. Filleting marks.

V Marks produced due to human gnawing.

During Neolithic Period the tools used for the above works were mostly stone tools and bone tools .Relatively green bones were fractured and shaped into such tools that could have performed one or more jobs like hunting, piercing, butchering skinning and perforating for marrow. Such multipurpose tools have been found in large numbers from the excavations at Gufkral. Stone tools like polished axes and adzes were generally employed for butchering and cutting.

I. *Butchering marks*:— (Fig. 1 —4, 14, 20)

During butchering a hunted or captive animal, marks are produced as a result of cutting and chopping. Butchering marks generally occur at the same location on the bone, specimen after speciman. Nature of these marks also depend on the nature of tools used. Cut marks made as a

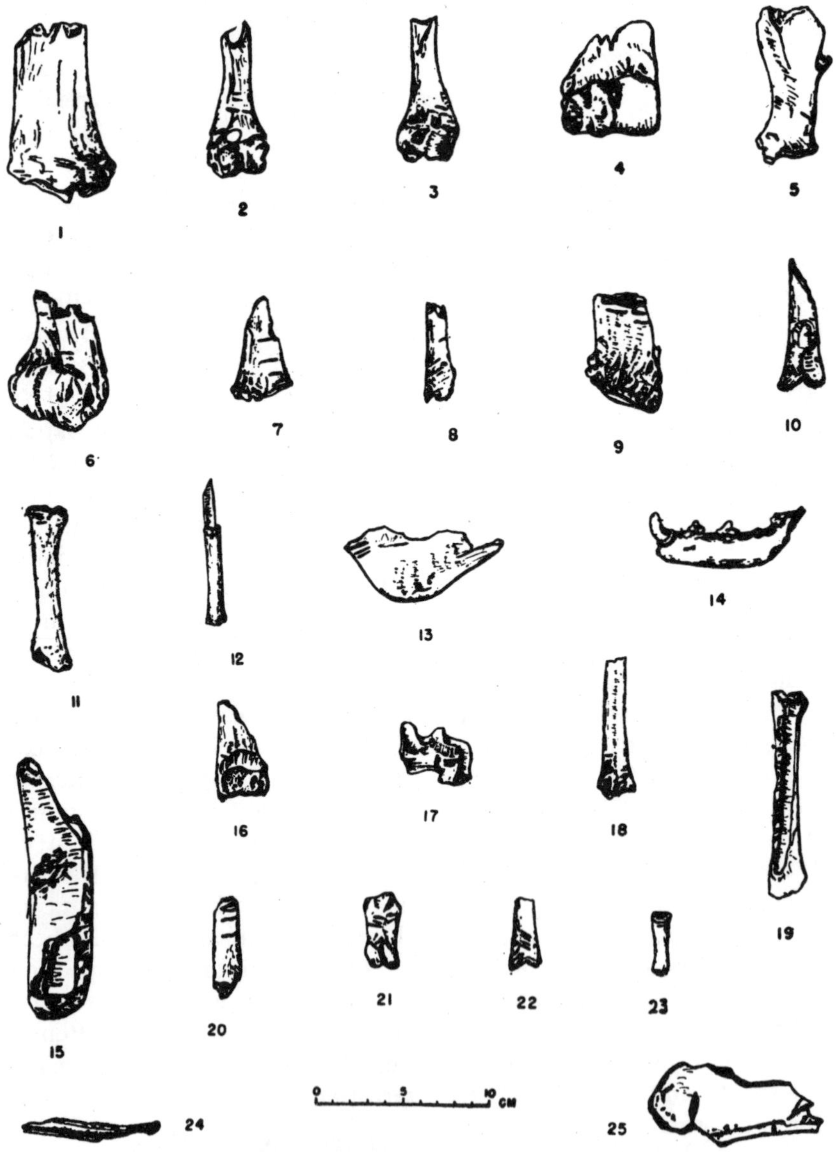

Fig. 1 : Cut marks on animal bones.

result of use of metal tools are very thin, almost hairline in size and are generally long and obliquely placed, leaving an overlapping small 'shelf' of bone. Marks from stone tools are generally short and occur in groups of parallel marks and have rugged appearance and do not appear through the contours of the bone as the pressure with which stone tools are used is not great.

Butchering marks generally occur at the points of the joints. In the specimen from Gufkral a large number of distal ends of humerus have been found to have transverse cut marks across the lower part of the coronoid fossa and the obecranon fossa. They are generally common on the obecranon, mostly running across the process. These marks also occur on the mandibles, antler bases and scapula.

1. *Distal end of humerus of Bos* (XD4, Qd1, Layer 6): showing transverse cut marks across coronoid fossa on anterior surface, caused during the process of dismembering. (Fig. 1-4)

2. *Ventral view of right half of mandible of wild dog* (XD1, Qd1, Layer 8) showing vertical deep cut mark on canine tooth. Probably caused while butchering (Fig. 1-14)

3. *Dorsal surface of rib of goat* (XD1, Qd1, Layer 6): showing vertical cut marks produced while butchering. (Fig. 1-20)

II. *Skinning marks*:— (Fig. 1-9, 17, 18, 21, 23)

Cut marks resulting due to skinning process generally encircle a bone at a particular point. Such marks have been noticed on the shafts of upper and lower limb bones like tibia, shaft of metatarsals, phalanges and tail bones. Skinning marks could also be observed on the skull, particularly around the base of the antler, horns and around the mandibles. If the skin is to be used as clothing then careful skinning marks are found around the phalanges, antlers and chin area of mandible.

1. *Base of antler of Himalayan Ibex* (XM2, Qd2, Layer 2): showing deep cut marks. One of the marks is just at the base where as others, more deep and encircling the antler are a little above the base. They are indicative of skinning process and have been caused with a metal tool as is evident from the fact that they are quite deep, running along the contours of the antler and small 'shelf' of bone have chipped off. (Fig. 1-9)

2. *Navicular cuboid of cattle* (XD3, Qd1, Layer 7): showing transverse sharp cut marks across anterior and lateral face caused during dismembering or skinning. The marks cover almost half of the circumference of the bone. The marks have been caused by sharp stone tools like celts. (Fig. 1-17, PI.—I.

3. *First phalanx of capra* (XD1, Qd1, Layer 8): showing transverse sharp cut marks near the distal end on the anterior surface. These cuts have been derived during the process of skinning. Normally such marks are caused on the phalanges when great care is taken to skin out the foot, particularly for obtaining skin from which covering for foot can be made .

4. *Proximal half of metatarsal of capra of tender age* (YD1, Qd2, Layer 9): showing transverse cut marks on the margin of lateral face as a result of skinning activity. (Fig. 1-18)

5. *Second phalanx of capra* (XM2, Qd2, Layer 3): showing horizontal and oblique cut marks both on ventral and dorsal surface, caused as a result of skinning process. Marks are short and deep and it is evident that they have been caused by stone tool such as celt. (Fig. 1-21)

6. *Coccygeal vertebra of goat* (XD4, Qd1, Layer 5): showing a series of deep cut marks on the dorsal surface of the proximal end. Four parallel cut marke of varying length are indicative of skinning activity. They have been caused by a sharp stone tool like celt. (Fig. 1-23, PI. II)

7. *First phalanx of capra* (XD2, Qd2, Layer 8): showing large number of slightly oblique transverse cut marks above the dorsal surface, caused as a result of skinning. The bone has also been severely gnawed by the scavenging animal due to which on the left side towards the ventral surface crenulated edge has been produced and linear close scoring marks could also be seen, produced due to dragging of the teeth across the compact tissue. While gnawing, the bone has also been fractured almost longitudinally in order to obtain marrow. It is apparent that the scavenging animal (dog, wolf, etc.) feasted on it as soon as it was thrown after man has consumed the flesh.

III. *Dismembering marks*:— (Fig. 1-1,2,3,5,6, 11.13.22 25,)

Since dismembering of parts involves disarti

culation cut marks are generally found near points of articulation, such as removal of the head from the neck and mandible from the skull. If the mandible is not dismembered immediately after death, later on it requires serval strokes to seperate it as the carcass becomes more rigid and as a result, more cut marks are observed on such bones.

Other parts that possess dismemberment marks are vertebrae, ribs, sternum, pelvis, sacrum, femur, tibia, tarsals, metatarsals, scapula, humerus, radio-ulna, carpals, metacarpals and phalanges.

1. *Proximal part of radius of Bos* (YD1, Qd1, Layar 4): showing transverse cut marks on the dorsal margin of radial tuberosities produced while dismembering the parts. As dismemberment consists of disarticulation cut marks are associated with points of articulation. That these were produced as a result of dismembering process is clear as they occur on the articular surfaces, on the end of the long bones. These marks show characteristic features of those produced by stone tools as they do not follow the contours of the bone and occur in groups of parallel marks unlike those produced by metal tools which are generally very thin and long and leave an overlapping small 'shelf' on bone that remain in place. (Fig. 1-1, PI.III)

2. *Distal part of humerus of red deer* (YD5, Qd3, Layer 5): obliquely oriented vertical cut marks above and across the corono'd fossa on ventral surface. Marks produced while dismembering. Congential perforation has been caused in the region of obecranon fossa through coronoid fossa. Thin bony membrane between the two fossae has totally disappeared. This modification in this region of the humerus is generally caused as a result of excessive use of the forearms in hazardous conditions like running and jumping fast. (Fig. 1-2).

3. *Distal part of humerus of dog* (XD3, Qd1, Layer 7): showing horizontal cut marks between lateral supra condylar ridge and radial fossa. These marks appear to have been caused during dismemberment process. On the lateral supra condylar ridge *scoring* marks are clearly visible. These scoring marks have been caused as a result of dragging the teeth across relatively compact bone by gnawing animal. (Fig. 1-3)

4. *Iliac bone of dog* (XM2, Qd2, Layer 3): ventral view showing a deep cut mark near iliac crest and three cut marks on tuber coxae reg.on produced during dismemberment. (Fig. 1-25)

5. *Scapula of sheep* (XD4, Qd2, Layer 5): oblique transverse marks on the neck of scapula produced during dismemberment. (Fig. 1-5)

6. *Distal end of humerus of Bos* (XD1, Qd4, Layer 7): showing cut marks on anterior, medial and lateral surfaces along and around the coronoid fossa, caused during dismembering the parts. (Fig. 1-6)

7. *Distal end of left humerus of Bos* (XD2, Qd2, Layer 3): showing horizontal cut marks across the coronoid and radial fossa as well as on the medial surface caused during dismembering or filleting.

8. *Radius of capra* (XD5, Qd2, Layer 7): showing transverse cut marks on anterior margin of radial tuberosity caused during dismembering. (Fig. 1-11)

9. *Lateral view of mandible of sheep* (XM2, Qd2, Layer 2): Transverse cut marks on the inferior surface of the mandipular condyle. Produced by stone tools while dismembering it from the rest of the skull. (Fig. 1-13)

10. *Proximal end of tibia of an young capra without the condyles* (YD1, Qd2, Layer 2): showing oblique cut marks on the lateral surface, caused during dismembering. (Fig. 1-22)

IV. *Filleting:*—(Fig. 1-7,12,15,16,24)

Filleting is the process associated with dismembering when the dismembered parts are further segmented for storage and/or for finally preparing the kill for consumption. In this process the appendages are removed from the long bones etc. So that it becomes easier to remove meat from the parts. Filleting marks are mostly longitudionally oriented on the bones on which they are caused so that the bone could be easily pulled free from the meat and could be served from muscle attachments. Filleting process produces only superficial scratch marks unlike deep cut marks produced butchering or skinning. They are generally inclusters on irregularly shaped bones like radio-cubitus, lateral side of the tibial crest etc.

1. *Proximal parts of radius of Bos* (XD4, Qd1, Layar 7): showing transverse marks on the dorsal surface near proximal extremity. The marks

are produced in the process of disarticulation of parts during secondary butchering action. On the ventral surface of the radial tuburosity gnawing marks could also be seen.

2. *Proximal part of radius of capra* (XD2, Qd2, Layer 6): showing transverse cut marks on the shaft region below the tuberosities produced due to filleting. (Fig. 1-7, PI. IV)

3. *Distal half of radius of capra of tender age* (XD2, Qd1, Layer 3): showing cut marks almost in the centre of the shaft region produced as a result of secondary butchering or filleting.

4. *Distal half or radius of fowl* (XD1, Qd1, Layer 2): showing cut marks in the centre of the shaft produced while filleting or preparing for the meal. (Fig. 1-12)

5. *Shaft fragment of long bone of cattle* (XD5, Qd3, Layer 2): ventral surface shows deep cut marks from where chipping has also taken place as a result of filleting. These appear to have been caused as a result of percussion impact at the time of preparing kill for consumption or storage. These marks are the results of use of sharp me al tool, as the cuts are deep, sharp and oblique allowing chips of bone to flake out. The ventral surface of the shaft is also pitted and scured by animal teeth. (Fig. 1-15)

6. *Distal part of humerus of capra* (XD1, Qd1, Layer 8): showing marks all along the portion particularly on the medial supra condylar ridge. As a result of sharp cut, major portion of trochlea, capitulum and lateral epicondyle have been chopped off. These are caused during the process of secondary butchering while making it ready for cooking or roasting. (Fig. 1-16)

7. *Shaft of long bone of fowl* (XD,2 Qd2, Layer 5): Distinct cut marks as a result of filleting. (Fig. 1-24)

8. *Spinous process of thoracic vertebra of ibex* XD1, Qd1, Layer 8): displaying longitudional cuts on the dorsal surface near the apex. The cuts are as a result of filleting during preparation for roasting.

9. *Fragment of rib* (XD3, Qd1, Layer 9): showing vertical cut marks produced while secondary butchering.

10. *Shaft fragment of long bone of red deer* (XD3, Qd2, Layer 8): exhibiting a series of cutmarks on the lateral surface as a result of filleting. Due to the heavey blow of the stone celt a portion of bone has also chipped off. The fragment also contains several tooth marks which were caused apparantly when the bone was gnawed in green condition.

V. *Gnawing and breaking for marrow:—*

During consumption, like animals man is also required to gnaw and break the bones in order to obtain marrow. In case of man it is always the green bones that is subjected to this process. The bones cracked by man do not show crenulated edges as in case of *animal cracked bones*. The marrow containing bones are hit in mid shaft and generally exhibit spiral fracture with angular profile.

NON-HUMAN ACTIVITY

1. *Tooth marks:—*

While feasting on the thrown parts, scavenging animal like dogs and wolves leave various marks on the scavenged materials. As these animals main implements are the teeth, we do get various kinds of modifications on bones produced by teeth. Almost all the skeletal parts are scavenged and they bear varying degree of modifications depending on their hardness. Teeth produce (a) punctures (b) pits (c) scares and (d) furrows

a) *Punctures:—*When the animal starts gnawing, due to impact of tooth ,a portion of the bone collapses leaving impression of the tooth (P1. V). In case of thin bones the tooth pressure makes holes in cancellous bone and at times creates crenulated edges (P1. VI). Gnawing proceeds from soft to hard bone.

b) *Pitting:*— When the bone being gnawed is harder, it will not collapse and instead exhibit only shallow depressions in the form of pitted surface (P1. VII).

c) *Scoring:*— When relatively compact bone is gnawed by turning it round, the surface of the bones get scarred, exhibiting lineal marks normally following the contours of the bone. These marks are generally transverse to the long axis of bones. (P1. VIII)

d) Furrowing:— Furrowings are generally results of leasure chewing of bones by dogs etc. They show repeated jaw action and produce undulations on the harder surface after removing softer tissue (P1. IX)

Apart from these, there are other modifications caused by animals on the bones. Animals first attack ends of long bones as it is easier to chew away the soft articular ends and reach the medullary cavity (P1. X). They also crack the bone shaft with their strong teeth. In an attempt to reach marrow, they often produce channeled breakages. The process of excessive gnawing may result in pitted and scarred bones, bones with chipped edges, bones with highly polished and rounded edges giving impression of 'pseudo-tools'. Soft bones like scapula produce crenulated edges as a result of gnawing.

Apart from these, there are other factors like trampling, variations in pressure and temperature etc. that cause modifications in the bones.

e) *Pathological modifications:*—At times modifications in bones in the form of outgrowths,perforations, twisting etc. may take place as a result of accidents, malnutrition,and hazardous conditions of life. Such cases have been noticed in some bones from the site. A case of congenital perforation has been described in example 2 under dismembering.

1. *Second phalanx of capra* (XD2, Qd2, Layer 5): showing two bony outgrowths, one on the dorsal surface and another, a minor one, on left lateral surface. These craggy mass of bony outgrowths are pathological abnormalities which might have been caused due to some severe injury. The outgrowths indicate that the injury was not fatal and the bony parts of the individual were still in the process of growth. These bony outgrowths resulted in growth of fibrous bands of hallucis and brevis muscles around the outgrowths .As the growth on the dorsal surface is quite big it might have caused some difficulty for the animal to walk and the sheep/goat might have limped. (P1.XI)

2. *Femur of a bird* (YD1, Qd2, Layer 6): The left lateral surface shows two distinct tiny bony outgrowths on the outer margin of the shaft. These outgrowths are pathological abnormalities which might have been caused due to some injury when the bony parts were still in the process of growth. These outgrowths would have hardly caused any inconvinience to the owner except little pain. (P1. 11B)

ACKNOWLEDGEMENT

I am deeply thankful to the Directorate and to Dr. K.D. Banerjee for providing all the facilities to complete my observations.. I am thankful to Shri A.S. Stevenson who worked hard ungrudgingly at the site. My thanks are due to Shri J.S. Dubey for the line drawings and to Shri Pyara Singh for the excellent photographs. For the final type script I am thankful to Ku. Jayashree Baokar. Photographs are by the courtesy of the Archaeological Survey of India.

REFERENCES

Binford, L.R. 1981, *Bones: Ancient and Modern Myths*, New York.

Cornwall, I.W. 1956, *Bones for the Archaeologist*, London.

Foley, Robert 1982, A reconsideration of the role of predation on large mammals in tropical hunter-gatherer adoptation., *Man*, Vol. 17, No. 3; pp. 393—402, London.

Hesse, Brian 1982, Slaughter patterns and domestification: The beginning of pastoralism in Western Iran, *Man*, Vol. 17, No. 3; pp. 403—417, London.

Issac, G.L. 1978, The food-sharing behaviour of protohuman hominids. *Scientific American* 288, pp. 90—109.

Jones, P.R. 1980, Experimental butchery with modern stone tools and its relevance for Palaeolithic archaeology, *World* Archaeology 12(2). pp. 153—165.

Sisson, S. 1967, *The anatomy of the domestic animals*, Tokyo.

Wells, Calvin 1964, *Bones Bodies and Diseases*, London

Significance of Animal Fossils in the Prehistoric studies of the Upper Mahanadi Valley, Central India

R.P. PANDEY
Deccan College, Pune

INTRODUCTION

Palaeontological studies of the Quaternary period are of great importance. The significance of these studies increases when the fossils are found in association with archaeological material in the stratigraphical context. Although the fossil evidences were recorded from the Siwaliks (Falconer and Cautley 1849) and Narmada (Princep 1832:466-468) in the thirties of the last century these were effectively correlated with the archaeological remains in the stratigraphic context perhaps for the first time by De Terra and Paterson (1939) in different parts of India. This team not only recorded the discoveries but also tried to build up a comprehensive history of the palaeoenvironment. After this classic work several river valleys of peninsular India were explored from the similar point of view and many of them have yielded palaeontological remains along with archaeological material in the stratified deposits.

The major peninsular rivers like the Narmada (Khatri 1966; Supekar 1968; Badam 1976 and Joshi *et al* 1978), the Godavari (Joshi *et al* 1966; Rajaguru 1972; Corvinus *et al* 1973 and Joshi *et al* 1980) have been explored and have yielded stone Age material along with animal fossils. Some tributaries of Godavari such as the Ghod (Kajale 1978) and Manjra (Joshi *et al* 1981:67-94 and Badam 1980) have recently given rich palaeontological and archaeological remains. The Krishna Valley however, needs intensive studies. Though the Stone Age sites in this valley are numerous (Joshi 1955 and Pappu 1974), the fossiliferous sites associated with cultural material are only few and are Hagargundi (Paddayya 1969:12-14), Nittur (Ansari 1970:1-7), and Dhond (Corvinus *et al* 1972/73:53-69). Recently some plant fossils with Middle Palaeolithic tools have been discovered at Wajjal, in district Gulbarga (Korisettar *et al.* 1976/77:62-65). Besides these major peninsular rivers some northerly flowing rivers of M.P. and U.P. like Son (Sharma 1980) and Belan valleys (Dassarma and Biswas 1976) have been brought to light for the rich archaeological and faunal wealth.

Apart from these river valleys, several caves have been unearthed in the Kurnool area, Andhra Pradesh. These caves have yielded varieties of Pleistocene faunal remains of mammals, asses, reptiles, amphibians and stone tools (Foote 1884: 200-208, Cammeade 1927:1-12 and Murty 1974: 196-230 and 1975:132-138). The fossils found during the explorations of the upper Mahanadi by the writer provide further information not only on the ancient fauna but to some extent also on the palaeo-environment (Pandey 1978, 1980-1981 and 1982, Joshi *et al* 1980:47-64).

The Mahanadi is one of the largest rivers of peninsular India and after traversing various landforms in parts of Madhya Pradesh and Orissa, debouches into the Bay of Bengal near Cuttack on Orissa coast. The river flows between two great peninsular rivers: Narmada and Godavari and is fed by several smaller rivers. The important among them are the Seonath, the Hasdo and the Jonk. The region experiences typcial monsoonal rainfall and can be classed as sub-humid (Thornthwaite 1933:433-40).

SITES AND STRATIGRAPHY

The faunal material of vertebrate and invertebrate fossils has been discovered from the Seonath river, a major tributary of the Mahanadi. The animal fossils have been found from the four localities: Nandghat (Bilaspur), Simga (Raipur), Somnath (Raipur) and Rajnandgaon (Rajnandgaon). while the fresh water molluscus have been traced only at Simga. The animal fossils come from the basal gravel (Pebble conglomerate) stratigrphically lying below almost at the present river level. These gravels unconformably rest over the shale rock and composed of bigger pebbles of shale, quartzite and silica group of minerals. This horizon in the valley has also yielded Middle Palaeolithic tools and fossils. The molluscan shells have been collected over the pebbly gravel (gravel II) stratigraphically lying over the previous gravel (gravel I). They lie over the banks about 3-4 m above the present river bed and are composed of comparatively smaller pebbles than the gravel I. This gravel yields freshwater molluscan shells along with Upper Palaeolithic tools Due to long exposure and continuous rains, gullies have been formed over these gravels and sometimes tools and molluscan shells could be picked up from the river bed also. In the present paper only the details of vertebrate palaeontology are given.

THE FAUNAL MATERIAL

The fossils in the Mahanadi have been collected from the lower gravel in the river bed alongwith the Middle Palaeolithic tools and sometimes they were found *in situ* especially at Nandghat and Simga. A few fossils in the collection have got some amount of rolling due to transportation for some distance and some have got thick cement coating over the enamels and the body of the teeth. Among all the sites, Nandghat has given the richest fossil evidence and the Simga is next in order. The sites namely Somnath and Rajnandgaon have yielded only a few specimens.

The faunal collection includes *Equus namadicus, Equus caballus, Equus asinus, Bos sp., Bos namadicus, Bos indicus, Bubalus bubalis* and *Ovis/Capra* in the form of isolated lower and upper teeth, vertebrae, astragalae, limb fragments and numerous unidentifiable parts. The site-wise distribution of the species is as follows:

SPECIES	LOCALITIES			
	Nandghat 20°01' N 81°48' E	Simga 21°37' N 81°42' E	Somnath 21°34' N 81°48' E	Rajnandgaon 21°06' N 81°02' E
Equus namadicus	+	—	—	—
Equus caballus	+	—	—	—
Equus asinus	+	—	—	—
Bos sp.	+	—	—	—
Bos namadicus	+	+	—	—
Bos indicus	+	+	+	—
Bubalus Bubalis	+	—	—	+
Ovis/Capra	+	—	—	—

The fossil elements found at different sites are listed in Table 1 and the measurements of Equdae and Bovidae are given in Tables 2 and 3

TABLE 1

C. No.	*Family*	*Species*	*Sites* Nandghat	Simga	Somnath	Rajnandgaon
	Equdae					
NDG—8		*Equus namadicus* (Right upper M_1)	+	—	—	—
NDG—1		*Equus caballus* (Left upper P_2)	+	—	—	—
NDG—2		(Left upper P_4)	+	—	—	—
		Equus asinus				
		(Right Lower P_4)	+	—	—	—
		(Left upper M_1)	+	—	—	—
	Bovidae					
		Bos sp.				
		(Right upper M3)	+	—	—	—
		(Part of theoraice vertebrae)	+	—	—	—
		Bos namadicus				
NDG—6		(Right upper M2)	+	—	—	—
		(Left upper M2)	—	+	—	—
		(Astragalus)	+	—	—	—
		Bos indicus				
NDG—4		(Right Lower M1/2	+	—	—	—
SMG—3		(Right Lower M2	—	+	—	—
SMG—10		(Right lower P3)	—	+	—	—
SMG—9		(Left Lower molar)	—	+	—	—
SMG—2		(Left lower M1/2)	—	+	—	—
SMG—1		(Left upper M1)	—	—	+	—
SMG—5		(Right upper M2)	—	+	—	—
NDJ		(Right upper M3)	+	—	—	—
		Bubalus bubalis				
RDN—2						
NDG—18		(Left lower M3)	+	—	—	+
NDG—12		(Left lower M1)	+	—	—	—
		Ovis/Capra				
NDG—14		(Right lower M3)	+	—	—	—

TABLE 2
Measurements in mm of the dentition of Equus sp.

No.	Species	Length	Breadth	Thickness	Prefossette	Postfossette	Protocone	Metaconlid	Metastylid
NDG—1 (LUP4)	Equus Caballus	26	25	55	11×5.5	10×6.5	11×5.5		
NDG—9 (LUP2)	Equus caballus	34	21	55	14×5	10.5×6	8×6		
NDG—8 (RUM_1)	Equus namadicus	22	23	35	11×5	9×5	9.5×5		
NDG—3 (LUM_1)	Equus asinus	20	21	34	9×4.5	8×5	10×5		
NDG—2 RLP4	Equus asinus	23	14	65	—	—	—	6×4	5×4

REMARKS ON THE FAUNA

Equdae:

This species has been represented by some isolated teeth of *Equus namadicus, Equus caballus* and *Equus asinus*. These are generally right and left molars and premolars and have been found only at Nandghat in the Mahanadi valley. Distribution of various horses from the different parts of India is given in Table 4.

A number of species of Equdae have been discribed from India. The most common among them are *Equus sivalensis* of Northwest India and the *Equus namadicus* from Narmada and other parts. The *Equus namadicus* was described by Falconer and Cautley (1849) from the upper Pleistocene level of Narmada. Mathew (1949) Colbert (1935) and Hooijer (1949) thought the Narmada and Siwalik species are the same and the Narmada species may be progressive form of the Siwalik horses. Except for the slight differences in the skull (skull of *Equus namadicus* is larger and broader) there are no morphological differences in the asteological parts. After the statistical study of the Pleistocene Equade, Badam (1979) supports the fact that the *Equus namadicus* may be a survival from the Siwaliks having migrated to the central Indian plains after a considerable lapse of time.

Bovidae:

The *Bos* is the most common species and comes from all the localities except Rajnandgaon in the valley. This is also the most prolific species in the Indian Pleistocene deposits. They are generally *Bos namadicus, Bos aculiforns* and *Bos indicus. Bos aculeforms* is reported from the early Pleistocene sediments in the Siwaliks. In the stone Age culture, there are reports of *Bos namadicus* from many sites (see Table 5). However, in the Mesolithic cultures generally *Bos indicus* have been found but at Langhnaj (mesolithic) and Mohenjodaro (chalcolithic). There are reports of *Bos namadicus* respectively by Clutton Brock (1965) and Sewell and Guha (1931 : 649-763) which indicate the large geological range of the species right from Pleistocene Holocene periods. At various sites such as Kalegaon, Nevasa (Sankalia 1952), this species has

TABLE 3

No.	*Species*	*Length*	*Breadth*	*Height*	*Prefosseette* L×B	*Postfossette* L×B
SMG—8 LUM2	Bos namadicus	33	23	49	11×5	10×5
NDG—6 RUM2	Bos namadicus	34.5	20	51	2	12.5×5
NDG—10 RUM3	Bos indicus	23.5	17	48	11×5.5	9×6
NDG—4 RLM1/2	Bos indicus	30	12	69	12.4.5	10.5×4
SMG—7 RUM2	Bos indicus	28	16	57	12×6	10.5×5
NDG—7 RUM3	Bos indicus	21.5	17	41	2	12×8.5
SMG—15 RUM2	Bos indicus	29	19	52	10×5	10×6
SMG—1 LUM1	Bos indicus	24	17	65	1	8×6
SMG—9 LLm	Bos indicus	29	12.5	62	10.5×2.5	12×3.5
SMG—3 RLM2	Bos indicus	26	15.5	45	9×2	8×2
SMG—10 RLP3	Bos indicus	18	11	39.5	?	?
NDG—5 RUM3	Bos sp.	32	21	58	12.5×7	10×6
RDG—15 LLM3	Bubalus bubalis	35	13	6.3.5	10×4	9×3
RDN—2 LLM3	Bubalus bubalis	35	12	61	11×4	11×5
NDG—12	Bubalus bubalis	18	16	30	9×3	9×3
NDG—14 RLM3	Ovis/Capra	20	7	39	6×2	6×3

been found in association with Middle Palaeolithic tools. This species is characterised by a broad forehead and sideward pointing of horns and a hump (Badam 1973:21-40) and has given rise to the living cattle of India *Bos indicus*.

Bubalus, found only at Nandghat and Rajnandgaon is represented by lesser bone material than the *Bos*. In many cases because of the isolated nature of the teeth, it cannot be distinguished from *Bos*. However, wherever the complete vertical ramus has been found, we can definitely assign the material to the species. In the early Pleistocene two species of Bubalus have been found namely *Bubalus palaindicus* and *Bubalus platyceros*. The former is supposed to have given rise to *Bubalus bubalis* which is the foundation of the domesticated form from various sites. Some scholars however, believe that it may be treated

TABLE 4

Age	Culture	Locality	Species	Remarks
LATE	Upper Palaeolithic	Kurnool (A.P.)	*Equus asinus* *Equus* sp.	*Equus* sp. has resemblance with those of Ghod valley
PLEISTOCEN	Middle Palaeolithic (M.S.A.)	Meshvo (Gujarat)	*Equus asinus*	
		Ghod valley near Inamgaon (Maharashtra)	*Equus* sp.	
		Nevasa (Maharashtra)	*Equus* sp.	*Equus palaeonus* is synonym of Equus namadicus
		Mula Valley near Khupti (Maharashtra)	*Equus* sp.	
		Susunia (U.P.)	*Equus namadicus*	
		Narmada (M.P.)	*Equus namadicus* *Equus palaeonus*	
MIDDLE	Lower Palaeolithic (E.S.A.)	Narmada (M.P.) Godavari (Maharashtra)	*E. namadicus* *E. palaeonus* *E. namadicus*	Equus sp. was found opposite Hathiwell section on river Pravara near Nevasa along with lower Palaeolithic and Middle Palaeolithic tools.
		Nevasa (Maharashtra)	*Equus* sp.	
		Ariyalur (Tamil Nadu)	*E. namadicus*	Ariyalur is a Middle Pleistocene site. No stone tools have been found here.
EARLY	No tools	Karewas (Kashmir) Siwaliks (Punjab)	*E. sivalensis* *Equus* sp. *E. sivalensis* *E. cautleyi*	No stone tools. *E. cautleyi* is considered synonymus with *E. sivalensis.*

only as a semi-domesticated form because of its frequent inbreeding with *Bos gourus.* A new species of *Bubalus* has recently been discovered from Maruvattoo in Tamil Nadu which has been named as *Bubalus maruvattoorensis* (Ghose *et al* 1972:97-102).

TABLE 5
DISTRIBUTION OF *BOS* AND *BUBALUS* SP IN INDIAN QUATERNARY DEPOSITS

Age	*Culture*	*Locality*	*Species*: *Bos*	*Species*: *Bubalus*	*Remarks*
Holocene	Mesolithic	Adamgarh (M.P.)	*Bos Indicus*	*Bubalus bubalis*	All the fossils except *Bos Namadicus* are domesticated. *Bos namadicus* has also been reported from excavations at Langhnaj (Clutton-Brock, 1965) and Mohenjodaro (Sawell and Guha, 1931)
		Bagor (Rajasthan)	*Bos Indicus*	*Bubalus bubalis*	
		Tilwara (Rajasthan)	*Bos indicus*	—	
		Langhnaj (Gujarat)	*Bos Indicus* *Bos namadicus*	*Bubalus bubalis*	
Late	Upper Palaeolithic	Kurnool caves (A.P.)	*Bos/Bubalus* sp.		
QUATERNARY PLEISTOCENE	Middle Palaeolithic	Paimar valley (Bihar)	*Bos* sp.	*Bubalus* sp.	The age of the sites is based faunal and cultural findings, however at Ariyalur only fauna has been taken into consideration for assigning the age of the site, since no tools have been recovered from Ariyalur
		Belan Valley (U.P.)	*Bos* sp.	*Bubalus* sp.	
		Narmada (M.P.)	*Bos Namadicus*	*Bubalus bubalis*	
		Godavari (Maharashtra)	*Bos* sp.	—	
		Pravara —	*Bos* sp. *Bos namadicus*	—	
		Mula Valley —	*Bos namadicus*	*Bubalus bubalis*	
		Purna —	*Bos namadicus*	—	
		Ghod Valley —	*Bos* sp. *Bos namadicus*	*Bubalus bubalis*	
		Manjra (A.P.)	*Bos namadicus*	*Bubalus bubalis*	
		Krishna (Karnataka)	*Bos* sp. *Bos namadicus*	-	
		Ariyalur (Tamil Nadu)	*Bos* sp.	*Bubalus Moruvatteorensis*	(no tools)

Contd. on next page

Contd. from pre-page

Age	*Culture*	*Locality*	*Species*		*Remarks*
Middle	Lower Palaeolithic	Narmada	*Bos namadicus*	*Bubalus palaindicus*	
		Godavari (Maharashtra)	*Bos* sp.	—	
			Bos namadicus		
		Pravara —	*Bos* sp.	—	
			Bos namadicus	—	
		Krishna (Karnataka)	*Bos namadicus*	—	
Early		Karewas (Kashmir)	*Bos* sp.		(no tools)
		Siwaliks (Punjab)	*Bos acutifrons*	*Bubalus platyceros*	
				Bubalus palaeindicus	

On the basis of some characters this species is much larger in form than the fossil *Bubalus palaeindicus* (Narmada and Godavari Valleys) and the present day ***Bubalus bubalis.*** It is, however, than smaller *Bubalus platyceros* (Upper Siwaliks) which is known to be much larger than the other known buffalos. This species is also much shorter than *Bos acutifros* (Middle and upper Siwaliks) and slightly less than those of *Bos namadicus* (Narmada and Deccan river valleys).

As regards sheep and goat, it is very difficult to precisely identify them in the absence of the skull. The relation of the sagittal sutures to the coronal sutures is very important in identifying the two species. In the present collection however, we have got only an isolated tooth, hence we have put it as *Ovis/Capra.*

The distribution of bouides upto the Mesolithic is given in the chart.

DISCUSSION

On the basis of cultural material of Palaeolithic and Mesolitic, it can definetely be said that the upper Mahanadi was a centre of early man right from Lower Palaeolithic to Mesolithic times.

The fosssils are useful in determining the approximate age of the associated cultures but their collection in the present case is very small. Taking into consideration the similar fossil evidences from Madhya Pradesh and Maharashtra, the fossils found in the Mahanadi indicate an Upper Pleistocene age. They are also well dated by a series of 14 C dates in Western India (Rajaguru and Hegde 1972:69-79). The recent investigations in the central Godavari have revealed the antiquity of Middle Palaeolithic cultures in the range of 40,000 years B P. Since no radiometric determination is yet possible for the Mahanadi valley, the absolute date of the cultures as well as the associated fossils cannot be precisely determined.

On the basis of this fossil assemblages, some deductions can be made about the climate and ecological conditions that prevailed at the Middle Palaeolithic stage. The cattle *(Bos, Bubalus, Ovis/Capra)* and horse *(Equus)* are indicative of a scrub type of vegetation of wooded grassland probably savannah forests and hard ground surrounding watersheets in the valley. Thus when the alluvial plain of the upper Mahanadi and the Seonath was covered with thick vegetation, varieties of animals must have roamed freely in the upper Mahanadi valley.

ACKNOWLEDGEMENT

The writer is grateful for the advice and encouragement received from Dr. G. L. Badam, Palaeontologist, Deccan College, Pune, in the studies of fossil material from the Mahanadi valley.

REFERENCES

Ansari, Z.D. 1970, Pebble tools from Nittoor, Mysore State *Indian Antiquary* 4 (1—4).

Badam, G.L. 1973, Pleistocene Fossil studies. *Bulletin of Deccan College Research Institute,* 33 (1—4).

* Badam, G.L. 1976 Quaternary palaeontology of the Central Narmada Valley and its implications in the Prehistoric Studies, call, on the *Palaeontological Studies in the Southern Region,* Geological Survey of India, Hyderabad.

Badam, G.L. 1980, Quaternary Faunal Remains from the Manjra valley, India Paper presented at the Seminar on Indian Prehistory, Allahabad.

Cammiade, L.A. 1927, Prehistoric Man in India Kurnool Bone caves. *Man in India* 7 (1).

Colbert, E.H. 1935, Siwalik mammals in the American Museum of Natural History. *Transections of American Philosophical Society* (NS) 26: 1—401.

Corvinus, G., S.N. Rajaguru and G.G. Mujumdar 1972/73, Some observations on the Quaternary of Western Maharashtra (India) Quarter 23/24.

Clutton Brock, J. 1965, Excavations at Langling: 1944—63, 2 The Fauna, Deccan College Ser 27.

De Terra, H and T.T. Paterson 1939, *Studies on the Ice-Age in India and Associated Human Cultures* Washington: Carnegie Institution of Washington.

Dassarma D.C. and S. Biswas 1971, *Quaternary Deposits of the Balen Sloti valleys, Allahabad District Uttar Pradesh*, Proceedings of 6th Indian Colloquum Peierepalaeontology and Stratigraphy.

Falconer, H. and P.T. Cautley 1949, *Fauna antiqua sivalensis Part 9* Equidae, Cameledae and *Siratneruum*. Landon Smith, Elder & C.

Foote, R.B. 1884, Mr. H.B. Foote's work at the Bitla Surgam Records Geological Survey of India 17: (4).

Ghosh, R.K., S.N. Paul and L.D. Saha 1972, A new Pleistocene Buffalo from Tiruchirapalli District, Tamil Nadu, India. *Journal of Zoological Society of India* 24 (1), 2.

Joshi, R.V. 1955, *Pleistocene studies in Malaprabha Basin*, Poona, Dharwar.

Joshi, R.V. G.L. Badam and R.P. Pandey 1978, Fresh Data on the Quaternary Animal fossils and Stone Age cultures from the Central Narmada Valley. *Asian Perspectives*, 21 (2).

Joshi, R.V. G.L. Badam and R.P. Pandey 1980, Late Pleistocene Animal fossils and Stone cultures in the upper Mahanadi valley, *The Eastern Anthropologist* 33 (2).

Joshi, R.V. P.P. Bopardikar & S.A. Sali 1976, Animal fossils and Stone Age tools from Gangapur on the Godavari River (Nasik District, Maharashtra State)*Current Science* 35 (13).

Joshi, R.V., R.S. Pappu, A.R. Marathe and R.P.Pandey 1980, Excavation at Wadoli-Waghodi. A Middle Palaeolithic site on the High Level Gravel of the Godavari River, Bulletin of *Deccan College Research Institute*, 39 (1-26).

Joshi, R.V., S.V. Chitale S.N. Rajaguru, R.S. Pappu & G.L. Badam 1981, Archaeological studies in the Manjra valley, Central Godavari Basin. *Bulletin of the Deccan College Research Institute.* 40.

Kajale, M.D. 1978, *Bio-archaeology of the Ghod valley, Maharashtra* Unpublished Ph.D. thesis, University of Poona.

Khatri, A.P. 1966, The Pleistocene Mammalian Fossils of the Narmada River valley and their Horizons, 9.

Korisettar, R., M.D. Kajale, S.N. Rajaguru and K. Paddayya 1976/77, On the occurrence of Plant Fossils along with Middle Palaeolithic tools at Wajjal, Dist. Gulbarga, Karmataka *Bulletin of the Deccan College Research* Institute 36 (1-4).

Mathew, W.D. 1929, Critical observations upon Siwalik mammals, Bulletin of American Meseum of *Natural History*, 53.

Murty, M.L.K. 1974, A late Pleistocene cave site in Southern India, *Proceedings of American Philosophical Society*, 1118 (2).

Murty, M.L.K. 1975, Late Pleistocene Fauna of Kurnool caves South India. In Clason A. I. (ed.) *Archaeozoological Studies*. New York Holland Publishing companey.

Paddayya, K. 1969, Hagargundi: A fosseliferous Middle Stone Age site on the Bhima river, Journal of Asiatic Society Bengal, 11 (1-4).

Pandey, R.P. 1978, Prehistoric Investigations in the Upper Mahanadi valley, Central India. Presented in International Symposium on Recent Advances in Indo-Pacific Prehistory, Pune.

Pandey, R.P. 1980, Geomorphology and Prehistory of the Upper Mahanadi valley, Central India, *Bulletin of the Deccan College Research Institute*, 39.

Pandey, R.P. 1981, An attempt of estimating settlement characters during Stone Age in the Upper Mahanadi Region Central India. Presented at Joint session of Society for Prehistoric and Quaternary Studies and Indian Archaeclogical Society, Waltair.

Pandey, R.P. 1982, Archaeology of the upper Mahanadi valley, unpublished Ph. D. thes.s, Poona University.

Pappu, R.S. 1974, *Pleistocene Studies in the Upper Kashmir* Basin. Poona Deccan College.

Princep, J. 1932, Note on the Jabalpur Fossil bones *Journal of Asiatic Society of Bengal*, 1.

Rajaguru, S.N. 1968/69, Some New Fossil Discoveries from Western Maharashtra *Puratattva*:2.

Rajaguru, S.N. and K.T.M. Hedge 1972, The Pleistocene stratigraphy in India, *Archaeological Congress and Seminar Papers:* (ed) S. B. Deo, Nagpur.

Sankalia H.D. 1952, *The Godavari Palaeolithic industry* Poona: Deccan College Monograph Series 10.

Sewell, R.B.S. and B.S. Guha 1931, Zoological Remains: In Marshall, J., *Mohenjodaro and the Indus Civilization* 2: 649-763, London, Arthur Probosthain.

Sharma, G.R. 1980, *History to Prehistory: Archaeology of Ganga Valley and Vindhyas*, Allahabad

Supekar, S.G. 1968,*Pleistocene Stratigraphy and Prehistoric Archaeology of the Central Narmada Basin* Unpublished Ph.D. thesis, Poona University

Thornthwaite, C.W. 1933, *The climates of Earth* Rev 23: 433-40.

The Authors of the Indus Seal Texts or The Indus Seal Motifs

DR. M.N. GUPTA, FAMS[1]

"we commemorate great events or honour outstanding persons by means of coins, sculpture and now postage".

(Paul Younger. Introduction to Indian Religious Thought. 1972).

I. INTRODUCTION

A logical intellectual point of view against the theory of animistic belief prevalent in the course of the Indus Valley Civilization (IVC), of some historians and archaeologists, is presented below.

A seal is defind as a stamp or die engraved with some device, motto or image, used for making an impression and sealing is an act of confirmation, ratification of the authority and keeping secure or secret the sealed object. The Indus seals conform to this definition and display an inscription in the upper quarter and an animal motif in the lower three-fourth quarter of the register.

The very controversial use of animal motifs (about seven: unicorn, two types of bulls, buffalo, elephant, tiger, rhinoceros, leaving aside the antelope, goat and hare and fabulous and composite forms) on 1441 seals (Mahadevan), has lead to declaration of zoolatary and animism by various authors which is absurd. The context in which these iconographic objects are used has not been properly understood. An icon is defind as a sign or a symbol containing a point-by-point resemblance to the object it depicts (eg. an engraving or picture of a bull or elephant). This is explained in detail with reference to the Indus seal motifis later on.

The specific vision that these animals symbolise has to be comprehended. They symbolise corporality, solid flesh and ornamental decoration.

2. THE REAL FACT.

Their presence or portrayal can not be explained by Vedic liturgy, still less by Vedic religion. It is hard to believe or imagine a statue of God of Fire (Agni), Ushas, Maruts or Varuna (wind). As a matter of fact there is no record of Vedic Icons or Vedic temples in Harappa, Mohenjo-Daro, Kalibangan or Lothal. Fire places have, however, been found in Kalibangan and Lothal. Domestic fire in a Vedic home was a sort of a temple in itself.

3. PRE-AND POST INDEPENDENCE GOVERNMENT OF INDIA SEALS.

The use of animals as a heraldic device conforms to the use of the rampant UNICORN and LION on either side of a crown and the inscription 'Dieu et mon droit' (God is on my right), as a Govt. of India seal during the British regime. Our post-independence National Emblem (seal) is the replica of the Capital (top portion of Ashoka's pillar at Sarnath) and depicts three sitting lions with open mouths, (the fourth lion in Ashoka's pillar is missing), a bull on the right and a horse on the left in the upper register of the seal and an inscription (a quotation from the Mundak Upanished) in the lower quarter register.

This is a departure from the Indus style where the inscription is in the upper register.

A seal so inscribed becomes a synthesis of literature, ornamentation, art of adornment with heraldic animal figures, celebraitng the authorship of the various Indus (Vedic ?) sages and seers (the authors of the seal inscriptions) and producing finally an object of imposing quality, excellence and elegence. The identification of various seal animals with these authors is most difficult. We have no biographical account of these authors. All this, however, convincingly expresses the priestly Indus authorities under whose directions the seal texts weree inscribed. The seals were objects of practical utility, preserved by the teacher (ACHARYA) and the student (Brahmacharin) and the symposiasts at various PARISHADS, alike in the course of their studies and discussions.

4. UNICORN.

The most common charge—the unicorn (on 1159 seals) is the earliest use as a heraldic sign on a seal of antiquity in any script in the world. The use of animal motifs as a heraldic sign has never been conceived by any previous decipherer. Aristotle has ascribed the unicorn to India. Their use in this context is without any risk of confusion and functions best.

Almost nothing is known of the earliest or the latest Indus lexicographer (except possibly YASKA). But we can form a fairly clear idea of the identity from the shape and form of the seal animal and their aim, function and achievement from the seal vocables (when deciphered). The seven sages in the Veda may have been animated on the seals (?), which however does not fit the context.

The use of the rebus principle is evident in these seals. The arms of the city of Oxford show an ox crossing a ford. The pictures of the animals bear an allusion to the name of the Indus seer and his heraldic symbol, likewise. These symbols are necessary for identification—a prerogative of the ruling class, a sign of noble rank. The quotation at the beginning of this paper supports the theme expressed above.

5. ANTHROPOMORPHIC MOTIFS.

Mankind has always felt compelled to surround itself with legends, riddles, mystical forces and the like. The several anthropomorphic motifs (On about 525 seals), make the first contribution to the presentation of these legends etc.. which survive on the fertile soil of popular credulity as they attract and hold the imagination of listeners.

The engraved animal figures constitute not only the most ancient aesthestic heritage in the strictly artistic form, but also possess uncommon sublimity and grace, remarkable vigour and originality with an unsurpassed intensity of expression of the art of Harappan engraving.

The group of seals with mythopoeic engravings would require a different treatment for their interpretation, so also the texts which carry avian (bird) signs, used in a symbolic way.

The engravings of these animals carry a feeling of sincere and intense devotion of the scribe and thus emphasises their value.

6. ANIMAL WORSHIP AND THE VEDA.

Animal worship was never at the root of vedic religion. "Vedic worship is aniconic. It uses no symbols besides what is found in vedic poetry, and ritual. As no material image is used, the vedic poet can easily identify one Deva with another. (A.C. Bose). "The religion of the Veda knows no idols. The worship of idols in India is a secondary formation, a later degradation of the more primitive worship of ideal gods". (Max Muller). In the vedic religion totemism has very little to adduce in its support. The Rig Veda is full of figurative expressions and often likens gods to animals. The Indus seer was not refractory to the idea of being represented as a bull. The earliest allusion to the bull is in RV. 4.58.3 ("catvari srnga trayo asya padah....) There is difference between theriomorphism and animal worship. Vedic Gods were often conceived therio-morphically and did not require the use of an image. These animals are not religious symbols or cult animals even today. Though there was anthropomorphic conception of the gods, no images were made or worshipped.

Bull is a symbol of creative power. The PURUSA SUKTA (R.V. X. 90.) describes PURUSA as an animal, a symbolic description. * The term vrsabha is very often applied to gods, but especially to Indra as expressing mighty strength and fertility (RV.ii.I2.I3)—"The mighty seven reined bull, who let the seven streams to flow.........he, O men, is Indra." There is no totemic ritual connected with any animal in the Veda and there is no animal sacrifice. The imagination of Indus seers deified natural objects into personified Gods. Likewise animals in the Indus valley were elevated to the ranks of seers, sages and divines, for portrayal on the seals and endowing them with power and authority, so early in the history of Indus civilzation. A process of concrete personification from nature is evident behind most Rigvedic conceptions. A human entity can likewise, in reverse, be identified with any other natural (animate or inanimate) object. The resulting personification will therefore obscure the original reference. The authors of the Indus texts were real human personalities. If they are portrayed on the seals as living animals, it is a process in reverse, a poetical identification, an abstraction (animation) by the Indus scribe. The animals are references to the concrete. The animation is not on the anthropomorphic lines. The scribe transformed the concrete human authors into an animated engraving probably because of his being an engraver *par excellence*. and a lover of other animate beings (animals and birds).

The original basis of Rig-vedic Gods is some nature form on which anthropomorphic features are superimposed. In the Indus seals the basis is vedic seers and divines on which animation is superimposed. The activities, the functions and the qualities of the animals parallel with the activities, qualities and the functions of these seers, although this animation is translucent or opaque or hidden, it can still be perceived and argued. A human basis is visible in the tranquil pose of these seal motifs.

The Indus seer, a worshipper of the Goddess of Learning or VACH, or God of Learning VACHASAPATI (Atharva Veda. I.I.I.), knew full well that God cares not to ask the name of HIS votary, not only denied to himself the privilege of pronouncing his own name on the seal, but preferred to be shown in the garb of another object of creation—an animal, (next to man), an easily identifiable living being. The Indus seer did not care what he looked like when animated (as in a present day cartoon). The Indus scribe was interested in a way of expressing the essential qualities of the animal (described later) that satisfied him so thorough ly that the animal symbol was used many centuries, the life of IVC. The scribe also found in these animals a source of inspiration for displaying his dexterity in the art of engraving and presenting and preserving the message of Indian seers. He engraved the animal figures as if it was of an existing animal.

The various animals are those that help to create beauty in the seals, create reality and help the mind to form an image of the unknown Indus seer. The beauty of the beasts has often been admired along with human beauty as in Atharva Veda, XII. I. 25. The animals have been portrayed in their tranquil form, in all tenderness and sublimity in the single moment of an action, presenting at the same time the whole image of the real animal. The majestic rendering of the humped bull has a monumental strength out of all proportion of the small field available. The seal animals are a perfect iconographic representation of the animals in their natural form. His minuteness of the observation of the physical details (given later) of the portrayed animals alone could bring out their beautiful form which have gone to enrich the beauti of his art. The beauty and the sublimity of the Brahamani Bull, the Unicorn and the Elephant, and their tranquil forms are not easy to describe but it is a thing to be seen and eyed to be feasted upon.

The most striking and the most complete aspect of a quadruped is its profile. Mammals and birds are also shown in side view as in the Egyptian hieroglyphs. Their forms have arisen out of the artist's pleasure in his work, his creative satisfaction and consciousness of his skill to meet the requirements of pure utility (as seals) and the material in whcih he worked (soap stone, faience) to convert practical shapes (bovine and avian) into artistic imitations. No avian signs are seen so engraved on the lower register of these seals; these symbols are used only in the writing of texts. It is to the credit of the Indus engraver, that his is the earliest extant engraving of these animals to have given fit expression to this *beaute supreme*.

There is apparent an intimate unity of the Indus seer with the animal. Engraving like painting is concerned with tranquil forms (Turner's paintings). The chisel and hammer of the Indus scribe are physical objects, but the chiseled animal arouses an unique sprituality, authorship and aestheitic delight in the mind of the spectator when he sees vedic vocables inscribed along the top of the seal. The crude clay toys (animals, birds, figurines) of the Indus period bear no comparison to the beautifully carved animals on the seals. These seal engravers were specialists and not the common potters who made toys for the children.

The use of animal figures on the seals as heraldic signs representing Indus sages and seers is a novelty unknown in other ancient civilizations. The oval cartouche on Egyptian monuments contains the name or title of a sovereign or deity, It is not a ! eraldic sign in the correct perspective. The use of animal symbolism served to disguise the name of the Indus seer and thus he was spared the pain on seenig the seals being trampled under the feet of ignorant people. Almost all books belonging to the early literature of India are anonymous (Sir. S. Radhakrishanan). The animals retain more accurately and fixedly their external character which gives distinict personality to the various Indus seers and reveal their idenification and human traits in unambigous terms. The animals give personality to the sages by their anthropomorphical presentation, physical prowess and virility.

All mythological representations on the seals depict an earlier stage of thought and religious development (anthropomorphism) whcih got arrested for 2000 years after the dissolution of IVC, when the large intaglio seals began to be manufactured. Conjectural pre-historic restoration of such Indus texts, unsupported inferences, strange analogies and guesses from words in the Dravidian Etymological Dictionary have no place in working with Indus seals. Tht animal epithets blend exquisitely with the spiritua-lity of the seers, who-so-ever they were. It is quite intricate to find the original nature of the Indus seer, but we can see through these animal figures their trasparent character and physical nature after scrutinising the seal animal in which they are garbed. The Indus seer was careful to consider that in his being represented as an animal there was no probability of the seal being used as a votive object or an object of reverence and adoration by any worshipper in the future.

7. THE INDUS SEAL ANIMALS.

I. UNICORN. A fabulous animal with the body of a horse, the hind limbs of a deer, a lion's tail and essentially a single long horn on its forehead. Once thought to be native horse to India. It figures frequently in heraldry and was adopted by James I, king of Scotland (1424—1437) as the symbol of Scotland on the Royal arms. (The Great Encyclopaedia of Universal Knowledge). In its best form it is seen in text No. 1038 (MIC. Pl. CIV. 38). It is engraved on 1159 seals (MJD-747, HRP-239, CHD-43, LTL-76, KLB-45, Other sites-6 West Asia-3), i.e. the largest number of seals, followed by the short-horned bull with lowered head over trough (95 seals).

II. RHINOCEROS. The rhino family (Rhinocerotidae) is nearly 60 million years old. Its typical characters are : massive barrel like build, thick and solid bones, short and stumpy legs, with three toes (odd-toed ungulate-hoofed animals). The Indian horned rhino, (Rihnoceros Unicornis) is safe in its habitats—Assam, West Bengal and in Nepal (Himalayan foot hills). The horn is a mass of agglutinated hair, is not connected to the skeleton at all, and can be knocked off by a hard blow. The skin is very thick and raised into strong definitely arranged folds; very large pointed incisors and a single nasal horn. It is covered with tubercles. The more the tubercles, the older is the animal. It is best seen in seal No. 1342 (MIC. Pl. CXI. 342) and No. 2651 (FEM. PL. XCIX. 651)' on 39 seals. Its sense of sight is poorly developed. Its blundering gait gives the impression of a clumsy animal, still it is agile and can manage short bursts of high speed. Rhinos seldom go out of their way to attack.

It is quite long lived—almost 70 years. Their breeding rate is low. Gestation period is 16 to 19 months. They love to wallow in marshy mud—holes, in congregations. They feed from late afternoons throughout the night. Fossil remains have been found in the Shivaliks. Many superstitions have been built around its horn (aphrodisiac properties) in Nepal, Burma, Malaysia and Thailand. Unicorn tales might have originated from the Indian Rhino (E.P. Gee). It is the largest and most powerful terrestrial mammal, except the elephant. It is fierce when provoked. Rhino is quite common on terracotta sealings and copper tablets with two or one rhino figures. The animal disappeared in later Indian iconography.

III. ELEPHANT. In the Veda, the elephant is a symbol of royal splendour, and Indra is "as it were an elephant": The name AIRAVAT sounds like a matronymic appelation—son of Iravati, and name of RAVI (river), along whose bank stood Harappa. Of the two living species, the Indian (Elephas maximus) is more intelligent and easily capable of being domesticated. The males as a rule have tusks, the tusks of the female being only small when there are any. It is seen on 55 seals. It is best seen on texts Nos. 1369 and 2648. Tht elephant is a symbol of purity because it is supposed to bathe in rivers at full moon, and is a symbol of gentleness.

IV. BULL. Rig Veda. 4.58.3. (quoted in para 6 above). Three varieties are depicted on Indian seals: Bull with long horns-5 seals, short-horned bull-95 seals, Humped Bull-54 seals (Zebu bull with hump-back, dew-lap and U-shaped horns). The short-horned bison or gaur (MIC. PL. CX-308 to 326. etc.) and the Brahamani bull or Zebu (BOS Indicus) adorn a large number of seals (154 in all). 'VRSABHA' regularly denotes a 'bull' in the Rigveda (1.94.10, 160.3, VI.46.4). The humped bull with the dew-lap is the animal most beautifully carved on seal. No. 1337.

The crocodile is a symbol of all that is evil. It is very often depicted with a fish caught in its long jaws. Every one is quite familiar with the ferocious qualities, the agility and its nature of prowling in the dark, and in engaging in constant duels with human beings.

The UNICORN seals are the predominant seals forming about 50% of all the seals. The Indus seer who is stylised as an unicorn was probably the latest and the most learned seer to start the collection of the vocabulary of the seals, like YASKA, the etymologist, in his NIRUKTA and NIGHANTU. His identity will be revealed only when decipherment reveals the words, which like borrowals in NIGHANTU will also reveal the names of the authors who were his predecessors (i.e. the other animals), which seems an impossibility at this stage, and thus have faded into an almost impenetrable obscurity.

If the seal animal is used as an 'upama' (simile) for the particular seer, the expression must be very near to the truth. This mode of expression is in line with the large scale use of 'figures of speech' (Gonda. G.) in Vedic poetry. Their beauty cannot fail to obtain appreciation from everybody who beholds them. The seal animals were teachers whose authority was adequate to secure its acceptance in the vedic pathshalas.

In the seals the Indus seers have left 'a part of themselves as a heritage to us', as such, 'they are a part of that which we call our glorious past': They are not only word-builders and word selectors, but makers of the Indus culture and civilization. The religious power in the RISHI families was hereditary. This accounts for the preponderance of bull, rhino, elephant and unicorn seals, and their currency and use over a number of generations during the millenium of the IVC.

The seal animals, plants, swastika and avian signs and heraldic animals in Indus script could not be known to post-Indus artist for over 3000 years, as they lay burried in the ruins of these cities after the dissolution of IVC. They do not appear on Asokan edicts of the 4th century B.C.

8. SYMBOLISM.

"Mankind it seems has to find a symbol to express itself. Indeed, expression is symbolism" (Whitehead). There is difference between sign and symbol. "Symbolism is the recognised key to that mental life which is characteristically human and above the level of sheer animality...It is the starting point of all genuinely intellectual growth" (Langer S.K.). "Sign is dependent on sense impression, symbol is rooted in ideation" (Satya Prakash Singh). The content of a symbol is a concept, The concept of the Indus scribe has a proper denotation and adequate and correct connotation—a semantic content of a symbol which is rational on the analogy of the Vedic quotations. The signs in Indus script are, "designative or indicative of the sounds of the Indus language and substitutional for those use in Indus numeral system—both being conventional containing a particular meaning." A symbol is not necessarily a picture...it is metaphorical or analogical which is the very essence of the symbolic function." (Urban W.M.[9]). According to the classification of Urban of various symbols, the Indus seal motifs are of the intrinsic or descriptive type, as they are animation of the Indus Text authors, while the avian symbols are of the insight type. These avian symbols are artificial as shown else where.

The proper psychological ground for the selection of animal symbols, has been provided comprehensively by the Indus scribe. As such these symbols are not pictorial.

It is from this integral view point that the present scientific research has been made and the related principles have been evolved. Obviously, the Indus symbolic mode of express on is adopted out of the necessity of communicating an idea of an entirely unfamiliar range of experience of the Indus seer, in familiar terms as seen in Vedic literature. They are an inevitable necessity in the realization of that Vedic Reality. In all fields of knowledge, however, symbols have a definite purpose over and above sheer expression. We must be capable of discovering the value invested in these symbols. by the Vedic seers, centuries back, or even by the pre-Vedic people many millennia earlier., cosequently the symbol has an air of reality in these texts.

9. CONCLUSION.

Mahadevan's or Parpola's concordances provide a proof of an attempt at the preparation of a lexicon like. that of the NIGHANTU of Yaska (Lakshaman Sarup). The Indus seal vocables, in my opinion have a parallel in Nighantu and Nirukata collection, and made for exegetical purpose as a teaching aid Textual analysis of these texts have confirmed my hypothesis of sanskritic origin of these texts connected with Vedic literature. Proofs of which are provided amply in later pages.

I have advanced enough arguments in favour of the seal animals being the disguised authors of the seal inscriptions. I have approached the subject without any pre-conceived opinions and bias, but I must wait for further phonological evidence (in the second Volume of my book) and be careful not to force my research results into a false direction by premature dicta. If my interpretations are considered as presumptuous readings and thoughts, they should be done with an open heart and in a charitable spirit to rejoice in the truth whereever it can be found.

The Indus seal animals are no artistic representations of magical beliefs of the Harappans. They have a specific message to convey and a definite event or sequence of events to describe. They do not display the phenomena of magic, demonology and idolatory, mystical creed and doctrine, and phallic and serpent worship (except the practice of fire ritual in individual homes). In the design of the animals the artist has capriciously given what attitude pleased him when copying from nature, the immense grandeur of the Brahmani bull and the unicorn are an example. These motifs accompanying the inscriptions do not indicate zoolatary, but is a heraldic symbol of the authority under whose direction the text words were picked out for engraving for the use of posterity.

REFERENCES

Mahadevan I. The Indus Script, texts, Concordance and tables. 1977.

Bose A.C. Hymns from the Vedas. 1963. p. 24.

Max Muller.: Chips from a German Workshop. Vol. I. p. 38.

Gonda J. Similies in Sanskrit Literature.

Kimmo Koskenniemi and Asko Parpola.

i. Materials for the study of Indus script. A concordance to the Indus Inscriptions. 1973.

ii. Corpus of Texts in the Indus script. 1979.

iii. Documentation and Duplicates of the Texts in the Indus script. 1980.

Lakshman Sarup. The Nighantu and the Nirukta. The oldest Indian Treatise on Etymology, Philology and Semantics. 1962.

Whitehead A.N. Symbolism. Its meaning and effect Cambridge. 1928. p. 73.

Langer. S.K. Philosophy in a new Key. Newyork. 1954. p. 21-23.

Satya Prakash Singh. Upanisadic Symbolism. 1981. p. 11

Urban W.M.. Language and Reality. London, 1939. p. 406, 424.

Neo-chalcolithic remains at Rangai (Vidisha)

M. D. KHARE

The decipherment and publication of Heliodors pillar inscription in 1908-09 made the ancient city of Besnagar(also known as Vidisha, internationally famous. Ever since, the city has been attracting the attention of archaeologists. Lake (1910) and Bhandarkar (1913-15) brought to light a few Buddhist and Hindu remains. But the extensive and scientific excavations were conducted by the author on behalf of the Archaeological Survey of India during 1963-65 and 1975-77, traced the antiquity of the site to the chalcolithic period, the upper phase of which was found to be contemporaneous with the Painted Grey Ware culture. Of the early historic remains, an elliptical temple assignable to 4th-3rd century B.C., a huge palace complex and a fortification wall constructed in a criss-cross pattern, after the fashion of wooden palisades, besides many other structures of religious and secular nature, are noteworthy.

Besnagar is one of the very few ancient cities, the remains of which are still more or less 'intact'. It lies about 3 km. to the north-west of Vidisha on Ashoknagar road, within the triangular confines of the two rivers Betwa on the east and south and Bes on the north, further defended by a 10 m. high fortification wall on the west, running north-south to a distance of more than a km. Thus occupying a very strategic position, from where many roads went in different directions, notably to Pataliputra, Sravasti, Broach, etc. Naturally enough, it became a prosperous and populous centre of trade and commerce, providing great impetus to artistic and architectural activities before and during the early centuries of the Christian era.

The excavations conducted during 1963-65 proved rewarding because the contemporaenity of chalcolithic and P.G.W. cultures was noticed here for the first time. But it was also evident that the chalcolithic remains were confined only to the two sites BSN I and IV, which are on either side of the river Betwa. No other part of the ancient city yielded any chalcolithic remains.

Therefore, it was decided to explore and excavate horizontally a chalcolithic site, which was likely to be outside the ancient city but on the banks of the river Betwa and yet not very far from the township. From the information furnished by V.S. Wakankar, a single culture site near a small village, known as Rangai and situated midway between Sanchi and Vidisha was subjected to excavations during 1975-77. It is an extensive mound with slopes on all sides but the slope of south and south-east sides being more marked. The river Betwa flows to the west and south at a distance of about 300 m. The surface finds consisted of a fragmentary neolithic celt, plenty of raw material for neolithis and microliths besides chalcolithic pottery. It is not unlikely that the village Rangai still retains its name after the people, who were well-versed in painting pottery during the chalcolithic period.

Trenches A—H, each measuring 5x5 m. were laid on the southern slope of the site, but digging was confined to treuches B, F, G and H only.

In the early stages of the excavations here, the site was taken to be a neo-chalcolithic site, for 2.25 m. thick deposit yielded the material of this single culture. But it was at the fag end of the work that pre-pottery microlithis were also found in two stratified deposits.

Pd-IA: A control pit measuring 1x1 m. yielded pre-pottery microlithis from a pale brown compact deposit lying over loose sandy clay. Looking into the variety of the raw material, like chalcedony, quartz, jasper, agate, etc. it appears that there was neither a particular choice of material nor the systematisation of tools, which were irregular in shape and lacked sophistication. All these were found between the depth range of 9.00 m. to 9.25 m. from the surface.

Pd-IB: There was a sterile layer of about 5.50 m. over which was found another deposit ranging in thickness from 40 cms. to 60 cms. and yielding non-geometric and a few geometric microliths, without retouch. These tools have also not been associated with pottery. A floor of burnt brick jelly was exposed in this level. Systematisation appears to have come out of the earlier (I.A.) rudimentary forms, as is evident from the use of sophisticated tools like po nts and triangles. About 300 microliths, cores and flakes have been collected from both the phases of this period.

Pd-II: About 50 cms. thick sterile layer separates this period from Pd. I.B. Divisible into three sub-phases, it yielded typical chalcolithic material consisting of microlithis, painted black on red, white painted and plain black and red, fine grey—both thick and thin and coarse red wares, terracotta bulls and ivory pendants. A neolithic celt, triangular in shape and of thin section, the only copper rod and a majority of beads come from the upper levels, though neolithic pottery, a few sherds with simple incised designs and finger nail impressions (rope design), continued up to the mid-levels, below which the variety of beads and abundance of terracotta bulls are noteworthy. A particular type of graffiti mark (inverted Z), though occurring mostly on the black and red ware, is also occasionally noticed on other wares as well.

The black and red ware is usually of thick section and medium fabric. Its blackness is confined to the interior only and does not extend to the exterior. The only type met with is a wide-mouthed shallow basin. It forms about 25-30% of the total assemblage. A thin and fine black and red ware is also represented but rather feebly. In addition to the painted bands in white, post-firing incised marks, also on the interior, except in one case where it is on the exterior, are also available in some cases. Surprisingly the graffiti marks are identical in all cases.

The red ware, which is about 60-70% is usually thin, fine, well fired and treated with a very pleasing variety of black on red designs, consisting of bands, loofs, filled triangles and squares, bulls with long and curved horns, cross hatchings, leaf pattern, etc. Thick and coarse red ware forms about 10%. Though not well fired and has often grey to black core section with sand and grift in the paste, in certain cases it carries incised wavy lines over pale brown surface. The shapes represented in this ware are thin *lota* types, invariably painted, a few shallow bases and deep bowls with straight sides, also slipped on both sides and neolithic urn types. A fragment of a channel spout has also been picked up from the middle levels of this deposit. Another noteworthy type is a very small lamp type with a pinched wavy rim.

Grey ware, whether thin, medium or thick is invariably fine and forms 5-10% of the total assemblage. Usually it is of medium thickness and carries simple bands in brown. In one or two cases, the painting appears to have been in black pigment. A few instances of highly smoothened black surface have also been noticed. The usual shape is the *lota* type as in the red ware.

The other components of this culture are a large number of small beads of paste and terracotta bulls with long horns, prominent hump, short legs and very delicately carved tail.

The entire pottery, except the neolithic vases, which are turned on a slow sheel, has been made of fine clay on a very fast wheel and well fired. The plain red ware has a sturdy appearance.

The microlithic industry of this per od has two distinct traditions of slender ribbon blades and short blades, representing chalcolithic and neolithic characteristics as in pottery.

Three floor levels have been noticed here Each floor consists of a thin layer of hard pale brownish earth, occasionally treated with lime or brick jelly. A large number of post-holes varying in size from 8-12 cms. in diameter and forming circular or rectangular plans have been noticed. The posts of mid levels were strengthened with lumps of clay (thickness 6-7 cms. and diametre 40-50 cms.). A part of the habitation appears to have been burnt. In another part, a groove of a thin bamboo(?) stick was also traced.

The foregoing account shows that the chalcolithic people inhabitated this area for several years, but long after the disappearance of the pre-pottery microlith using people. The earliest chalcolithic occupation is contemporaneous with Kayatha II, which has been dated to 19th-18th century B.C., while the latest as revealed from the finds of 1963-65, with the Painted Grey Ware using culture, assignable to the beginning of the Ist millennium B.C. The other facts, which emerge are; the chalcolithic folk appear to have settled on the right bank of the river Betwa. The neolithic pottery has a greater affinity with that of South India. The use of fine grey ware, with occasional painting in brown pigment in one site and the contemporaneity of P.G. Ware with the last phase of this culture in another, has added new dimensions to the Central Indian Chalcolithic complex.

Recent Advances in Protohistoric Gujarat

SUMAN PANDYA

Gujarat can be clearly defined as a separate region which stands apart from the Indian subcontinent. It is the only region having variables in land forms, precipitation, vegitation cover, soil and rivers etc. The large sea-coast broken by rivers, rivulets, and creeks offer safe anchoring for native ships. At its north-east and east it is bounded by the hill-ranges dressed with dry to moist deciduous forest covers. The greater Rann of Kutch, a vast waste-land, at the north and Arabian sea with the two gulfs border at the west.

In 1936, Father Heras had proclaimed protohistoric significance of Gujarat, particularly of Saurashtra. Latter on excavations at Rangpur, Lothal, Shrinathgarh (Rojdi) and some other sites provided some good information. However, a clear picture of protohistoric Gujarat did not emerge.

Gujarat has a large number of Harappan and Harappan affiliated sites. Except typically Harappan settlements like Lothal, Kotdo (Khadir) where Harppan traditions are dominant, most of the sites are small to medium in size, highly concentrated over a fluvial or coastal soil usually near flowing sweet water course. They do not yield typically Harappan elements to label them as Mature Harappan sites. To some extent our hunts for Mature Harappan materials, may have ignored the elements of those who had inhabited Gujarat prior to the Harappans. Excavations at Rangpur is one of the examples. Here the first excavation (Ghurye, 1939, pp. 3—12) showed some Harappan affinities, others denied and link with the Harappan (Dikshit, 1950. pp. 3—35), as most of the materials differed from those of the Sind Harappans. Yet, Rao excavated it as full-fledged Harappan town (Rao, 1963. pp. 205). Based on this, he formulated some thought provoking hypothesis such as Harappan migrations of the flood-refugees from Sind, degeneration of the Harappan culture at Rangpur, evolution of a new culture of Lustrous Red Ware and its spread over the large area of the India etc. Rao deserves our congratulations for the tireless, enthusiastic archaeological operations he has carried out in Gujarat, yet his interpretations of the Rangpur material are some-what misleading. Even at Rangpur along with the Harappan traditions different (Non-Harappan) traditions were appearing later on surpassing the Harappans. The ceramic traditions, lithic blade-tools, some stone weights, even architecture and cultivation of spiked millet etc. suggest existence of some local chalcolithic and nomadic cultures prior to the Harappans which continued along with Harappans. Compared to these materials even the Harappan traditions are limited, appearing only in Rangpur period II A, gradually dsiappearing. For highlighting the Harappans, probably non-Harappan traditions are ignored. For a while if we forget terminology such as Mature, Degenerate, Devolved and Evolved Harappans etc. it becomes clear that in Gujarat Mature Harappan traditions are very limited. What I think is that Rangpur was already in existence prior to the Harappan. A few Harappans either from Lothal or from other places (not flood refugees, please) might have come to Rangpur and settled down gradually mingling with them.

P. P. Pandya (Pandya, 1954. pp. 1—12), has reported some twelve microlithic sites in Junagadh and Jamnagar districts. The material consisted of parallel-sided flake-blades and cores of agate, chalcedony etc. Aliabada, Bhangol, Modpur etc. are reported as factory sites. Even scrapers of agate and jaspar have been collected from Harappan listed sites of Akru, Alau and Bhimpatal. Short parallel-sided blades of chalcedony and fluted cores come from Vaniawader also. In fact, there are good numbers of sites having such tool-types, Some of them do not show Harappan affiniy. Chert blades come in very few numbers. Even at Rangpur only one chert blade has come. However, so far, no full-fledged microlithic habitation has been looked for.

A few typically Harappan type beads come from Rangpur. Pear-shaped, flat at top and bottom T.c. beads are most common, gradully they are increasing. Terracotta beads come from Somnath also. They seemed to be net sinkers for fishing in moderate to still waters.

Coming to the architecture, except in period II-A at Rangpur through-out all the periods mud-walled houses with post-holes have been constructed. They are present in period II-A too. At Somnath, houses are found built with no foundations or had shallow ones. If the Harappans had enough time and knowledge to manufacture typically Harappan standard bricks, at many sites raw material was available in plenty. Prof. Dhavlikar has now identified a building complex having very small rooms with very thin walls as a ware-house (like Lothal 1) (Dhavlikar, 1982. pp.). They are non-Harappan in nature.

At Lothal copper was known to pre-Harappans. At Rangpur the peacock motifs engraved on the copper celts are typically non-Harappan.

The weights and seals, sealings are identical for this issue. At Rangpur in period II-A along with stone weights only two typcial cubical weights of agate are collected. Gradually stone weights are increasing with great variations in styles and standards. Now circular, rectangular, ovoid and elliptical weights are common. In shape and standard, it is difficult to accept them as Harappan weights.

A large number of seals and sealings come from Lothal only. A seal has come from Kotado (Pandya, 1982. pp. 127—130), Khirsara, Deshalpur etc. Compared to Kutch, except Lothal, no seals or sealings have been reported from any sites of Gujarat. Therefore, it is high time to explore this composite nature of cultural assem- of local chalcolithic and nomads with Harappan- blage with a view to ascertain the settling down inspirations having some degree of econo-cultural tie with them.

There is very little geographical distance between Kutch and Sind. Now, we have some scientific information showing the Ranns under Navigable shallow sea providing easy communication marine routes between Sind and Kutch. In present state of researches it is difficult to accept hypothesis of flood refugees from the Sind and the Harappans as immigrants in Gujarat. These easy, short marine routes (Gupta, *et al.* 1980, pp. 39—46), hospitable environment and resources in form of agricultural produce and raw materials such as agate, carnelian ochre etc. must have attracted the Harappans to Gujarat to colonize at some strategic points such as Lothal, Kotado etc. Rest of Gujarat might have come under some degree of econo-cultural tie only. As being a next-door neighbour, Kutch had more chances to receive inspirations, ideas and influence from Sind, therefore, more Harappanisation than Saurashtra and mainland of Gujarat. Soundar Rajan, Joshi and Chitalwala's archaeological excavations have provided us with some valuable information on Kutch. However, composite nature of the assemblage, its relations with Sothi and Rajasthan, fortifications of the sites etc. still remains in dark.

Lothal surrounded by three sub-regions seems to have typical geographical location, to collect and redistribute the raw materials and manufactured items. It was built over silty clay rich loam which could produce rice and wheat without irrigation.

The discovery of some sixteen chalcolithic sites near Lothal in Bhalbara area and some others in Omkar river valley shows that Lothal was surrounded by these feeder villages which must have some economic ties with Lothal. Unfortunately as the material is not dated by scientific determinations it is difficult to postulate their economic relationship further.

Possehl also worked in Gujarat, especially in Saurashtra region (Possehl, 1980). However, his evaluation and interpretation of the archaeological assemblages are highly hypothetical based on surface evidences and Rao's undated periodizations of Rangpur. He has computated the assemblage, and correlated and identified it as Rangpur II-A, II-B, II-C and III etc. In Gujarat most of the sites are very much disturbed by constant ploughing and by river floods and rains. In such circumstances surface collection won't help much.

Possehl's hypothesis, which is in circulation, explains how and why the number of sites increased through time as a result of extensive agriculture, a type of cultural shift. Mostly relying upon Rangpur ceramic typological sequences he has postulated that there are only four Mature Harappan sites (Rangpur period II-A) in Gujarat, (except Kutch). This is because the Harappans arrived and settled down only on wheat growing alluvial soil like that of Sind. The Harappan Pastoral nomads, who were making frequent trips to the peripheral regions of the Indus civilization (as cited by Possehl; according to Fairservice as there was critical need for pastur in Sind in urban phase), were link between the nuclear regions of Kutch and these colonised Harappans. After abandonment of Mohenjo-daro etc. (urban phase) in Sind, these pastoral Harappans settled down resulting in increasing number of sites i.e. of Rangpur Period II-B and II-C types. These Harappans took up cultivation of spiked millet, a type of cultural shift from wheat growing to the dry farming.

Looking from this angle the problem seemed to be different. As mentioned earlier the Rangpur excavations and cultural periodizations have limitations. Therefore in the interpretations of the cultural assemblages of Gujarat, particularly of Saurashtra, it is difficult to depend upon Rangpur periodizations. Gujarat, even Saurashtra, is a very vast region having some better and larger sites than Rangpur. Surprisingly Koth has not revealed ceramic or any other traditions identical to the Rangpur period IIA.

In the mainland of Gujarat, in Bhalbara region of Cambay taluka, a good number of chalcolithic sites have been discovered and some of them were excavated by the M.S. University of Baroda under the leadership of Prof. R.N. Mehta (Mehta, 1982. pp. 167—174). These sites are located on alluvial soil of Oxbow lake, an abandoned meander of Sabarmati. The cultural assemblage is not like of those of period II A of Rangpur.

Spiked millet is heat and hot-loving, draught tolerant, quick growing, short duration (50 to 60 days) fodder crop. Before flowering it contains very high protien and is the most suitable crop for dry farming in semi-arid regions. It can be grown in varieties of soils including alluvial; spiked millet grows well in 250 to 8000 mm. precipitation P.A. and in 35°c to 40°c temperature zone (Relwani, 1979. pp. 9—12).

Originated either from Africa before 5000 B.C. or in India (undated) spiked millet seems to be ideal crop in semi-arid regions like Gujarat particularly of Kutch, most of Saurashtra and north Gujarat. Even today it grows in most of these areas. Great millet which is also an ideal fodder crop grows in similar condition except it is less tolerant to heat and temperature. Frequent showers are good for them.

It is probable that spiked millet was known to local inhabitants of Gujarat, particularly of of Saurashtra prior to the Harappans. Their economic pattern might be a mixed one based on limited agriculture on fluvial soils and domestication of cattles, sheep, goat etc. A good number of bones of humped cattle (*Bos indicus*) buffaloes *(Bos babulus)*, Sheep *(Ovis-vignei)* goat *(Capra hircus aegagrus)* pig *(Sus scrofa cristatus* etc. have come from all the levels of Rangpur. Some of them also come from Kanpur and other sites. Bones of humped cattle come in good numbers along with their young ones. Zebu, buffaloes and pigs were consumed for food. A hoof impression of a cattle like animal has come from Oriyo Timbo also (Possehl's team per com). These domestic cattle might have subsisted on grass-lands and the fodder crops. In fact, cattle are mostly domesticated on alluvial and medium black soils of fodder crop-growing regions like Sind, Punjab, Uttar-Pradesh, Gujarat etc. (Pandya, 1980. pp. 172—177). Rich protien contained fodders make them sturdy and healthy. In fact no pasture land is required for such regions as domestication of cattle is associated with agriculture. It is significant that cattles and sheeps, goats etc. played an important role in protohistoric Gujarat. The Harappan inspirations might have accelerated process of this mixed economy resulting into growth of prosperity and population increase.

Rice germinates and grows successfully in water or sub-merged conditions. Clay silt loam and inundation conditions are ideal for rice. Wheat is well adapted to steppe climate grown in slit loam soil in 15°c to 20°c temperature (winter) during vegetation period. As it is short rooted crop it is well grown in semi-arid regions if irrigation is provided. Barley differs only in soil. It can be grown in poorer, even salty soils and cool temperatures. Here it is emphasised that a different crops such as wheat in Indus plain, barley at Kalibangan, rice at and around Lothal and spiked millet at Rangpur, some herbs at Surkotada etc. indicate different climatic and physiographic conditions rather than a cultural shift and population change. Therefore, a word of caution may be said, when we take crop patterns as cultural indicators. Variation in site numbers may not be directly related to cultural shifts and population change.

In Gujarat, particularly in Saurashtra, there are places associated with Lord Krishna and Yadavas. Mahabharata epic and Harivansha give detailed accounts of Lord Krishna. Yadavas and their migration to the capital of Dharavati and geographic information of area around. In Rajasthan also a few places are associated with Lord Krishna. Excavations at Dwarka first under leadership of Prof. Sankalia, and then by Shri S. R. Rao have failed to link the present Dwarka with Lord Krishna's Dwaravati. Somnath excavations also could not throw any light on this issue. Now, in the age of experimental sciences we are in position to investigate this problem afresh.

Somnath excavations have provided a very significant creamic sequence. Here the Prabhas ware appears with all its shapes and designs and in profussion. Stratigraphically it is succeeded by Lustrous Red Ware, Coarse Red Ware and Historical period. It is spread over in area around Somnath and in Bhadar valley upto Shrinathgarh (Rojdi). Though the few shapes are common with the Harappans, yet, thd tradition is identically of non-Harappan. Even the architecture, the amulet, an obsidian blade flake etc. are non-Harappan in nature. Therefore, a point may be raised for labelling the Prabhas culture as a sub-Indus one. Even C-14 dates from Somnath is somewhat contemporary to the Harappans (Agrawal, 1982.pp.192-193). Stratigraphy and typology have great significance; still have limitations too.

Sedimentological studies of coastal Saurashtra and the Greater Rann of Kutch have showed that during the Holocene period, the Ranns were an arm of the present Arabian sea. (Gupta, pp.201-205). Geomorphological investigations have revealed remnants of ancient river channel, sand bars and braided chanels of a big river falling into the Greater Rann of Kutch (Roy; Merh. 1977 pp. 195-200). Just northwest of the Khadir island Landsat images have showed that the present Ghaggar was a mightier river, having present Yamuna and the tributaries of the present Indus bringing water for her (Yash Pal,*et al.* 1980. pp.317-331) Though these events are not dated they indicate that in Holocene period the geography of Guparat was more different than today : Kutch being an island and two major rivers falling into it interlinking Kutch, Rajasthan and Sind. It is possible that such a situation might have continued even in Mahabharata period interlinking Dwarka (Western coast, Saurashtra?) With the Hastinapur, via this short, open marine-cum-land route following the river banks of Saraswati and Chautang (Yamuna).

There are some important evidences indicating that Lothal was located on a creek which was an extended part of the present Gulf of Cambay (Pandya, 1982). In fact, geomorphological information shows a big wide channel interlinking the Little Rann of Kutch with the Gulf of Cambay. Even today excess water of the Rann empties into the Gulf through this channel-(Pandya 1981. -pp. 6-30). Was Saurashtra an island during the period of Indus civilization too?

In fact, geomorphology and geography of western part of India has gone through considerable changes. Faunal and floral remains coming from number of protohistoric sites do not suggest climatic change but a different landscape having more vegetation cover and the faunal remains.

In summing up I would think that though protohistoric research is gaining good ground in Gujarat, yet the progress is very slow. Except in one or two cases multi-disciplinary approach is absent. Traditional excavations still rule the scene. Scattered archaeological operations at selected sites could paint a local picture, models and hypothesis may be built. Yet, it won't provide complete picture of protohistoric Gujarat. As its geographical locational significance as a recipient of number of peoples, geographical and geomorphological changes it has witnessed, this is a bit complicated region in a sense of cultural variations and changes. In fact, a long-term research strategy to reconstruct man/environmental relationship in forms of migrations, trade and commerce, subsistence and settlement patterns and changes etc. is a present need. Collaboration of a good group of scientists and integrated study of their findings would speed up the necessary research.

REFERENCES

Ghurye, G.S. 1939, "Two old Cities in Kathiawar", JUB Vol. 8 (New series) Pt. 1, pp. 3—12, Bombay.

Dikshit, M.G. 1950, "Excavations at Rangpur: 1947" BDCRI, Vol. II, pp. 31—35, Poona.

Rao, S.R. 1963, "Excavation at Rangpur and other explorations in Gujarat, AI, No. 18-19 pp. 205-207, Delhi.

Pandya, P.P. 1954, "Explorations in Halar and Sorath Districts, Saurashtra" JMUSUB, Vol.3; No.2; pp. 1-12, Bombay.

Dhavlikar, 1982

Possehl, G.L. 1980, Indus Civilization in Saurashtra; New Delhi.

Pandya, Suman. 1982, "Kotado: A Major Harappan Settlement in the Greater Rann of Kutch" in *Indian Archaeology, New Perspective,* pp. 127-130, ed. S.R. Sharma, Delhi.

Gupta, S.K., Pandya, Suman, 1980, "Kutch Harappans'; Their communication Routes: A discussion", Vidya, Vol. XXII (i), pp. 39-46; Ahmedabad.

Mehta, R.N. 1982, "Some Rural Settlements in Gujarat"; A contemporary perspective, ed. by Possehl, G.L. pp. 167-173 New Delhi.

Relwani, L.L. 1979, Fodder Crops and Grasses; pp.9-12; New Delhi.

Pandya, Suman, 1980, "Ecology of the Harappan Urban Centres of Gujarat", Recent Researches in Geology, Vol. 9, pp. 170-178; Delhi.

Agrawal, D.P. 1982, Archaeology of India, pp. 192-193.

Gupta, S.K. 1977, Holocene Silting in the little Rann of Kutch", in Ecology and Archaeology ed. by Agrawal, D.P., Pande, B.M. pp. 201-205; New Delhi.

Roy, Bhasker, Merh. S.S, 1977; "Geomorphology of the Ranns of Kutch", ibid, pp. 195-200.

Yash Pal, *et al.* 1980, "Remote Sensing of the "Lost" Sarasvati River", Proceedings of the Indian Academy of Sciences (earch and planerary science) Vol. 89, No. 3, pp. 317-331.

Pandya, Suman, 1982, "Protohistoric Floods at Lothal A critical study", Sri A. Ghosh Commemoration Volume (in Press).

Pandya, Suman, 1981, "Sabarmatina Pooras Karano; Samasyao", Ukel (Gujarati), pp. 6-30, Ahmedabad.

Copper Hoard Culture of India: A Reassessment

MAKKHAN LAL
Deccan College, Poona.

Since the first discovery of a copper harpoon at Bithur in Kanpur district in 1822 *(As. Res.* p.3) nearly one thousand copper objects have been found from different parts of India. As these copper objects have mostly been found in hoards, they are known as 'copper hoards'. The number of copper objects found in a hoard varies between 1 and 47 except in the case of Gungeria, in M.P. where 424 pieces were found in a single hoard. Except in the case of Saipai, (*IAR* 1971-72:46-47) in Etawah district, Uttar Pradesh where a harpoon was found in excavation, at all other sites copper objects of the 'copper hoard' typology came to light while ploughing a field, digging a canal or making a road.

In 1951 Lal listed 34 copper hoard sites. Since then the number has gone up to 86. Of these 5 sites came from Haryana, 6 from Rajasthan, 33 from U.P., 19 from Bihar, 6 from West Bengal, 7 from Orissa, 8 from Madhya Pradesh and 1 from Karnataka (Fig. 1). The total number of objects from these sites are 959. This figure does not include objects from Kiratpur, Chandausi, and Pariar as the exact number is not known (Table No.1).

Main Types and their Probable Use

1. *Celts*:

Celts are of three types:

(a) Flat Celt:
(b) Shouldered Celts
(c) Bar Celts

These three types of celts show a flat ventral and slightly convex dorsal side. The flat and shouldered celts were probably used for cutting wood and for hunting animals. On the basis of use marks on the edge Agrawal (1971:198) suggests that bar celts were used for mining ores.

A study of 12 celts (flat and shouldered type) by Thapliyal and Shukla (1974) and Lal (1979) shows that celts have regular depression marks (varying in number) on one surface. Thapliyal and Shukla (1974) suggest that these depression marks may be the trade mark of smiths.

Smith (1905:238) suggested their use as currency like Irish gold and silver ring money. Agrawal (1971: 199) thinks that they were units of weight for smiths.

Harpoons

Harpoons are of two types.

Type 1: They are cut from a thick sheet of copper and hammered. They have 4-6 oblique barbs on each side spaced equally on the two-third length of blade. Besides they have a holed lug or forked hook on the stem.

Type 2: These are cast in double mould and have a long spear blade with generally two but sometimes three or four pairs of incurved barbs (Fig. 2.1). They have a well developed midrib and are superb examples of craftsmanship.

Antennae Swords

Antennae swords consist of a blade of 45-50 cm. in length and a hilt in one piece. The mid rib in the blade is quite prominent. The most remarkable feature of swords is the hilt which bifurcates like the antenna of an insect.

Antennae swords imply military element. They may have been used in killing game also.

Hooked Swords

Hooked swords are like antennae swords except that in place of antenna there is a forked hook on the steam (Fig.3.3).

Anthropomorphs

Anthropomorphs are large and massive objects. Forearms are incurved and sharpened on the outer edge, and legs are plane. The arms are thinner than the head which was further thickened by beating from the top (Fig. 3.4). The length of anthropomorphs varies between 25 and 45 cm. and breadth between 30 and 43 cm. In all cases except one the length of anthropomorph is more than its breadth.

Tiny (from 4 to 10 cm.) anthropomorphic figurines resembling hoard specimens are worshipped in the Ganga-Yamuna doab region as *Shani* God. It is, therefore, quite possible that copper hoard anthropomorphs were also objects of worship. In northeast Asia anthropomorphic figurines symbolize ancestors who are regarded as defenders of race (Gupta 1965).

Double-Axes.

These are made by cutting away almost circular pieces from the sides of an oval sheet. Only three specimens of double-axes are known. They come from Bhangarapir, Orissa. Of the three specimens two have both ends sharpened while the third has only one end sharp.

Type Distribution of Copper Hoards

On the basis of typology the copper hoard area can be divided into three zones.

Zone A

Zone A comprises Bihar, West Bengal and Orissa. This zone is characterised by the occurrence of (I) Flat celts (II) Shouldered celts (III) Bar celts, and (IV) Double-axes.

Zone B

Zone B comprises of Uttar Pradesh and Haryana. In this type finds are: (I) Anthropomorphs (II) Antennae swords (III) Hooked swords, and (IV) Harpoons, besides the types I, II and III of Zone A.

Zone C

Zone C comprises Rajasthan. The type finds of this zone are: (I) Flat celts, and (II) Bar celts.

Technology of Copper Hoard objects.

Smith (1905) mentioned the result of the analysis of 4 objects: one celt from Jabalpur, one sword from Fatehgarh and two harpoons (Locality not known). All these objects showed 3.38 to 13.3 percent of tin. The Bisauli anthropomorph showed 0.66 percent of nickel (Lal 1951 : 24). The chemical analysis of three celts from Bargunda (Gupta 1971) shows that one celt was of pure copper whereas two had one percent of alloys (alloy metal not mentioned). Five objects (Shahabad celt, Shahabad fragmentary harpoon, Kamdera celt, Dhanbad celt and Durgama celt) were analysed by Agrawal (1971 : 171). These samples showed that they were made of pure copper.

Agrawal and his colleagues (Agrawal *et al.* 1974, 1978) carried out analysis of 41 copper hoard objects. Of these 32 objects came from 12 sites in Uttar Pradesh and 9 from 5 sites in Bihar. Following is the number of different objects:

Celts	—	33	(24 from U.P. and 9 from Bihar)
Bangles	—	2	(from U.P.)
Anthropomorphs	—	1	(,, ,,)
Spear heads	—	2	(,, ,,)
Harpoons	—	2	(,, ,,)
Swords	—	2	(,, ,,)

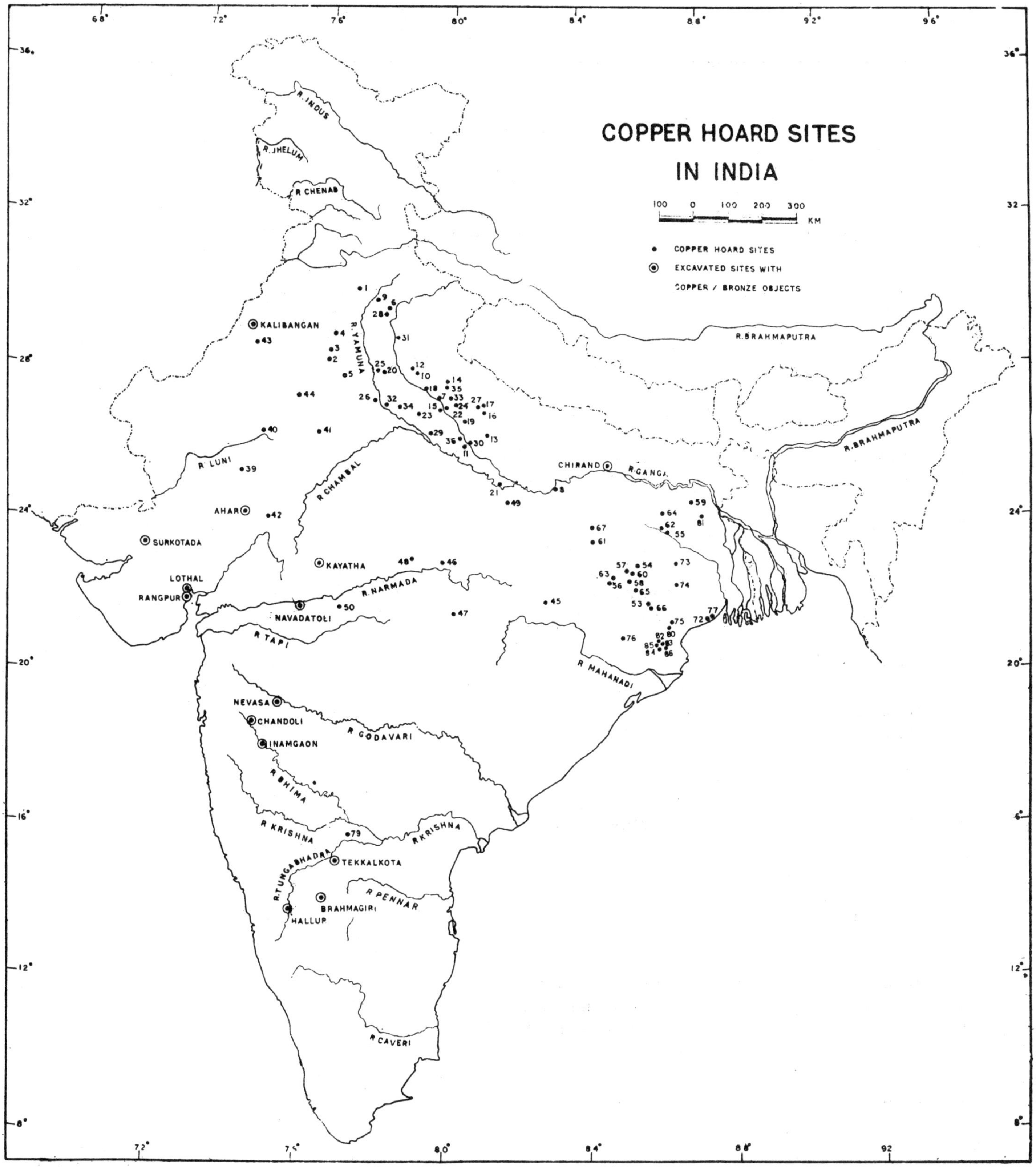

COPPER HOARD SITES
IN INDIA
100 0 100 200 300
KM
COPPER HOARD SITES
EXCAVATED SITES WITH
COPPER / BRONZE OBJECTS
R. INDUS
R. JHELUM
R. CHENAB
R. YAMUNA
R. BRAHMAPUTRA
R. GANGA
R. CHAMBAL
R. LUNI
R. NARMADA
R. TAPI
R. MAHANADI
R. GODAVARI
R. BHIMA
R. KRISHNA
R. TUNGABHADRA
R. PENNAR
R. CAVERI
KALIBANGAN
CHIRAND
AHAR
SURKOTADA
LOTHAL
RANGPUR
KAYATHA
NAVADATOLI
NEVASA
CHANDOLI
INAMGAON
TEKKALKOTA
BRAHMAGIRI
HALLUR

TABLE 1. List of sites of Copper Hoards and

			Copper				
S. No.	Locality	District & State	Flat celt	Shouldered celt	Bar cent	Hatchet or Parsu	Double edged axe
1	2	3	4	5	6	7	8
1.	Chandigarh	District H. Q., Haryana	—	—	—	—	—
2.	Dadri	Mahendragarh, Haryana	1	—	—	—	—
3.	Mitathal	Hissar, Haryana	1	—	—	1(?)	—
4.	Pauli	Jind, Haryana	—	—	—	—	—
5.	Rewari	Gurgaon, Haryana	4	—	—	—	—
6.	Bahadarabad	Saharanpur, U.P.	6	1	—	—	—
7.	Baheria	Shahjahanpur, U.P.	—	—	—	—	—
8.	Balua	Varanasi, U.P.	—	4	—	—	—
9.	Bargaon	Saharanpur, U.P.	—	—	—	—	—
10.	Bisauli	Badaun, U.P.	1	—	—	—	—
11.	Bithur	Kanpur, U.P.	29	7	—	—	—
12.	Chandausi	Moradabad, U.P.	—	—	—	—	—
13.	Deoti	Lucknow, U.P.	1	—	—	—	—
14.	Dhaka	Shahajahanpur, U.P.	—	5	—	—	—
15.	Fatehgarh	Farrukhabad, U.P.	—	—	—	—	—
16.	Gandhauli	Sitapur, U.P.	6	3	—	—	—

Copper-Bronze Implements of Protohistoric India

Hoard Types

Ring	Anthropomorphic figure	Harpoon	Artennae sword	Hooked sword	Place where lodged	Reference
9	10	11	12	13	14	15
4	—	—	—	—		IAR 1970-71 : 7-8
—	—	—	—	—	State Museum of Archaeology, Jhajjahar, Haryana	Gupta 1971
1	—	2	—	—	,,	Suraj Bhan 1969: 1—5
7	—	—	—	—	,,	Dikshit 1968: 49
—	—	—	—	—	,,	Dikshit 1968: 49
1	—	—	—	1	,,	Lal 1953: 91
—	—	1	1	1	Kausambi Museum, Allahabad	*IAR* 1966-67 : 43-44; Sharma 1971-72: 42-43
—	—	—	—	—	Bharat Kala Bhawan, Varanasi.	Dikshit 1968: 50
2	—	—	—	—	,,	*IAR* 1963-64 : 57
—	3	1	—	—	One Anthropomorphic figure in Muncipal Museum, Allahabad; the rest in Bharat Kala Bhawan, Banaras	Piggott 1944: 182; Lal 1951: 24—26
—	—	10	1	—	Indian Museum, Calcutta; State Museum, Lucknow, Muncipal Museum, Allahabad and Local Temples	*As. Res.* 1882:3; Anderson 1883: 395; Smith 1905: 232 and 1907: 53; Shastri 1915: 1—6; Lal 1951: 24; Lal 1979.
—	1	Several	Several	—	Sanskrit University, Varanasi: National Museum, New Delhi; Muncipal Museum, Allahabad.	*IAR* 1966-67: 81; Dikshit 1968: 50.
—	—	—	—	—	State Museum, Lucknow	Lal 1951 : 29.
—	—	—	—	—	State Museum, Lucknow	Lal 1951: 27-28
—	1	—	13	—	Indian Museum, Calcutta; National Museum of Antiquities, Edinburgh	*As. Res.* 1832: 624; Anderson 1883: 405—408; Smith 1905: 232.
—	—	—	—	—	State Museum, Calcutta Lucknow; Personal Collection of Misra Bandhu of Gandhauli	*IAR* 1956-57: 74, 1969-70; 38; Dikshit 1968: 50; Thapliyal & Shukla 1972: 98

Table contd.

1	2	3	4	5	6	7	8
17.	Hardi	Sitapur, U.P.	1	—	—	—	—
18.	Indilapur	Saharanpur, U.P.	1	—	—	—	—
19.	Kamalpur	Hardoi, U.P.	1	—	—	—	—
20.	Kiratpur	Bulandshar, U.P.	2	—	—	—	—
21.	Kausambi	Allahabad, U.P.	1	—	—	—	—
22.	Madanpur	Hardoi, U.P.	1	9	—	—	—
23.	Mainpuri	District H.Q., U.P.	2	—	—	—	—
24.	Majhadpur	Hardoi, U.P.	1	—	—	—	—
25.	Manpur	Bulandshar, U.P.	1	1	—	—	—
26.	Mathura	District H.Q., U.P.	1	—	—	—	—
27.	Nakarahiya	Sitapur, U.P.	—	4	—	—	—
28.	Nasirpur	Saharanpur, U.P.	2	2	2	—	—
29.	Niorai	Etawah, U.P.	—	—	—	—	—
30.	Pariar	Unnao, U.P.	1	1	—	—	—
31.	Rajpur Parsu	Bijnor, U.P.	9	—	1	—	—
32.	Sadabad	Mathura, U.P.	16	—	—	—	—
33.	Sahabad	Hardoi, U.P.	4	1	—	—	—
34.	Saipai	Etah, U.P.	—	—	—	—	—
35.	Sarthauli	Shahjahanpur, U.P.	—	—	—	1	—
36.	Sheorajpur	Kanpur U.P.	—	—	—	—	—
37.	?	Hardoi, U.P.	1	—	—	—	—
38.	?	Etawa, U.P.	—	—	—	—	—
39.	Elana		1	—	—	—	—
40.	Khardi	Nagaur, Rajasthan	7	—	1	—	—
41.	Nandlapura	Jaipur, Rajasthan	—	—	6	—	—
42.	Padaliya	Chittorgarh, Rajasthan	6	—	—	—	—
43.	Savarniya	Bikaner, Rajasthan	2	—	—	—	—
44.	Ganeswar	Sikar, Rajasthan	58	—	—	—	—
45.	Balpur	Bilaspur, M.P.	2	—	—	—	—
46.	Dabakia	Jabalpur, M.P.	—	—	1	—	—

9	10	11	12	13	14	15
—	—	—	—	—	State Museum, Lucknow	Lal 1951: 27.
—	—	—	—	—	State Museum, Lucknow	Lal 1951: 29.
—	—	—	—	—	,,	Shastri 1915: 4
Several	1	—	—	—	,,	*IAR* 1969-70: 38
—	—	—	—	—	British Museum, London	Smith 1905: 232.
—	—	—	—	—	Deccan College, Pune	Misra 1976
6	—	—	—	—	Indian Museum, Calcutta;	*P.A.S.B.* 1968: 251—62 Anderson 1883: 403.
—	—	—	—	—	State Museum, Lucknow	Lal 1951: 29.
—	—	—	—	1	,,	Shastri 1915: 4.
—	—	—	—	—	,,	Cunningham: 16
—	—	—	—	—	State Museum, Lucknow	Dikshit 1968: 50
—	—	1	—	1	Gurukul Kangari Museum, Hardwar	Dikshit 1968: 47
—	—	1	—	1	Royal Society of Antiquaries, Copenhagan	*P.S.A.S.* 1870: 293, 300; Anderson 1883: 396.
—	—	Several	—	—	Local temples	Fuhrer 1891: 168; Smith 1907: 53.
—	—	6	—	—	State Museum, Lucknow	Smith 1905: 231, 234
—	—	—	—	—	,,	Srivastava 1973: 41.
—	1	4	1	12	National Museum, New Delhi,	*I.A.R.* 1966-67; 81; Gupta 1965: 2-3.
—	1	1	—	2		*IAR.* 1970-71: 38; Lal 1971-72: 47.
—	—	1	—	5	State Museum, Lucknow	Lal 1951: 28-29.
—	3	—	—	—	,,	*Ibid* p. 29
—	—	—	—	—		Gupta, 1971
—	—	1	—	—	British Museum, London	*Ibid*
—	—	—	—	—	Directorate of Archaeology & Museums, Govt. of Rajasthan	Agrawal, 1979
—	—	—	—	—	Jodhpur Museum, Jodhpur	*IAR* 1960-61: 66
—	—	—	—	—	Dept. of Archaeology, Rajasthan	Parmar, 1977: 63-64.
—	—	—	—	—	,,	Times of India dated 27-8-1977; Agrawal 1979: 91.
—	—	—	—	—	State Museum of Archaeology, Jhajjhar, Haryana	Dikshit, 1968: 49; Gupta 1971; *IAR* 1968-69: 69
—	—	—	—	—	Department of Archaeology, Rajasthan	Agrawal 1978: 123.
—	—	—	—	—	Personal collection of Shri Pandey Lochan Sharma of Bilapur villate	Gordon 1958: 142
—	—	—	—	—	—	*IAR* 1961-62: 99

Table contd.

1	2	3	4	5	6	7	8
47.	Gungeria	Balaghat M.P.	Several	Several	Several	—	—
48.	Kelsi	Sagar, M.P.	3	—	—	—	—
49.	Pondi	Rewa, M.P.	5	—	—	—	—
50.	Ramjipura	Nimar, M.P.	1	—	—	—	—
51.	?	Jabalpur, M.P.	1	—	—	—	—
52.	?	Chhota Nagpur, M.P.	1	—	—	—	—
53.	Andheri	Singhbhum, Bihar	—	6	—	—	—
54.	Bandua	Ranchi, Bihar	1	—	—	—	—
55.	Bargunda	Hazaribagh, Bihar	1	—	—	—	—
56.	Bartola	Ranchi, Bihar	21	—	—	—	—
57.	Bichana	Ranchi, Bihar	1	—	—	—	—
58.	Bordogaon	Singhbhum Bihar	—	3	—	—	—
59.	Chadsai	Santhal Paragana, Bihar	—	2	—	—	—
60.	Dargama	Ranchi, Bihar	5	—	—	—	—
61.	Hami	Palamau, Bihar	6	—	17	—	—
62.	Kaharbari	Hazaribagh, Bihar	—	3	—	—	—
63.	Kandera	Ranchi, Bihar	2	—	—	—	—
64.	Kaushaya	Monghyr, Bihar	—	1	—	—	—
65.	Kera	Singhbhum, Bihar	—	1	—	—	—
66.	Kolabarty	Dhanbad, Bihar	—	6	—	—	—
67.	Saguna	Palamau, Bihar	1	—	—	—	—
68.	?	Hazaribagh, Bihar	3	—	—	—	—
69.	Various	Manbhum, Bihar	27	—	—	—	—
70.	?	Ranchi, Bihar	2	—	—	—	—
71.	?	Ranchi, Bihar	2	—	—	—	—
72.	Chatla	Midnapur, West Bengal	—	1	—	—	—
73.	Kulghera	Purulia, West Bengal	—	3	—	—	—
74.	Tamajuri	Midnapur, West Bengal	—	1	—	—	—
75.	Bhangarapir	Mayurbhanj, Orissa	—	1	—	—	3

9	10	11	12	13	14	15
—	—	—	—	—	Indian Museum, Calcutta; National Museum Dublin; British Museum, London, National Museum of Anticuities Edinburgh.	*PASB* 1970: 131; Anderson 1883: 414—25; Reed 1920: 182-83; Smith 1905: 233 ff.
—	—	—	—	—	Central Museum, Nagpur	Gupta 1971.
47	—	—	—	—	Muncipal Museum Allahabad; Office of the Superintendent of Archaeology, Vindhya Pradesh	Lal 1951: 22-23.
—	—	—	—	—	—	*IAR* 1962-63: 99; Krishna 1966: 197
—	—	—	—	—	—	*PSAS* 1874: 691
—	—	—	—	—	Patna Museum, Patna.	Gupta 1971
—	—	—	—	—	Ibid "	*Ibid*
—	—	—	—	—	"	*Ibid*
1	—	—	—	—	Madras Govt. Museum, Madras	Foote 1916: 164
—	—	—	—	—	Patna Museum, Patna.	Coggin-Brown 1915: 127-28.
—	—	—	—	—	"	Roy 1915: 422
—	—	—	—	—	"	Gupta 1965; 68—77; Dikshit 1968: 50.
—	—	—	—	—	"	Gupta 1971
—	—	—	—	—	Patna Museum, Patna.	Roy 1915: 239
—	—	—	—	—	"	Roy 1916: 482-83.
—	—	—	—	—	"	Gupta 1971.
—	—	—	—	—	"	*Ibid.*
—	—	—	—	—	Indian Museum, Calcutta	Mukherjee, 1935: 517 ff
—	—	—	—	—	Patna Museum, Patna	Gupta 1971.
—	1	—	—	—	Patna Museum, Patna & State Museum, Lucknow	*Ibid*
—	—	—	—	—		Coggin-Brown 1915: 125-26.
—	—	—	—	—	Indian Museum, Calcutta	*PASB* 1971: 231; Anderson 1883: 392—95.
—	—	—	—	—	"	Campbell 1916: 392—95
—	—	—	—	—	Patna Museum	Gupta 1971.
—	—	—	—	—	"	Gupta 1971.
—	—	—	—	—	Dept. of Archaeology, West Bengal.	*IAR* 1965-66: 68.
—	—	—	—	—	Directorate of Archaeology Govt. of West Bengal	*IAR* 1971-72 : 51.
—	—	—	—	—	Indian Museum, Calcutta	Anderson 1883: 485-86; Smith 1905: 5.
—	—	—	—	—	Shouldered celt in Patna Museum, Double axe. one each in State Museum, Lucknow.	Goggin-Brown 1916: 386-87; Gupta 1971.

Table contd.

1	2	3	4	5	6	7	8
76.	Dunria	Pal Lahara, Orissa	—	3	—	—	—
77.	?	?	—	—	—	—	—
78.	Agavibani	Midnapore, West Bengal	—	2 2 Celt fragments 4 unfinished selts	—	—	—
79.	Kallur	Raichur, Karnataka	2	—	—	—	—
80.	Parihati	Midnapore, West Bengal	—	—	1	—	5
81.	Bhaktabandh	Bankura, W. Bengal	—	2	—	—	—
82.	Khiching	Mayurbhanj, Orissa	—	2	—	—	—
83.	Kshetra	" "	—	2	—	—	—
84.	Baghada	Mayurbhanj, Orissa	—	—	—	—	1
85.	?	" "	—	2	—	—	—
86.	?	" "	—	1	—	—	—

Atomic absorption spectrometric analysis of 27 objects from Uttar Pradesh shows traces of tin in all specimens whereas nickel 0.005 to 0.453%, iron 0.0037 to 0.4768%, arsenic 0.1361 to 7.844% and lead 0.0038 to 2.432% are present (Agrawal *et al.* 1978: Table 1). Alloying of arsenic was deliberate. The closed casting of pure copper is quite difficult and harpoons and swords show that their casting was done in closed moulds. Arsenic was added to facilitate casting and make the metal hard.

A comparative study of impurity patterns of copper hoard objects from U.P. and Bihar has been carried out by Agrawal *et al* (1978: 43, Table 2 and 3). In spectrophotometry analysis not a single object from Uttar Pradesh shows the presence of tin whereas it is present in Rakha ore (Agrawal *et al.* 1978: Table 3).

Metallurgy

Metallographic analysis of some objects shows that besides alloying copper—hoard—smith knew the process of annealing and coldwork (Agrawal *et al.* 1978: 45-46). The objects were made both in open and closed moulds. Celts were generally cast in open moulds whereas swords and harpoons were cast in closed moulds.

Relationship between Copper Hoards, Late Harappans, OCP and Aryans

On the basis of typological analysis of copper hoards, celts and axes from Harppa and Mohenjodaro and similar objecs found in Egypt, Sardinia, British Isles, Greece and Transcaucasia, Heine-Geldern (1936, 1956) propounded that copper hoards belong to Aryans who came to India sometime between 1200 and 1000 B.C. Lal (1951) in his detailed typological analysis and critical assessment of Heine-Geldern's view showed that none of the copper hoard types have been found in Egypt. Sardinia, Transcaucasia etc.

Piggott (1944) first supported Aryan theory of Heine-Geldern but later changed his view and assigned the copper hoards to the Late Harappan people (Piggott 1950). Hoard objects, OCP and Late Harappan pottery at Bahadarabad and

9	10	11	12	13	14	15
—	—	—	—	—	State Museum, Lucknow; Patna Museum, Patna.	Gupta 1971; Lal 1951: 29.
—	1	—	—	—	Brooklyn Museum, U.S.A.	Chakrabarty 1977: 68.
11	—	—	—	—	Dept. of Archaeology, W. Bengal.	Times of India Dec. 3, 1976.
—	—	—	3	—	Hyderabad Museum, Hydera-bad	Annual Rep. Arch. Dept. of H.E.H. The Nizam's Dominion for 1937—40 (Calcutta 1942) pp. 22—24.
—	—	—	—	—	Dept. of Archaeology, University of Calcutta,	Nag and Chakrabarty 1980: 97—100
—	—	—	—	—	Directorate of Archaeology Govt. of West Bengal	Nag and Chakrabarty 1980: 97—100
—	—	—	—	—	Baripada Museum, Orissa.	Mohapatra 1964 : 45—47
—	—	—	—	—	,, ,,	,, 1964 : 45—47
—	—	—	—	—	,, ,,	,, 1964 : 45—47
—	—	—	—	—	,, ,,	,, 1964 : 45—47
—	—	—	—	—	,, ,,	,, 1964 : 45—47

a broken anthropomorphic figure from Lothal led Sharma (1962) to conclude that OCP and copper hoards were only the Late Phase of Harappan Culture.

The typological analysis of Harappan copper objects and those of copper hoards gives completely different pictures. The flat celts are the only common link between the two. The distinctive Harappan types are razor, arrow-heads, barbed fish hooks, and curved blades whereas copper hoards are distinguished by harpoons, antennae swords, and anthropomorps. The metal analysis of Harappan implements shows that tin was alloyed in copper from 1 to 23% to 7.84%.

Dikshit (1968), however, believes that the mid rib in harpoons and swords of copper hoards evolved due to the contact between Harappans and copper hoard people living in Haryana, Uttar Pradesh and Rajasthan. He does not specify from which Harppan object midrib in copper hoard objects evolved. But this theory cannot be sustained since only one copper hoard type, namely, harpoon is known by a single example from the surface of the mound at Mitathal.

Before the excavation at Saipai, copper hoards were never found in a stratigraphic context. At copper hoard sites of Bahadarabad, Nasirapur, Rajpur Parsu, Baheria, Kiratpur, and B sauli OCP was found.

Considering these evidences Lal (1951) associated copper hoards with OCP which was obtained from Hastinapura, Bisauli and Rajpur Parsu. From Saipai (*IAR* 1970-71: 46-47) OCP and a copper harpoon were found together in stratified deposit. Lal assigned this ceramic tradition and copper hoards to the people who inhabited the doab before the arrival of Aryans. The area of copper hoard distribution is at present known to have been occupied by Austo-Asiatic speaking Mundas, Santhalas and other tribes belonging to the Proto-Austroloid group of Indian population which probably migrated to India from southeast Asia (Mukharaji and Chakrabarty 1964). The Austro-Asiatic languages spoken in Burma and by Khasis in northeastern India would provide likely link to indicate the route which Mundas had taken on their migration to eastern and central India. It is also possible that eastern Austronesian tribes, forefathers of Mon Khmer and linguistically associated with Mundas, (Bongard-Levin 1957) independently developed the use of metal. Recent research shows that in Thailand the use of bronze started in 4th millennium B.C. and iron in the Middle of second millennium B.C. (Solheim II 1978). The northeastern India has been considered as an integral part of southeast Asia during neolithic period (Gupta 1963). So in all probability Mundas who migrated to India with the knowledge of metallurgy sometime between 3000-2000 B.C. were the authors of these hoards.

In Vedic literature also we find references about the Aryans encountering certain native tribes whom they called *nishadas,* having short stature and flat nose (*anas*). Most probably these native tribes were Mundas and other Austroloid tribes.

NOTE:

After this article was written and typed I received a comunication from Dr. S.P. Gupta and Dr. D.K. Chakrabarty regarding the occurrence of 16 harpoons, 7 celts, 2 chisels, 7 swords and a hooked rod 'all typical Gangetic valley specimens'. These were acquired in November 1982 from a place called Mallah in Ghana sanctuary near Bharatpur area of Rajasthan. These objects are now in the possession of Directorate of Archaeology, Rajasthan. Since nothing has been published about them so far, it is not possible to add and more information.

Dr. D.K. Chakrabarty informs also about the occurrence of a shouldered-celt from a place called Peura in Sabang P.O. in Midnapur district. This celt was acquried in late 1982 and is now in the Indian Museum, Calcutta. Nothing is yet known of the circumstances of the discovery.

In spite of my best efforts to see and examine the copper hoard objects kept in Jhajhjhar Museum and yet unpublished, I failed. But I feel that this should not affect the analysis and conclusions I have presented here; because, as Prof. B.B. Lal pointed out in Delhi conference 1982, these objecs were bought in Rewari market and their find spot is not known. Thus their value lies in increasing the number of objects rather than contributing anything new towards the understand of the culture.

ACKNOWLEDGEMENTS

I greatfully thank Prof. V.N. Misra for kindly going through the manuscript and suggesting several improvements and to Drs. S.P. Gupta and D.K. Chakrabarty for sending me the information about new copper hoards.

REFERENCES

Agrawal, D.P. 1971, *Copper Bronze Age in India.* Delhi: Munshiram Manoharlal.

Agrawal, D.P., R.V. Krishnamurthy, S. Kusumgar and M.B. Sarin 1974, Alloying in Copper hoards. *Bulletin of Archaeology and Museums in U.P.* 14: 14—18.

Agrawal, D.P., R.V. Krishnamcrthy and S: Kusumgar 1973, New data on the copper hoards and Daimabad bronzes. *Man and Environment.* 2: 40—46.

Agrawala, R.C. 1978, Copper celts and an Indus arrowhead from Kulhade-Ka-Johad, District Sikar, Rajasthan. *Man and Environment.* 2. 123.

Agrawala, R.C. 1979, More copper finds from Rajasthan. *Man and Invironment.* 3: 91-92.

Anderson, J. 1883, *Catalogue of Archaeological collections in Indian Museum* Vol. II. Calcutta.

Bongard-Levin, G.M., and D.V, Deopic 1957, K. problem proiskhozdeniya norodov Munda. *Sovetskaya Etnogratia.* 1: 46—50.

Campbell, A. 1916, A note on the occurence of copper celts in Manbhum. *Journal of Bihar and Orissa Research Society. 2. 85-86.*

Chakrabarty, D.K. 1976, An anthropomorph in the Brooklyn museum, New York. *Man and Environment.* 1: 68.

Coggin-Brown, J. 1915 Notes on two copper axes. *Journal of Bihar and Orissa Research Society.* 1: 127-28.

Coggin-Brown, J. 1915, Note on a copper celt found in Palamau district. *Journal of Bihar and Orissa Research Society,* 1: 125-26.

Coggin-Brown, J. 1916, Further relics of copper age. *Journal of Bihar and Orissa Research Society.* 2: 386-87.

Cunningham, A. 1871, Mathura. *Archaeological Survey of India Report.* 3: 13—15.

Dikshit, K.N. 1963, The copper hoards in the light of recent discoveries. *Bulletin of Ancient In-*

dian History and Archaeology. 2: 43—50.

Foote, R.B. 1916, *The Foote Collection of Indian Prehistoric and Protohistoric Antiquities, Notes on their Ages and Diseribution.* Madras: Madras Government Museum.

Fuchs, S. 1980, The origin of Mundas. *Anthropos.* 75: 286-87.

Fuhrer, 1891, *Monuments and Antiquities of N.W. Provinces and Oudh, Allahabad:* Government Press.

Gordon, D.H. 1958, *Prehistoric background of Indian Culture.* Bombay: Bhula Bhai Memorial Institute.

Gupta, P.L. 1968, Prehistoric copper implements from Bardugua. *Journal of Indian Museums,* 21-24: 77.

Gupta, P.L. 1971, Copper hoards in India. Paper presented at 28th Intrnational Orientalists Congress, Canberra.

Gupta, S.P. 1963, Indian copper hoards : The problem of homogenity, stages of development, origin, authorship and dating. *Journal of Bihar Research Society.* 49: 147—66.

Gupta S.P. 1965, Further copper hoards, a reassessment in the light of new evidence. *Journal of Bihar Research Society.* 51: 1-7.

Heine-Geldern, R. 1936, Archaeological traces of vedic aryans.*Journal of Indian Society of Oriental Art.* 4: 87—113.

Heine-Geldern, R. 1956, The coming of the Aryans and the end of Harppa civilization *Man.* 56: 136—40.

Krishna, C. 1966, Copper celt from Ramjipura, District East Nimar. *Bulletin of Deccan College Research Institute.* 25—197.

Lal, B.B. 1951, Further copper hoards from the Gangetic basin and review of the problem. *Ancient India.* 7: 20—39.

Lal, M. 1979, New copper hoards from Bithur, Kanpur district, Uttar Pradesh. *Archaeological Studies.* 4. 34—37.

Lal, M. 1982, *Early Human Colonisation Patterns in the Ganga-Yamuna Doab.,* unpublished Ph.D. Thesis, Poona University.

Misra, V.N. 1976, New copper hoards from Madnapur, district Hardoi; Paper presented at Annual Conference of Indian Archaeological Society, held at Jaipur.

Mohapatra, G.C. 1964, Prehistory. pp. 1—54. In Sahu, N.K. (ed.) *Utkal University History of Orissa.* Vol. I. Bhubneshwar: Utkal University.

Mukherjee, G.N. 1935, Prehistoric copper celts. *Indian Historical Quaterly* 11: 517—28.

Nag, A.K. and D.K. Chakrabarty, 1980, Copper hoards from West Bengal, *Puratattva,* 9: 97-100.

Naik,A.V. 1943, A note on the copper swords from Kallur. *Bulletin of Deccan College Research Institute.* 4: 76-78.

Parmar, B.M.S. 1977, A copper hoard from Nandlalpura, district Jaipur, Rajasthan; *Man and Environment.* 1: 63-64.

Piggott, S. 1944, Prehistoric copper hoards in Ganga basin., *Antiquity.* 17: 173—82.

Piggott, S. 1950, *Prehistoric India,* Harmondsworth: Penguine Books.

Reed, C. 1920, *Guide to the Antiquites of the Bronze Age in British Museum.* London: British Museum.

Roy, S.C. 1915, A note on some remains of ancient asuras in the Ranchi district. *Journal of Bihar and Orissa Research Society.* 2: 481—84.

Roy, S.C. 1916, Relics of copper age found in Chhota Nagpur. *Journal of Bihar and Orissa Research Society.* 2: 481-84.

Sharma, G.R. 1971, Excavations at Baheria. *Puratattva.* 5: 42-43

Shstri, H. 1915, Recent addition to our knowledge of the copper age antiquities of Indian empire. *Journal of Asiatic Society, Bengal.* (new series). 11: 1—7.

Smith, V.A. 1905, Copper age and the prehistoric bronze implements of India. *Indian Antiquary.* 229—44.

Smith, V.A. 1907, Copper age and the prehistoric bronze implements of India supplement *Indian Antiquary.* 36: 53—55.

Srivastava, A.K. 1973, Treasure trove finds from Mathura. *Bulletin of Archaeology and Musems in U.P.* 11-12: 37—41.

Suraj Bhan, 1969, *Excavations at Mithathal, Hissar;* Kurukshetra: Kurukshetra University.

Thakkar, H.A. 1977, The technical and cultural study of Madnapur copper hoard axes, unpublished M.A. Thesis. Department of Ancient Indian History, Cclture and Archaeology. Baroda University, Baroda.

Thaplyal, K.K. and Shukla, S.P. 1976, Copper celts with circular depressions some observations. in U.V. Singh (ed.) *Archaeological Congress and Seminar Papers.* Kurukshetra. Kurukshetra University. pp. 98—101.

Wheeler, R.E.M. 1959, *Early India and Pakistan,* London: Thames and Hudson.

Plant Economy in Ancient Sringaverapura Phase–I (*C.* 1050–1000 B.C.)

K.S. SARASWAT
Botany Department, D.S. College
Aligarh

INTRODUCTION

Professor B.B. Lal and K.N. Dikshit have recently carried out the archaeological excavations at Sringaverapura, an ancient site on the bank of the river Ganga in Allahabad district of Uttar-Pradesh (24° 47′and 25° 47′ N, and 81° 9″ & 82° 21′ E) under the joint auspices of Indian Institute of Advanced Study, Simla and Archaeological Survey of India, New Delhi, as part of National project 'Archaeology of Ramayana sites.' It was done with the view to determine the cardinal facts of the chronology of Ramayana age. The huge epic of Ramayana which is probably lesser ancient than Mahabharata, relates the story of Rama, prince of Kosala (Oudh) and is also regarded by religious people as a storehouse of historical events. Literary tradition being almost the only source, the results obtainable are very meagre and wanting in precision. The history can not be divorced from chronology and that the investigation of facts incapable of chronological arrangement, lies outside the historian's province. Thus the scientific interpretation of the scanty material relics recovered through the archaeological excavations, will provide the direct evidence to reconstruct the history of Ramayana age culture at Sringaverapura.

The plant remains of cultivated assemblage discussed in the present paper have been discovered from the deposits of earliest phase of human settlement, characterised by a Red Ware Industry which is associable with Ochre Colour Ware dating back to C. 1050—1000 B.C. (Lal and Dikshit, 1981). The finds will capture the interest of archaeologists as well as the botanists, because the study of fragile and deceptive plant remains will provide the informations about agricultural economy that the Sringaverapura inhabitants were then practicing.

MATERIAL

The material was collected from a 30-60 cm. thick deposit of yellowhis clay just above the natural soil, labelled as Layer 19E in archaeological trench—SVP—1, YA3—Qd—3. The clay samples showing the superficial impressions of plant remains, were collected by the author under the direction of excavators. The embedded plant material consists of the wood charcoals, a few bits of woody tissue in deteriorated state, very limited number of fragile, carbonised seeds and grains and numerous leaf fragments of microscopic nature.

The grain impressions on the potsherd surface were also investigated. One of the sherds revealed a few textile fibres adhered inside a pit on its surface.

For comparative study, I had at my disposal some authentically identified material of extant plants obtained from Central Rice Research Institute. Cuttack and I.A.R.I. New Delhi.

Table No. 1 shows the nature of plant-remains selected for the study along with the archaeological numbers. The study of wood charcoals has not been included in the present paper.

TABLE NO. 1
Showing the nature of plant materials

S. No.	*Archaeological Number*	*Material*
1.	SVP-1 YA3-Qd.3 Layer (19E)	One complete seed and two broken pieces in the carbonised and deteriorated state of preservation.
2.	—Do—	Single carbonised cereal grain.
3.	—Do—	Some tender fibres of brownish colour, attached to minute pieces of carbonised seed
4.	—Do—	Two potsherds showing the impressions and marks of grains and husks.
5.	—Do—	Fragile husk and leaf fragments of microscopic nature, visible only under a magnifying lens.

METHODS

The nature of the plant material embedded in the mud determines the technique that had to be applied to bring out the detailed morphological and anatomical structure.

The grains and seeds embedded in the mud were repeatedly washed in water and treated with 5% glacial acetic acid for 2-4 hours depending on the condition of preservation to loosen the clay particles adhered to the surface of carbonised material. The material was then washed in water and cleaned with the help of soft camel-hair brush under a steriobinocular.

To recover the minute and microscopic leaf and husk peels, the bits of clay showing the superficial marks of the plant materials were sorted out under a magnifying lens. The desired clay pieces were treated with 10% glacial acetic acid for about 8-12 hours. The next step was to centrifuge the clay bit by bit in water for about 5 minutes. As a result the minute peels got dislodged from the clay particles and came up to float on the surface of water. They were collected under a steriobinocular, dehydrated and brought to absolute alcohol, and carefully mounted in canadabalsam.

The textile fibres were dislodged from the potsherd with the help of pointed forceps and a needle and transferred to 2% glacial acetic. The fibres easily got rid of mud particles by the repeated acid treatment. Dehydration was carried out in gradual series of tertiary-butyl alcohol and mounted in canadabalsam for the microscopic study.

The potsherds when examined under a steriobinocular microscope, revealed the characteristic husk marks and the grain impressions included here in this paper.

RESULTS

The results of botanical study have been given under different headings as given below:

SESAME, *Sesamum* sp.
SVP-1, YA3-Qd3. Layer (19E).
Figs. 1 & 2.

The lot consists of three seeds, one complete and other broken ones. The complete seed measures 2.5 mm in length and 1.5 mm. in width.

They are flattish and somewhat ovate in shape. Seed surface is smooth. Under a steriobinocular the presence of feeble marginal line is noticed on the flat surface of seed in all the three samples.

The flat and ovate shaped small sized seeds are regarded to belong to sesame species (Purseglove, 1974; Nagar, 1976). The comparision of the seeds under investigation with the extant sesame seeds shows the close resemblance in all the respects and therefore, the ancient seeds have been identified as such.

The faint marginal line as revealed by the carbonised sesame seeds, has been regarded as the diagnostic feature of *Sesamum indicum* L. (Martin and Barkley, 1961), the only cultivated species in India (Purseglove, 1974) for the source of sesame oil. It would, therefore, appear that the material under investigation belongs to *Sesamum indicum* L. (Family Pedaliaceae).

The sesame, also known as Beniseed, Gingelly and Til, is an important oil-seed corp in India.

BARLEY, *Hordeum* sp.
SVP-1, YA3-Qd.3. Layer (19E)
Fig. 3

The single elongated caryopsis measures 6 mm. in length and 3 mm. in breadth. The embryo rests on the elongated end of almost flat dorsal side. The ventral side has a longitudinal furrow originating from the base of grain and widening towards the upper end. The grain is enclosed within the thick husk showing longitudinal striations under a steriobinocular microscope.

Taking into consideration the morphological features revealed by the ancient grain, i.e., the elongated caryopsis with flat dorsal side, dorsally located embryo on the pointed end and the wide and shallow furrow on ventral side, which are diagnostic characters of *Hordeum* caryopsis (Chowdhury, 1963; Chowdhury and Buth, 1972; Saraswat, 1980), the author has been led to identify it as such. As the grain is enclosed in the thick husk, the Sringaverapura barley belongs to the hulled species of *Hordeum*.

The hulled species of barley is classified into two groups—two rowed and six-rowed forms depending on the number of fertile florets present per node of spike axis (Bor, 1960; Helbaek, 1960; Backer and Bakhuizen, 1968). Out of the three florets per node in two-rowed species, only the median floret develops in to the caryopsis and the rest being sterile, resulting in one row of caryopses on either side of the spike. While in six-rowed forms all the three florets are fertile forming three rows of caryopses on the either side of spike. The median caryopsis in this form is longer with a prominent bulge in the middle pushing the lateral ones outwardly. As a result, the lateral caryopses become asymmetrical and develop the characteristic twists on the ventrolateral sides.

The ancient grain from Sringaverapura shows the distinct twist suggesting that it is the lateral caryopsis of six-rowed *Hordeum* species (Chowdhury, 1963; Helbaek, 1964, 1966). All the wild and cultivated species of barley belong to the same potentially interfertile population and are grouped under one species, *Hordeum vulgare* L. emend. Bowden (Bakshi and Rana, 1974: Harlan, 1976). The Sringaverapura barley has therefore, been placed under six-rowed hulled *Hordeum vulgare* L. emend. Bowden., which is the predominently cultivated species.

COTTON, *Gossypium* sp.
SVP-1, YA3-Qd.3. Layer (19E)
Figs 4-9

The light to deep brown coloured fibres were located in a small pit of pottery piece (Fig. 4). under a steriobinocular, the fibres revealed the coarse nature. They were attached to the small pieces of carbonised seed coat. The exceedingly tender fibres used to break under a slight stress. However, it could be possible to obtain some permanent preparations for microscopic study.

The fibres are distinctly of two types the long and short ones. Some of the long fibres measure 10-16 mm. The long fibres are characteristically flat, having a lumen and twists throughout the length (Figs 7, 8 & 9) and a few short fibres are rounded in cross view and without any convolutions.

The long and short fibres on seed-coat surface and the flat, long fibres with convolutions, are the diagnostic features for the identification of true cottons of commerce i.e. the cultivated species of *Gossypium* suitable for spinning and turning into yarn (Carpenter & Leney, 1952; Hutchinson, 1959; Purseglove, 1974).

The long fibres are called as 'lint' or 'staple' and short ones, the 'fuzz'. The lint grows to a greater length and the deposition of cellulose is reduced forming a lumen, so that the hairs collapse and become flat on being dried. The deposition of cellulose is in spiral pattern and the change in the direction of deposition results in the formation of twists or convolutions. These twists permit the spinning of lint for the textiles. On the other hand, the wild *Gossypium* species are lintless with short and unconvoluted fibres.

The ancient cotton fibres from Sringaverapura reveal all the features of cultivated cotton, quite suitable for the textiles, it is therefore, identified as such.

There are four cultivated species of cotton with spinnable lint viz., the diploid Old World cottons *G. herbaceum* L. and *G. arboreum* L., and the tetraploid New World cottons—*G. barbadense* L. & G. *hirsutum* L. (Hutchinson, Silow and Stephens, 1947). The ancient cotton from Sringaverapura falls under the category of Old World cottons, it would therefore, be preferable to restrain the present study to only the Old World cottons.

Both the Old World species viz. *G. herbaceum* L. and *G. arboreum* L. fall under the 'genome—A' group of the conventional system of classification by Beasley (1942), based on cytological grounds. Though both the species are different from taxonomic point of view, yet there is no difference in the seed-coat anatomy and the hairs (Chowdhury and Buth, 1971). The cytological and anatomical approaches have their limitations to resolve the mystery of Sringaverapura cotton as to which species of Old World cottons it belongs, it has therefore, been placed under G. *herbaceum-arboreum.*

PADDY, *Oryza* sp
SVP-1, YA3-Qd.3. Layer (19E)
Figs 10-16

The study of rice in this lot is based on the impressions of paddy caryopses and the marks of husks (fertile glumes) on the potsherds (Fig 10), and the microscopic study of minute husk and leaf peels recovered from the soil (Figs 13, 14, 15 & 16).

The impression of caryopsis (Fig. 11) measures 7 mm. in length and 3.5 mm. in breadth. It shows the distinct fertile glumes i.e. the lemma and palea which cover the kernel. The lemma is characteristically boat shaped with convex outer surface and shows the longitudinal ribs on its surface. The rachilla or the stalk of the caryopsis is also clearly visible.

The impressions of lemma and palea, clearly exhibit the tissue under a binocular microscope, arranged in chess-board pattern (Fig. 12).

The presence of sub-equal lemma and palea with characteristic chess-board pattern of the tissues, is the important feature to identify the unknown caryopsis as belonging to *Oryza* species, in the grass family (Chowdhury and Ghosh, 1954-55; Musil, 1963; Chowdhury, Saraswat and Buth, 1977; Saraswat, 1980).

It is difficult to differentiate the cultivated rice from the wild one on the basis of grain impressions. In wild species, the caryopses are shattered before attaining the maturity while cultivated species does not do so. The rachilla in cultivated taxa is prominently developed having the swollen base to firmly attach the caryopses with the rachis. Luckily the impression of rachilla is quite clear (Fig 11) and shows the peculiarities of cultivated taxa. The Sringaverapura rice has, therefore, been identified as the cultivated species of *Oryza.*

There are two cultivated species of *Oryza, O. sativa* in Asia and *O. glaberrima* in Africa. Taking for granted the monophyletic evolution, the domestications of rice in Asia and Africa took place independently from a common wild, perennial progenitor which is still obscure and, probably, had existed in humid zone of Gondwana land before the continental drift (Shastry and Sharma, 1974; Chang, 1976 a, b). There is no evidence of any contact between Asia and Africa in the protohistoric times to account of the occurrence of *O. glaberrima* in Asia.

The immensity in the variations of rice crops has been regarded to have developed in India in four or five millennia. The domestication of rice is not strictly confined to the centres having diversity in its wild forms, the region having the vast variations in the cultivated forms, gives a more useful indication to the centre of domestication (Shastry and Sharma, 1974; Chang, 1976, a, b). Further the earliest direct evidence of domestication of rice known so far, at Neolithic Mahagara and Koldihwa (c. 7000-4500 B.C.) in Allahabad district (Sharma, 1980), supports the contention that North India is the ancestral home of cultivated rice.

In the light of above discussion, the Sringaverapura rice can safely be regarded as the cultivated *Oryza sativa* L..

The husk peels recovered from the soil revealed the squarish epidermal cells with thick and sinuous walls similar to the extant husk peels of *Oryza,* in all the anatomical respects.

In the leaf peels, the epiderimis consists of long and short cells (Fig 15). The long cells in the intercoastal region (between the veins) have thick and sinuous walls which are pitted. The short cells lie solitarily as well as in pairs. The paired ones are composed of cork cells and silica cells. The short cells over the veins, are arranged in rows and the cork cells and silica cells often alternate with each other...............(Fig. 16). The characteristic "Dumb-bell" shaped silica bodies inside the silica cells, are described as "Oryza-type" by Metcalfe (1960). The stomata with somewhat triangular and low-domed subsidiary cells, are arranged in rows and confined in the region between the veins. In all the anatomical details, the unknown leaf fragments exhibit the complete agreement with the structure of leaf peelings of extant paddy.

DISCUSSION

The knowledge of agricultural economy in the dim ages of past which lie beyond the ken of history, is attainable by the interpretations of results of archaeobotanical finds. The remains of the crop plants from the first occupational phase of Sringaverapura (C-1050-1000 B.C.) will significantly, give an idea of the highly developed agriculture achieved by early man. The plants of cultivated assemblage recovered consist of rice *(Oryza sativa* L.), barley *(Hordeum vulgare* L. emend. Bowden.), sesame *(Sesamum Indicum* L.) and cotton *(Gossypium herbaceum-arboreum* L.). The Sringaverapura mound is situated in the stretch of alluvial land in trans Ganga region, north of that river in Allahabad district. The area is fertile having the clay, loam and sandy-alluvial soils. The cotton can be cultivated on a variety of soils from light sandy soils to heavy alluvium. Sesame prefers sandy loams. It is not exacting in its soil requirements and does reasonably well on poor soils. It appears that the settlers at this place must have had the knowledge of the favourable conditions of soil and climate for the agricultural practices.

The plant remains will now be considered separately to show its archaeological significance in relation to some of the other finds.

The rice is the oldest crop of South-East Asia. North-East India, Northern Bangladesh and triangle adjoining Burma, Thailand, Laos, Vietnam and Southern China, are regarded as the primary centres of domestication of rice (Chang, 1976 a, b). Direct evidence of the early evolution of cultivated rices, is fragmentary and often controversial. Domestications of *Oryza sativa* in Asia and *O. glaberrima* in Africa, took place independently from a common ancestor which was present in Gondwana land before the continental drift (Chang, 1976 a, b). However, *Oryza 'perennis'* complex has also been regarded as the probable common progenitor, but indeed it is still obscure (Oka, 1974; Shastry and Sharma, 1974: Chang, 1976 a, b). In Asia, Oryza sativa has originated from a wild perennial species similar to *O. rufipogon,* via a wild annual *O. nivara* like form which is widely distributed in Deccan-plateau of India, S.E. Asia and Oceania. Numerous intergrading hybrids between *Oryza sativa* and its wild relatives, are widely distributed in the foothills of Himalays extending upto Mekong region suggesting the diffuse origin of rice in Asia (I.R.R.I., 1964; Harlan, 1969; Shastry and Sharma, 1974; Chang, 1975, 1976 a, b).

Recent excavations at Chopani-Mando and Mahagara in Belan valley within the hilly tracts of Vindhyan foothills, and Mahadaha and Koldihwa in Gangetic plains (Allahabad District, U.P.), have brought to light the earliest evidence of human settlement in Indian archaeological context. The sites have furnished the interesting evidence of human cultures from Epi-palaeolithic to Neolithic showing the transition from food gathering stage to the food producing stage. Rice was known and used in the area even in the advanced mesolithic culture represented by Chopani-Mando

(Phase III). Even though it was the wild rice, the evidence of the use of rice, is very important. As the evolution under domestication can not be older than agriculture (Hutchinson, 1974), the use of wild rice may safely be regarded to provide an indication for the beginning of agriculture. The evidence of cultivated rice (*Oryza Sativa* L.) has been obtained from Neolithic Mahagara and Koldihwa (C. 7000-4500 B.C.) This is the earliest evidence of rice cultivation discovered so far, in any part of the world (Sharma, 1980). Thus, the history of domestication of rice, now, goes back to seventh millennium B.C. suggesting that India is the ancestral home of rice.

In general, the evidences clearly indicate the considerable antiquity of rice, but indecisive as to the time and place. Outside India, rice has been reported from Sung-tse near Shanghai in China (C. 3500 B.C.). According to Julien, a historian, "It was reserved for the Emperor of China, Ching-nog, to sow seeds of rice at a particular ceremony (established about 2800 B.C.) in the beginning of cultivation season, and the sowing of less important kinds of grains was relegated to the princes of his family (De candolle, 1886). The recorded history of rice cultivation in China goes back to the third millennium B.C. A pottery from Thailand dated to 3500 B.C., bears the imprints of rice glumes (Chang, 1976).

It would be reasonable to say that in the light of present state of knowledge, Vindhyan Neolithic people emerged as the earliest farming community to cultivate rice in India at the time ranges between 7000-4500 B.C. For the detailed account of rice records from pre-and proto-historic sites, Vishnu-Mittre (1974) and Saraswat (1980) may be consulted.

The barley cultivation in Indian sub-continent has, evidently come from western Asia and can be followed with certainty, across North India and then south ward (Vishnu-Mittre, 1974; Bakshi and Rana, 1974). India's cultural and commercial contacts with West-Asia, Egypt, the Archaemenian empire and the Greco-Roman kingdom from pre-and proto-historic times, thrived due to commercial and trade relations. Barley came to India, either through the trade routes or alongwith the immigrating people, not only once but on several pre-historic occasions.

Barley was one of the earliest domesticated crops in Near-East. In the light of present knowledge on the evolution of barley so far revealed by the archaeological remains, the earliest barley used by man appears to be wild, two rowed *Hordeum spontaneum* koch. at Tell Mureybat (Syria) dated back C. 8050-7542 B.C. It continued to be found at Beidha (6800 B.C.) in southern Jordon and at Jarmo (7000-6500 B.C.) in Iraqi Kurdistan. The first record of domesticated barley was discovered at Tell Ramad in Syria (C. 7000 B.C.) which is identified as two rowed, hulled *H. distichum* L. (Renfrew, 1969; Harlan, 1976). The data reveals that *H. spontaneum* Koch, *H. distichum* L., *H. vulgare-nudum* L. and H. *vulgare* L. were cultivated, often as a mixture of two to three at different sites in Iran, Iraq and Turkey, alongwith the other primary crops as emmer-wheat, einkorn-wheat, flax, pea, vetch and lentil, from 6750 B.C. to 5000 B.C. (Renfrew, 1969; Chowdhury and Buth, 1972; Harlan, 1976).

In Indian sub-continent, barley was cultivated throughout the Harappan period (C.2300—1750 B.C.). The six-rowed, hulled *Hordeum vulgare* var. *hexastichum* was found at Harappa and it was referred to naked barley at Mohenjo-Daro (Marshall, 1931; Vats, 1940). The samples of barley grains recovered from pre-Harappan Kalibangan, consist of hulled as well as naked forms.

In the light of recent excavations at Mehragarh, an early Harappan site in Kachi plains of Baluchistan, the history of agriculture in north-western Indian sub-continent has gone back to sixth millennium B.C. The site has evidenced a gradual cultural evolution from phase-I (C. 6000 B.C.) to the beginning of mature Harappan culture at 2500 B.C. The phase-I at Mehragarh has revealed the interesting evidence of cereal cultivation. The cereals include two-rowed, six-rowed, hulled forms of barley & eincorn, emmer and bread wheats (Jarrige and Meadow, 1980).

It is evident that the cereal cultivation, often the mixture of two forms of barley *(Hordeum distichum* L. & *Hordeum vulgare* L.) along with einkorn *(Triticum monococcum)*, emmer *(T. dicoccum)* and bread-wheat *(T. aestivum)* as reported by Jarrige and Meadow (1980) at Mehragarh (Phase I), had been practised on the same identical pattern of West-Asia, from 6750 B.C.

to 5000 B.C. as at various ancient sites in Iran, Iraq, Turkey and Egypt. Thus, West-Asian agriculture took hold of vast land area upto Kachi plains of Baluchistan in north—West Indian sub-continent.

The Harappan culture has been extensively studied and is dated to the period between 2300-1750 B.C., but since there is extensive evidence of both an advanced agriculture and sophisticated textile craft, the Harappan evidently does not represent the beginnings of agriculture in Indian sub-continent (Hutchinson, 1974). Lal (1980) excavated at Kalibangan in Rajasthan, a pre-Harappan ploughed field. This is the earliest record of ploughed field excavated so far in the world, with some of the furrow-marks still intact. Not only the achievements of pre-Harappans but also those of Neolithic folks in Kachi plains of Baluchistan, seem to have been passed on to the Harappans. This conclusion may be drawn on the grounds of the facts that the crops of West-Asian cereals reaped by Harappans, have been recorded in the Neolithic agriculture at Mehragarh (C. 6000 B.C.). Wheat and barley were taken to cultivation in North-West Indian sub-continent right from the early neolithic times, much earlier to the Harappan period.

Next to Harappan period, Atranjikhera has provided the evidence of barley cultivation in Gangetic plains, over a quite long period of 1800 years between 2000-200 B.C. (Saraswat, 1980). The Neolithic site at Chirand (C. 1900-1400 B.C.) in Bihar, has revealed the hulled as well as naked forms of barley (Vishnu-Mittre, 1974). Sringaverapura (Phase I) has furnished an additional evidence of barley cultivation in Gangetic plains.

The sesame has been claimed to be the most ancient oil seed known to man since the remote past. It seems fairly definite that Sesame *(Sesamum indicum* L.) which is of very ancient cultivation, was first taken to agriculture in Africa and that it was taken at a very early date to India where a secondary centre of diversity developed Africa is the primary centre of origin due to the presence of diverse wild species in that region (Chandrasekharan and Parthasarthy, 1965; Purseglove, 1974; Nagar, 1976).

Arabs in pursuit of slaves in tropical Africa, perhaps, collected the sesame from there. On archaeological grounds the sesame was being cultivated in Palestine and Syria during the chalcolithic period, about 3000 B.C. (Nagar, 1976). Near East seems to have welcomed the sesame and that its name had reached Sumeria by the time of third dynasty of Ur (C. 2350 B.C.), though the way to Sumeria is not documented. Straoo (C. 54 B.C.-A.D. 24) states that it was the oil seed of southern Arabia and thrived well under the climatic conditions there (Burkill, 1962). Harappa (C. 2300 B.C.) far inland by river Ravi, has shown the seeds of sesame. Presumably, therefore, sesame was cultivated through the Indus civilization and possibly the agriculture of Sumeria had taken hold of fairly large part of North Indian sub-continent (Vats, 1940; Thompson, 1949; Burkill, 1962; Darlington, 1963). Next to Harappa, Sringaverapura (C. 1050-1000 B.C.) is the solitary site in India to provide the evidence of sesame *(Sesamum indicum* L.) in Gangetic plains.

The name of sesame (Til) appears in Vedic literature passes through Sanskrit and persists today. As a source of oil, its importance was so great that its name meant oil, the metonomy being from oil (Tel) to sesame (Til); and in that case all the other oil seeds raised would be secondary to sesame at the time when sesame obtained its name in the context of ancient civilizations in India.

Until, 1960, the only evidence of the use of cotton was given by Mohenjo-Daro. This knowledge was increased by the discovery of cotton fabrics associated with a necklace at Navasa in Maharashtra dating back to C. 1500-1000 B.C (Gulati, 1961) and cotton impressions on pottery at Rupar (C. 500 B.C.) in Punjab, situated in the foot-hills of Himalayas (Sankalia, 1970). Recently, in the light of discovery of cotton seeds at Mehragarh in Baluchistan, it has been surmised that cotton plant was native of Indus region and domesticated in early millennium of Harappan civilization for its fibres (Sheikh and Ashfaque, 1981). Now the discovery of cotton fibres at Sringaverapura has further increased the knowledge of cotton cultivation in Gangetic valley.

The earliest civilization to have spun and woven the cotton was the Harappan in Indus valley, now dated as 2500-1700 B.C. (wheeler, 1966). Gulati and Turner (1928) ascribed the Harappan cotton fabrics as belonging to *Gossypium arboreum.* The textile craft of Harappans was highly sophisticated and cannot be regarded as earliest in Indian subcontinent. Thus at the earliest agricultural levels yet discovered in Indo-Pak region at Mehragarh in Baluchistan and Nile valley in Africa, true cottons were already present. At about 2500 B.C., the cotton seeds were being fed to livestock at Egyptian Nubia in Nile valley before considerations of the need of textile craft could have induced man to introduce it from elsewhere (Chowdhury & Buth, 1971). The Nubian cotton exhibited the early stage of evolution from wild to primitive type of lint bearing cotton.

The wild *Gossypium herbaceum* var. *africamum* growing as perennial in South-Africa, is commonly, regarded to have been domesticated for the first time in southern Arabia and Syria where it gave rise to *G. herbaceum* race *acerifolium* (Hutchinson, 1959, 1974; Darlington, 1963; Purseglove, 1974: Phillips, 1976). The concept on the matter of origin of cultivated cotton, is changed now. The association between the wild and cultivated types, in morphology and distribution as well, is accounted for genetic circumstances of domestication and spread. The wild forms growing with the cultivated forms, have not been regarded as the escapes from cultivation, but are associates of cultivars (Hutchinson, 1970; Santhanam and Hutchinson, 1974). The wild and weedy forms have been reported to be associated with the primitive cultivated types of Old World cottons, growing on the field margins and abandoned clearings. In *G. herbaceum,* they are recorded from coastal area north-west of Karachi, through northern Baluchistan to South-Yemen, Ethiopia and Sudan and even to south of Sahara in West-Asia (Santhanam & Hutchinson, 1974), and in *G. arboreum* from Kathiawar, Gujarat, Khandesh & Deccan (Watt, 1907). In this light, the theory given by Hutchinson (1959, 1974), that *G. arboreum* arose under cultivation, is no more tenable and on evident grounds it may be surmised that both the Old World cottons were separately domesticated from the wild (Santhanam and Hutchinson, 1974).

On the above grounds of facts, *G. herbaceum* var. *africanum* may not be regarded to have contributed to the cultivated cottons as it is isolated in southern Africa. More plausibly, *G. herbaceum* race *acerifolium* growing wild in Arabia, was domesticated there for the first time, by ancient man. Undoubtedly, *G. arboreum* taken into cultivation by Harappans, was indigenous in India and was originally wild. It seems likely that it was in Gujarat or Sind that *G. arboreum* cottons were first brought into cultivation (Hutchinson, 1970, 1971; Santhanam & Hutchinson, 1974).

G. arboreum var. *indicum,* the most primitive perennial form in Western India is more closely related to *G. herbaceum* race *acerifolium* than other *arboreums* and therefore, must have been developed from it. Gossypium arboreum then spread to the Indo-Gangetic alluvial plains giving rise to perennial northern forms which extended throughout northern India; east wards to Burma, Indonesia giving rise to race *burmanicum* and westwards across southern Arabia, northern Sudan and southern Sahara to West-Africa giving rise to race *sudanense* (Purseglove,. 1974). Hutchinson (1949), discussing the cotton fabrics grown by the people of Meroe, an ancient kingdom in northern Sudan (650 B.C.-A.D. 350) suggested that they were made from *G. arboreum* var. *sudanense.* He, therefore, concluded that both the cotton and textile craft i.e.. the spinning and weaving were introduced, probably from India.

In the light of above discussion, the differentiated cultivated *arboreums* had already established in Indus basin and north-western India, much earlier to the introduction of cotton cultivation at Sringaverapura. The ancient cotton fibres from Sringaverapura, Phase-I (C. 1050-1000 B.C.) may safely be regarded to belong to *G. arboreum* L.

The Harappan civilization within Indo-Pak subcontinent encompassed a large area, may be four times as large as the area of ancient Sumer, from Saurashtra coast to Rupar in the foot-hills of Himalayas and up to the site of Satkagen-Dor near the Arabian sea on the Iranian border. Recently, more sites in northern Afghanistan near Shortuigai and another site as south as Daimabad in Ahmadnagar district of Maharashtra. The Harappan port-town of Lothal (2300 B.C.) at the head of the Gulf Cambay provided a harbour to the seafaring Harappans engaged in commercial trade of agricultural produce with peninsular India on one hand and the Indus valley & Sumer on the other, in the third and second millennia B.C. Such a large spatial extent of this civilization and its continuity over long span of period from 2500 B.C. to 500 B.C. (in Himalayan foot-hills) necessarily meant the inland trade routes.

In the light of ancient remains of crop plants revealed by Atranjikhera (C. 2000-200 B.C.) in Ganga-Yamuna Doab and Neolithic Chirand (C. 1900-1400 B.C.) in the vast alluvial tract of North-Bihar, near the confluence of Ghagra and Ganga, the cereal crops of rice, barley and wheat along with the pulse crops of gram, lentil, pea, khesari and mung *(Phaseolus)* which form the present crop economy in modern agriculture, were cultivated in northern India from second millennium B.C. to the end of first century B.C. (Saraswat, 1972, 1980; Chowdhury, Saraswat and Buth, 1977; Vishnu-Mittre, 1972, 1974, 1978). The plant economy at ancient Sringaverapura (Phase 1-C. 1050-1000 B.C.) is important and unique in the sense that in addition to the cultivation of rice & barley, it has provided the first evidence of sesame (Til) and cotton cultivation in Gangetic plains of North-India.

The most ancient literary tradition dealing with historical matter which is to be found in the sacred books of Brahmanas, Buddhists and Jains cannot be assumed to have taken shape earlier than 500 B.C. The story of epics is very much more ancient, necessarily obscure and uncertain, and refuses to be bound in chronological fetters. The Vedic literature of the Aryans gives much information on to the domestic life of the people including the idea about ancient agricultural economy. Another aspect of this study is to check-up the statements made in epics and Puranic literature. The direct evidence of plant remains from Sringaverapura, would be welcome for confirmation or otherwise of the statements made therein about the agricultural economy of Ramayana age.

ACKNOWLEDGEMENTS

The author dedicates this paper to respected Professor B. B. Lal whose services to Indian Archaeology, have been unparallely outstanding. I have nothing but praise for the help rendered to me in day-to-day discussions by my colleague & friend Dr. A.K.S. Chauhan, while the Mss was being prepared.

REFERENCES

Backer, C.A. and Bakhuizen, van Den Brink, R.C., 1968, *Flora of Java,* III. Noordhoff, Groningen.

Bakshi, J.S. and R.S. Rana, 1974, Barley; in *Evolutionary Studies in World Crops (Diversity and change in the Indian sub-continent),* ed. by Sir Joseph Hutchinson. Campridge Univ. Press: pp. 47—52.

Beasley, J.O. 1942, Meiotic chromosome behaviour in species, species-hybrids; haploids, and induced polyploids of *Gossypium, Genetics 27:* 25—30.

Bor, N.L., 1960, *The grasses of Burma; Ceylon; India and Pakistan-I.* Pergamon Press. Oxford.

Burkill, I.H., 1962, Habits of man and the origins of the cultivated plans of the Old World. In *Readings in Cultural Geography,* ed. by Wagner, Phillips L. & Marwin, W.M. The Univ. of Chicago Press.

Carpenter, C.H. and L. Leney, 1952, *382 Photomicrographs of 91 paper making fibres,* vol. XXV, No. 1. Technical Publ. No. 74 of the State University of New York, college of Forestry at Syracuse.

Chandrasekharan, S.N. and S.V. Parthasarathy, 1965, *Cytogenetics* and plant Breeding. P. Varadachary & Co. Madras.

Chang, T.T., 1975, Exploration and survey in rice. In *Crop genetic resources for today and tomorrow,* ed. by Frankel, O.H. & Hawke, J.G. pp. 159—165. Cambridge.

Chang, T.T., 1976 a. Rice Oryza sativa & O. glaberrima(Gramineae-Oryzeae). In *Evolution of crop Plants,* ed. by Simmonds, N.W., pp. 98-104. Longman: London & New York.

Chang, T.T., 1976 b. The origin, evolution, cultivation, dissemination and diversification of Asian and African rices. *Euphytica, 25:* 425—441.

Chowdhury, K.A., 1963, Plant remains from Deh Morasi Ghundai, Afghanistan. In *Anthropological Paper, 50:* 126—131. Am. Muse. nat. History, New York.

Chowdhury, K.A. and S.S. Ghosh, 1954-55. Plant Remains from Hastinapura (1950—52). *Ancient India;* 10 & 11: 121—127.

Chowdhury, K.A. and G.M. Buth, 1971, Cotton seeds from the Neolithic in Egyptian Nubia and the Origin of Old World Cottons. *Biol. J. Linn. Soc.,* 3:303-312.

Chowdhury, K.A. and G.M. Buth, G.M. 1972, 4;500 year old plant remains from Egyptian Nubia. *Proc. Indian Natn. Sci. Acad.* (B), *38* (1 & 2).

55—71.

Chowdhury, K.A. Saraswat, K.S. and G.M. Buth, 1977. Ancient Agriculture and Forestary in North-India. Bombay: Asia Publ.

Darlington, C.D., 1963. *Chromosome Botany and the Origins of Cultivated Plants.* George Allen & Unwin Ltd. London (Second Edition).

De Candolle, 1886. *Origin of cultivated Plants.* Hafner Publishers, New York (Second Edition, 1959).

Gulati, A.N., 1961. A note on the early history of silk in India. Tech. Rep. Archaeol. remain, 2: 55—59. Deccan College Res. Inst., Poona.

Gulati, A.N. and A.J. Turner 1928, A note on the early history of cotton. *Ind. Cent. Cotton Comttee., Tech. Lab. Bull., 17:* 1—10:

Harlan, J.R., 1969. Evolutionary dynamics of plant domestication. *Jap. J. Genet., 44* (Suppl.1). 337—343.

Harlan, J.R., 1976 Barley-*Hordeum vulgare (Gramineae-Triticinae).* In Evolution of Crop Plants, ed. by Simmonds, N.W., pp. 93—98 Longman: London 4 New York.

Helback, H., 1960. The Palaeoethno botany of the Near-East and Europe. In *Prehistoric Investigations in Iraqi Kurdistan,* ed. by Braid wood, R.J. and Howe, B., pp. 98—118. Chicago Univ. Press Chicago.

Helback, H., 1964. The Isca grain, a Roman Plant introduction in Britain. *New Phytol., 63:* 158—164.

Helback, H. 1966. Commentary on the phylogenesis of *Triticum* and *Hordeum. Econ. Bot., 20:* 350—360.

Hutchinson, J.B., 1949. The disscmination of cotton in *Africa. Emp. Cott. Grow. Rev:, 26.* 256—270:

Hutchinson, J.B., 1959. *Application of genetics to cotton improvement.* Cambridge: cambridge Univ. Press.

Hutchinson, J.B., 1970. The genetics of evolutionary change. *Indian J. Genet. Pl. Breed., 30:* 269—279

Hutchinson, J.B., 1971. Expl. Agric., *7:* 273.

Hutchinson, J.B., 1974. Crop Plant Evolution in the Indian subcontinent. In *Evolutionary Studies in World Crops* (Diversity and change in the Indian subcontinent), ed. by Sir Joseph Hutchinson. Cambridge Univ. Press. pp. 151—160.

Hutchinson, J.B., Silow, R.A.; & S.G. Stephens 1947, *The evolution of Gossypium and the differentiation of cultivated cottons.* Oxford University Press.

International Rice Research Institute (I.R.R.I.), 1964. *Rice genetics and cytogentics,* p. 274. Amsterdam.

Jarrige, J.F. and R.H. Meadow, 1980, The Antesedents of Civilization in the Indus Valley. Scientific American, 243: 102—110.

Lal, B.B. and K.N. Dikshit, 1981, Sringaverapura: A key-site for the Proto-History and early History of the Central Ganga Valley. *Puratattva, 10:* 1—7.

Marshall, Sir J., 1931. *Mohenjo-daro and the Indus Civilization-I:* 33. London.

Martin, A.C. and W.D. Barkley, 1961, *Seed Identification Manual.* Oxford & IBH Publ. Co., Bombay.

MctCalfe, C.R., 1960 *Anatomy of the Monocotyledons I-Gramineae.* Oxford : Clarendon Press.

Musil, A.F., 1963. *Identification of crop and Weed Seeds.* Agricultural Hand Book No. 219. Washington, D.C.

Nagar, N.M., 1976. Sesame—*Sesamum indicum.* In Evolution of Crop Plants, ed. by Simmonds, N.W., pp. 231—233. Longman: London & New York.

Oka, H.I., 1974. Experimental studies on the origin of cultivated rice. *Proc. 13th Intnl. Congr. Genet., 1:* 475—486.

Phillips, L.L, 1976. Cotton. In *Evolution of crop plants,* ed. by Simmods, N.W., pp. 196—200: Longman. London & New York.

Purseglove, J.W., 1974. *Tropical Crops-Dicotyledons* (Vol. 1 & 2 combined). London: ELBS & Longman Group Ltd.

Renfrew, J.M. 1969. *Tht archaeological evidence for the domestication of plants: methods and problems.* Proceedings of a meeting of the research seminar in archaeology and related subjects, by Ucko, P.J. and Dimbleby, G.W., Institute of archaeology, London. pp. 149—172.

Sankalia, H.D. 1970. *Some Aspects of Prehistoric Technology in India.* INSA, New Delhi.

Santhanam, V. and J.B. Hutchinson, 1974, Cotton *In Evolutionary Studies in World Crops (Diversity and change in the Indian Subcontinent),* ed. by Sir Joseph Hutchinson, pp. 89—100. Cambride Univ. Press.

Saraswat, K.S., 1972. *Anatomy of living and ancient seed plants—Plant remains from Atranjikhera* (C-2000-200 B.C.). Thesis submitted to

A.M.U. Aligarh for the degree of Ph.D. in Botany.

Saraswat, K.S., 1980. Ancient Remains of the Crop Plants at Atranjikhera (C. 2000—1500 B.C.) *J. Indian Bot. Soc.*, **59**: 306—319.

Sharma, G.R., 1980. *History to Pre-History—Archaeology of the Ganga Valley and the Vindhyas.* Allahabad.

Shastrv, S.V.S. and S.D: Sharma, 1974, Rice: In *Evolutionary Studies in World Crops (Diversity and Change in the Indian Subcontinent)*, ed. by Sir Joseph Hutchinson, pp. 55-61. Cambridge Univ. Press.

Sheikh, K.H. and S.M. Ashfaque, 1981, 'Cotton Rush' Led to Mohenjodaro Culture. *The Times of India (Daily)*, A UNI Press Release Dec. 10. 1981, with a note that the views are expressed in a book published by UNESCO.

Thompson, R.C., 1949. *A Dictionary : Assyrian Botany* London: British Academy.

Vats, M.S., 1940. *Excavations at Harappa*. Calcutta.

Vishnu-Mittre, 1972. Neolithic Plant Economy at Chirand, Bihar. *Palaeobotanist* 21: 18—22.

Vishnu-Mittre, 1974. Palaeoethnobotanical evidence in India. In *Evolutionary Studies in World Crops (Diversity and Change* in the Indian Subcontinent), ed. by Sir Joseph Hutchinson, pp. 3—30. Cambridge: Cambridge Univ. Press.

Vishnu-Mittre, 1978. Origin and History of Agriculture in the Indian Subcontinent. Jour. Human Evolution, 7: 31—36.

Watt, G., 1907. The wild and cultivated cotton plants of the World. London: Longmans.

Wheeler, Sir M. 1966. Civilizations of the Indus Valley and beyond. London: Thames & Hudson.

Stuccos in Central Asia and India : A Reapprisal

R. SENGUPTA

It appears that ancient Central Asian and Indian plastered sculptures have been rather loosely called as 'stuccos'. In fact, as there is no ancient mural painting in India executed in the fresco techique, similarly, no plastered image can be called as a stucco work strictly within its technical term. In a stucco work, powdered marble has to be used on lime-sand plaster so that the finished product when polished shines with a dazzling white surface. Powdered marble does not appear to have been mentioned in the available ancient Indian texts, to be used in the finishing coat of plaster on sculptures, nor has it been detected on any image so far.

The Italian word 'stucco' is said to have been derived from the old High German word 'stucchi' which stands for crust or coating. In lexicons it is further stated to be a plaster usesd for coating walls, making casts etc. One of them simply mentions that it is 'plaster' or 'cement' for covering exterior of walls, in imitation of stones, but with what material the 'plaster' or 'cement' is to be composed is not mentioned. One on Architecture and Building mentions 'Plaster when applied to walls in the usual way is a kind of stucco...' A book on history of Building Materials says, 'The term *stucco* is applied rather vaguely to renderings of lime, gypsum, or cement mixture applied as a coating to both internal and external wall surfaces...'

The term 'stucco' has thus neither been used uniformly nor appropriately to describe the actual nature of the material. Clay *(mrinmaya),* by connotation, is understood as unbaked *(apakva-mrinmaya)* clay and terracotta *(pakva- mrinmaya)* is the product obtained after baking clay in fire. The clay figures coated with plaster from Fondukitsan in (Afghanistan) are described by Barrett as of terracotta while Rawson prefers them to call as stucco figures. Verma says that it is difficult to indicate precisely how long this confusion has prevailed, but certainly it started from the beginning of the present century.

Verma has tried to sort out the confusion in his book on clay modelling. Although he has traced out the beginning of the image making in clay or lime-and-clay, to the 1st century A.D., the textual reference he has used are mostly from *agamas* of the medieval period, the earliest one is attributable to the 8th century and these are of no help in removing the misconception.

He has traced out from ancient texts that the word *sarkara* stands for lime-stone in the form of small stones or pebbles. For paste made of such stones, he cites the expression *kalka, sarkarakalka* and *ghati-sarkarakalka.* He considers the word *kankara* to be synonymous to *kadisarkara* of the Tamil literature and the Bengali word *ghuting* as a derivative of *ghatisarkara.* In northern India, kankar-nodules or pebbles have been know for its hydraulic properties and are in use since long. These pebbles or nodules are to be found in water-courses, *nullahs* or by the side of rivulets as quoted by him from textual sources.

Incidentally, it may be mentioned that the *kankar*-nodules are formed by sedimentation of fine particles carried by water and so contains a variable quantity of soluble salt for which reason in spite of its utility the Indian Standards Institution could not standarise it. Mughals were aware of its usefulness and have made extensive use of the material. The Archaeological Survey's Conservation Manual syas, 'Kankar being composed in part of clay does not, unless it happens to be unusually pure, require other substances to be mixed with it. For making lime, instead of ravines kankar is to be dug from fields and those containing clay from 8 to 30 per cent, are the best'.

To return to the point at issue, Verma does not call images made of *sarkarakalka* or limestone-paste as stuccos. He says, just because a material forms the bulk of a figure, it should not be the deciding factor to designate it. But it is the medium in which features are brought out should be taken into account. Since it is in stucco that the features are brought out. he feels that the figures so made should be called stuccos. He is well aware of the fact that such a definition of stucco is certainly not the solution. That is why he says if this criterian is not accepted, there will be only a handful of stuccos worked out in purely in stucco and the rest are to be called either clay-or stone-figures. Why should we not call a stone sculpture by that name, if it is not done in stucco method? If his criterian is to be accepted should we call the two Buddha colossi of Bamiyan, scooped out of the rock and the face done in plaster, as stuccos? Or the hundreds of small and medium sized clay images which adorned the interior of the Bamiyan caves be called stuccos? Personally, I feel that we should not alter the nomenclature of the age-old technique of stucco which is fairly well defined. I propose to come back to the point later.

Among the earlier scholars Stein and Marshall collected and excavated a large number of clay images which were inconsistently described in their reports. Marshall describes the sculptured figures from Sirkap of Parthian period, as being a composition of lime mixed freely with small broken stone and other foreign matters. Unfortunately in his voluminous descriptive report on excavations at Taxila, there is no information on chemical examination of stucco or lime nor any specific mention has been made of the type of lime and its proportion in relation to the other materials mixed with it. In respect of figures of later dates which he assigns to the Indo-Afghan school, he mentions that large figures were usually made of soft Kanjur stone and mud, but the head of the figures were made of a hard plaster. After the rough modelling the face was finished off by chiselling. A fine slip of lime or shell plaster was applied for eventual polychromy; for gilding red colouring was done as a ground work.

Two of my chemist colleagues in the Archaeological Survey of India have carried out in 1958 an examination of a mutilated painted head of a clay figure, collected by Stein from Karakhoto of Mongolia. The object is ascribed to a period between A.D. 1032 and 1226 and is called a stucco, following the prevailing practice. The clay with which the head was made was mixed with straw, husk and reed which materials were also found in the lowest layer of plaster on the Bamiyan Buddhas and walls of caves. Chisel marks were also observed on this head as mentioned by Marshall.

It appears that large heads had to be fashioned by modelling and chiselling while small images which were to be repeated and produced in thousands, according to the demands of pilgrims, to decorate the caves and exterior surface of stupa-walls were cast out of moulds. The two large Buddhas at Bamiyan were initially scooped out of the rock of the Hindu Kush mountain without the details. The face could not be carved out properly, so also the two projecting hands could not be brought out in stone. To model these portions, wooden armatures had to be used. Charred wood and charcoal were recovered by us from the hollow of the right elbow. On the back wall of the face also holes for wooden support and a chase behind the lower lip for a wooden beam, to serve as the base of the armature, were detected. This is to say that in making these two unusually huge images, the local artists followed the same technique as they used in making large images in that region.

The plaster on the face of the Bamiyan Buddha colossi was smooth but not polished to shine, nor the colour was applied when the plaster was wet. The plaster was made of gypsum, as was widely used in Central Asia, including the head from Karakhoto. The chemists found the gypsum on the karakhoto figure to be of an impure variety; though it had attained almost anhydrite quality, it had retained a fibrous lath-like particles. A thin layer of lime wash was applied on the plastered surface for painting the features of the face over a layer of fine clay. Ochre-colours were used as pigments with animal-glue.

In most of the Central Asian figures of Buddhist deities was used plaster made of gypsum ($CaSO_4 \cdot 2H_2O$), the use of which material was forbidden by Vitruvius for stucco work. In the report on the Karakhoto head the use of anhydrite binding material has been mentioned, a few words to elaborate this point is necessary in this context. Broadly speaking, lime as a binding material may be divided into two categories: one is gypsum which is calcium sulphate and the other is the commonly used lime in the form of calcium oxide. Low-burning gypsum generally used in building as mortar, is composed mainly of semi-hydrate gypsum and is obtained by thermal processing of gypsum rock, at temperatures of 130°-170°C. The product is also known as 'plaster of Paris'. High burning or anhydrite ($CaSO_4$) binding material is obtained by burning dihydrite gypsum at a temperature of 700°-1000°C to a complete loss of chemically bound water formation of anhydrous calcium sulphate. The common lime (CaO) when slaked in water (H_2O) becomes lime paste ($Ca(OH)_2$.

In the Russian part of Central Asia, gypsum has been used extensively and continued to be used till the medieval period. Bibi-Khanum Mosque at Samarkand, the great and ambitious work of Timur constructed in gypsum mortar, had collapsed due to the weakness of the binding mortar in brickwork. It is reported that after its completion when people used to go to the mosque for offering prayers, bricks used to drop from above. The monument is being restored at a great expense.

Useful information has been obtained by research works carried out by Russian scientists. Komar narrates the setting and strengthening of gypsum 'due to the intergrowth of very fine (of colloidal size) and poorly soluble crystals of dihydrate gypsum as they precipitate from a solution which remains oversaturated as long as the hydration of gypsum proceeds, owing to a high solubility of the starting substances. The increase in strength of the system generally ceases somewhat before semi-hydrate gypsum converts fully to dihydrate. Subsequently, hardened gypsum fails to gain strength and may even weaken somewhat as a result of partial failure of the structure due to internal stresses caused by the oriented growth of small crystals that are bound together by the intergrowth contacts and form an unbroken crystalline structure of hardened gypsum'.

For plastering walls, it appears Egyptians used a form of mortar mainly of calcined gypsum to level up the hollows and providing a hard smooth layer which could be painted. A sample of plaster from the pyramid Cheops was found to consist of 82% of calcined gypsum and about 10% calcium carbonate, probably derived from the impurities in the raw gypsum before it was burnt. It appears that from the early historical period in the Oriental countries a plaster in gypsum which was an approximation of stucco, was developed. In course of time this type of plaster, whether in gypsum or in lime, was also called stucco.

The Sassanian of Persia used gypsum in the palace at Ctesiphon (6th century). Abbasids of Baghdad used raw gypsum *(guch)* in ornamental designs at Samarra (9th century). At the Ibadite, capital of Sedrate, a Moslem city, (10th-13th cent). where sculptures executed in earlier Hellenistic traditions were blended with Oriental elements, local grey gypsum plaster called *'timchent'* was used. The craft of using gypsum plaster for decorative work had spread throughout the Near East and fall in three main classes of work, modelled in round or in three-quarter relief in statuary; incrusted and deeply carved on walls; and lastly slabs cast in pieces and carved or pierced to serve as window grills or balustrades.

The Italian Master Architect Vitruvius (1st century B.C.) narrates the actual form and character of stucco as meant and understood during his time. He says that for slaking of lime for stucco, best lime in lumps is to be used. Obviously he meant that calcium oxide (CaO) is to be used. In the next chapter dealing with stucco work on vaultings, he specifically recommends the use of powdered marble: as gypsum sets too quickly and does not dry uniformly, it should by no means be used. The mouldings on the soffits overhang very heavily and there is a danger of their falling, if gypsum is used. The stucco appears to be made of layers of lime and sand (which he calls 'sand mortar') with coatings of mortar made of powdered marble for polishing and painting. For faultless appearance of paintings or to make the surface dazzling white, as also to prevent shrinkage and development of cracks, Vitruvius advises three coats of sand mortar and as many of marble to be applied. At the same time he cautions that when only one coat of sand mortar and one of fine marble have been spread on, the thin layer is easily cracked for want of strength and it will not take on the brilliance created by polishing which it ought to have. He compares the essential quality of stucco with a silver mirror which takes a very high polish and reflects a brilliant and clear image when one looks at it. Secundas (1st cent. A.D.), following Vitruvius wrote, 'stucco always lacks brilliance unless the wall had received three coats of sand mortar and two of marble mortar'.

Vitruvius further mentions that the stucco plaster was so shining and beautiful that people stripped off old plaster from the old buildings in Rome, to use them as table-tops. The stucco plaster was as strong and rigid as a slab of marble is used on table-top. Any plaster whether in lime, gypsum or clay would not attain the qualities of stucco. It may be mentioned that in Italian gypsum is *gesso;* unburnt gypsum is *gesso crudo* and burnt gypsum or plaster of Paris is *gesso cotto.* Thus, Italians were explicit in their expression about the cementing materials used and there was no confusion whatsoever.

Doric Temples, made of a porous limestone used to be covered with a thin coating of stucco to fill in the cavities in the stone and also to render the uneven surface, smooth and for a refined look. In India too sculptures and other architectural members of cave-temples, scooped out of the vesicular Deccan trap, were plastered with a lime mortar for a fine finish. At Ajanta and Ellora (6th-13th Cent. A.D.) there are many sculptures with plaster on them. The sculptures of the main cave at Elephanta (7th cen. A.D.) were covered with a coat of bitumenous plaster, perhaps for protection against moisture and sea-salt, as the island is in the Arabian sea.

Leonardo da Vinci was aware of the beautiful sculptures of Elephanta and art-critics attribute Indian influence in some of his works. In one of his note-books he specifically mentions about a 'Map of Elephanta in India'. During the time of Leonardo (16th century), merchants from Milan and Florence were active on the Indian west coast. About the same time Raphael improvised and revived the stucco work in Italy and it became popular with the Mughals in India, though in a modified form and answering to some extent what Michelangelo used. Pirro Ligorio, an associate of Michelangelo mentioned their using lime made out of pure marble, as it is still done in the conservation of marble works of the Taj Mahal and other monuments.

In Italy, the improvised plaster was differentiated from stucco and was called '*intonaco*' and in Venice it was known as 'Marmorino'. Alvise Cornaro writes in 1560 that in Venice, near its Custom's House, a theatre should be built and its facade should be plastered with Marmorino becaus it becomes as strong as stone. Recent researches in the composition of marble-like intonacoes show that the second layer was made of fragments of stone and granules of microcrystalline marble bound together by lime and the third or outer layer was of marble dust with a binding medium. The surface was finished by the application of additives like wax, linen, oil etc. Thus though *intonaco* was an approximation of stucco, it was not called stucco to create confusion with the original technique of stucco.

The practice of polishing lime mortar has been traced back to 7000 B.C., at Jericho by Malinowski. Other examples come from Crete in Mycenaean and Minoan works (1500 B.C.); in a Greek cistern of Megara (500 B.C.) and the Roman aqueducts (100 A.D.). The Minoans used a mortar in which carbonated lime was as high as 95%. The mortar used is either unilayer or multi-layer but finely polished. As the result of polish, the mortar creates a dense capillary system at the surface and simultaneously accelerated the carbonation and/or the hydration process. The finely polished surface checks acumulation of dust on walls and sediments in cisterns and aqueducts. In a multi-layer stucco, the lowest layer of mortar acts for bonding, the carbonated one in the middle prevents shrinkage and the polished top surface assures impermeability and strength.

To recapitulate the qualities of stucco, as described by Vitruvius:

i) it is a particular technique in which the base layer (one or more) of plaster must be of lime (not gypsum) and sand;

ii) the upper layer (one or more) of mortar must be of powdered marble; and

iii) the surface of the uppermost layer must be highly polished to produce shine and brilliance.

In view of the specifications and nature of stucco mentioned above, it appears that the plastered sculptures under discussion would not qualify to be called as stuccos.

To be absolutely sure about its nature, an object may be put to scientific tests developed recently. It has been observed that (SEM) discloses the sizes, shapes and textures of the materials in the internal structures of a mortar with remarkable definition and minimum distortion. Although the same substance like lime may develop with quite different crystal habits in which the external shape and symmetry of the crystal do not correspond to its internal lattice type, SEM together with X-ray diffractometry and elemental analytical techniques complement and supplement the other to obtain spacies — specific information to understand the characteristics of the materials and technology used.

REFERENCES

Barrett D.—'Sculptures of Shahi Period' in *Oriental Art* The Oriental Art Magazine Ltd., Museum of Eastern Art, Oxford, (1957) Vol. III. 2, p. 57.

Biscontin, G. *et al.* 'Research on limes and intonacoes of the historical venetian architecture in *Mortars, Cements and Grouts used in the Conservation of Historic Buildings;* Rome (1981), pp. 359.

Davey Norman, *A history of Building Materials,* Phoenix House London (1961), pp. 112—115.

A Komar, *Building Materials and Components,* Mir Publishers, Moscow (1974) p. 115.

Lewin S.Z. 'X-ray Diffraction and Scanning Electron Microscope Analysis of Conventional Mortars', ibid, pp. 102a & 123.

Marshall John, *Taxila*, Cambridge (1951), Vol. II p. 513.

Marshall John, Conservation Manual, Calcutta (1923) pp. 48-49.

Malinowski R. 'Ancient Mortar and Concretes-Durability Aspects', Paper read in the International Symposium on Mortars, Cements and Grouts in the Conservation of Historic Buildings, held by International Centre for the Study of the Restoration and Preservaion of Cultural Property in Rome, November, 1981, p. 341.

Nagpal, J.C. and O.P. Agrawal, Examination and Preservation of Painted Stucco Head in the *Ancient India, Bulletin of the Archaeological Survey of India,* No. 15, 1959, pp. 94—99.

Rawson P. 'The Methods of Indian sculpture', *Ibid.,* (1958) Vol. IV, 4 p. 140.

Ramaswami, N.S. Indian Monuments New Delhi (1979) p. 45.

Sengupta R. Preservation and Conservation of Bamiyan', in Asian Culture, Bulletin of the *Asian Cultural Centre,* for *UNESCO*. Tokyo, No. 13, March, 1976, p. 11.

Sengupta R., 'Use of Dammar as a waterproofing medium for painting at Bamiyan' in *Indo-Asian* Culture, Vol. 17, No. 4, October; 1968.

Stein Aurel, Serindia, (Oxford. 1921), Vol. 1 p. 136.

Verma K.M. *The Indian Technique of Clay Modelling,* Santiniketan (1970), p. 111-12.

Vitruvius, *The Ten Books on Architecture Tr. Morris* Hicky Morgan; Dover Publications, Inc., New York (1960), pp. 206.

Technical Studies of Iron Implements from the Megalithic Site Tadakanahalli

O. P. AGRAWAL, HARINARAIN
& S. K. BHATIA
Natural Research Laboratory for Conservation
of Cultural Property, Lucknow

The dating of the first appearance of iron in India is still controversial. Before the excavations at Hastinapur, Alamgirpur, Kausambi, Ujjain and other sites where iron has been found in early phases it was thought that the iron objects from the megalithic graves of South India were the earliest. Wheeler dated the sites to 300 B C (Wheeler 1969) Excavations at Hallur conducted in 1965 and at Tadakanahalli in 1978 indicate that iron was known in India as early as 1000 BC. On the basis of the radio-carbon dating, the overlap phase of neolithic-chalcolithic ages at Hallur can be ascribed to circa 1000 B.C. (Nagaraja Rao 1978:19). According to Nagaraja Rao, the graves at Tadakanahalli are contemporary to the overlap phase of Hallur and, therefore, may belong to about 1000 B.C. (Nagaraja Rao 1981:25).

The excavations at Tadakanahalli yielded a number of iron objects including heavy axe, arrow heads, spear heads and knives from the graves.

Some of the iron objects found at Tadakanahalli site were received in our Laboratory for conservation and examination. Out of these, the result of examination of two iron implements and one axe is given in the following pages. These were examined in order to have a better understanding of their metallurgy and fabrication techniques. A brief description of the objects is to be found in Table I. The axe was rather heavy, weighing nearly 0.250 kg. The iron implements were thin but strong. The shape suggested that they were most likely cutting tools, e.g. the type used for cutting leather. All the objects were found tough and hard at the surface.

METALLOGRAPHIC EXAMINATION

All the three iron objects were found to be in an advanced stage of corrosion (mainly iron oxide) and no metal core was present in any of the objects save for only minute fragments of iron. This situation creates difficulties because, in the absence of metal, the micro-structure is not clear. We used the technique of examination of specimens at high magnification in the optical microscope, a procedure which allows us to detect the relic carbide structure. Samples were taken from iron implements with a diamond saw. The preparation of sample sections was done in the usual way including grinding, mechanical polishing and etching with 2% Nital (a mixture of nitric acid and alcohol). In most cases an acid mixture (Metal Handbook 1973) (92ml HCL, 5ml H_2SO_4. 3ml HNO_3) was also used for etching.

INTERPRETATION OF MICRO-STRUCTURES

1. *Iron implement; Laboratory No. Fe 56(1)*

Three small sections were taken from this implement at the zones a, b & c (Fig. 1). The section at 'a' after polishing was studied under the microscope. It was observed that the section was composed of several layers. Different layers were distinctly seen at 126 X and some metal crystals were also present in the layers (Fig. 2). After etching with 2% Nital solution, Ferrite and Pearlite structures, as well as slag inclusions were seen (Fig. 3). The presence of slag in the metal indicates that iron must have been extracted directly by the bloomery process and not from pig iron. (Tylecote 1980: 209; Wheelar and Maddin 1980: 115-116; Maddin and Muhley 1978: 113).

There are various processes of smelting iron. In the direct process (bloomery process) iron was smelted from its ores in the presence of charcoal at about 1200°C while the melting point of iron is 1540°C. The resultant product was in the form of a sponge rather than in a liquid form. The slag, i.e. iron silicate, is viscous at around 1170°C and is brittle below this point. It is removed by repeated hammering around that temperature. In this way iron was made free from impurities such as slag to some extent.

At this stage the iron was carburized by crucible method in which the sheet prepared from the iron is carburized by directly putting it into charcoal fire for some time. The process is also known as cementation, carburization or case hardening. Excess of carbon would result in brittleness in the steel, sometimes, too brittle for use. This excess carbon is removed by repeated heating and hammering.

In the indirect process of smelting (Hodges 1976:90; Needam 1980:570) pure iron melts around 1540°C. This much high temperature is easily reached with coal and forced air circulation in comparison to charcoal. After obtaining the pig iron from the blast furnace, the steel was being made by the process of direct decarburization of cast iron under a cold blast. Pig iron was remelted in a hearth with the forced air circulation which resulted in loss of excess carbon as carbon dioxide. The impurities as silica and others came to the surface during refining of the pig iron, which helped in their easy removal. The refined pig iron is quite malleable and could be easily forged into any shape.

It can, therefore, be concluded from our observations that the implements under metallographic examination were made by bloomery or direct process.

From zone b (Fig. 1), a 'V' shaped section was cut. After etching, the structure revealed martensite near the edge and relic carbide in the inner portion.

At the zone 'c' also, a 'V' shaped section was cut and examined under the microscope. In this case also several layers were seen in the structure. At 500 X, high percentage of carbon, martensite and Bainite were visible near the edge.

2. *Iron implement, Laboratory No. Fe 56(2)*

From this implement also 3 sections were taken from zones a, b & c.

The sample from zone a, after polishing and etching with acid mixture, showed a structure composed of several layers laminated together. In this structure the high carbon layers were near the edge. Relic pearlite was visible at high magnification in various layers in the inner portion of the object. Near the edge high carbon layers were seen having martensite structure.

The section from zone b, on examination at 126 X, revealed several layers with somewhat elongated slag inclusions (Fig. 5).

Relic pearlite was visible in the inner portion of the section from the zone c at 500 X. Examination was done after etching. In this section also, several layers, alternatively brighter and darker were seen. In one tiny metal crystal which had survived within the corroded layers, ferrite and pearlite structures were distinctly seen at high magnification of 1200 X. In other areas, relic carbide structure was noticed. Etching was done with 2% Nital.

3. *Iron axe, Laboratory No. Fe 54*

From this object, a section was taken from the area indicated at 'a' in Fig. 6. The section was polished and etched with the acid mixture. On examination at 126 X, it showed several layers, cracks and cavities. Some high carbon layers were also visible inside the section when seen at 500 X. Relic pearlite structure was visible all over the section.

INTERPRETATION AND DISCUSSIONS

It is apparent from the above observations that in all the three iron objects from Tadakanahalli—the two iron implements and one iron axe —both remnant pearlite and relic pearlite exist. This observation indicates the presence of steel (Reed Knox 1963:44-45).

Examination of sections from the three objects reveal the following features in their microstructures:

(i) Each object is composed of two or more definite layers.

(ii) The edge layer consists mainly of martensite which means that the objects had been hardened at the surface.

(iii) Inside the objects, layers of ferrite and pearlite are present.

(iv) As we move from the edge to the inner portion, the amount of pearlite and ferrite increases and the martensite decreases. However, in the case of the iron axe, the martensite layer again appears after some distance from the edge, i.e. martensite (high carbon) appears alternatively with low carbon layers.

It can thus be indicated that the cutting edge and the broad surface of the artifacts were of high carbon content (0.5-0.7% on the basis of metallographic examination). The presence of several layers in the sections indicate that the objects were prepared by forging togeher layers of wrought iron sheet which had been carburised[1] (Lang and Williams 1975:201-202) and hammered in the form of a compact flat bar (Smith 1957:46). On that, sheets of high carbon content were then forged. Thus a bar was obtained having several layers, of which some are low carbon content on one side and high carbon content on the other side. This bar was folded in such a manner that the high carbon content layers came to the two surfaces.

In the case of iron axe, it appears that the compact bar was prepared with high carbon content layers on both the sides with low carbon sheets in between. This bar was then folded and hammered to get the desired shape and length. In that manner the high carbon content metal will come not only on the surface but also inside the object. That explains the presence of high carbon content layer inside the iron axe.

Formation of martensite indicates that the artifact after forming in the desired shape was heated to redness (between temperatures 723°-910°C) and very rapidly cooled, i.e. quenched to attain the very tough surface. The steel acquired its full hardness only when heated above a critical temperature and cooled very rapidly.

It is also obvious that the objects were further heated (tempered at a low temperature below 723°C) for some time and then cooled in air to remove the brittleness, improve their cutting capability, wear resistance and to withstand impact of working, etc. This observation is confirmed by the presence of ferrite together with pearlite and martensite.

The layering technique of manufacture of tools provided a way by which a tool could be made strong on its working surface (Muhley el al 1977: 159; Lang and Williams 1975:199-200). The process also saved time for the smith. The carburization of a larger block of iron takes much more time than that a thinner iron sheet, several of which were joined together to get the required thickness.

Use of a number of carburized sheets gives internal as well as external strength and represents a technological advancement over the two-layered structure. It gives the required wear resistance to the surface as well as internal strength to the implement.

The micro-hardness test could not be performed as the objects were in advanced stage of corrosion.

Spectrochemical, analysis reveals the presence of copper in traces. Nickel, cobalt and titanium were found to be absent. The absence of nickel and cobalt ruled out the possibility of the use of meteoric iron for the preparation of these objects (Moss 1975:11).

CONCLUSION

This investigation lead us to the conclusion

that the blacksmith of Tadakanahalli had a gerat ability and craftsmanship. It is obvious that he had used two different materials deliberately and was fully conscious of their qualities. Heat treatment also had been done with great precision. furthermore, it is seen that the people even in that early age had great ability to obtain a superior cutting edge by quenching and tempering.

ACKNOWLEDGEMENT

We wish to thank Dr. M.S. Nagaraja Rao, Director of Archaeology and Museums, Government of Karnataka for kindly providing the specimens.

TABLE 1

Sl. No.	*Lab. No.*	*Object description*	*Site & cultural association*	*Thickness (average)*	*weight*
1.	Fe 56(1)	Iron implement	TDK Meg(II)	3.5 mm	12.5 gm
2.	Fe 56(2)	Iron implement	TDK Meg(II)	3.5 mm	9.0 gm
3.	Fe 54	Iron axe	TDK(1) Meg(II)	26 mm	1 kg 225 gm

REFERENCES

Wheeler, R.E.M. 1969, *Early India and Pakistan*, London.

Nagaraja Rao, M.S. 1978, *Progress of Archaeology in Karnataka*, Mysore.

Nagaraja Rao, M.S. 1981, *Madhu: Recent Researches in Indian Archaeology and Art History* New Delhi.

Metal Handbook 1973, *Atlas of Microstructures of Industiral Alloys* American Society for Metals, Ohio, U.S.A., Vol. 7.

Tylecote, R.F. 1980, Furnaces, Crucibles and Slags; The Coming of the Age of Iron (Yale University Press, New Haven & London.

Wheeler, T.S. and Maddin, R. 1980. Metallurgy and Ancient Man", *The Coming of the Age of Iron* (Yale University Press, New Haven & London.

Maddin, R. and Muhley, J.D. 1978, An Iron Dagger from Tomb 240 at Tell Fara South, *Levant*, British School of Archaeology in Jerusalem, Vol. 10.

Hodges, H. 1976, Artifacts, London.

Needam, Joseph 1980, The evolution of Iron and Steel Technology in East and South-east Asia, *The Coming of the Age of Iron* Yale University Press, New Haven & London.

Reed Knox, 1963, Detection of Iron Carbide Structures in the Oxide Remains of Ancient Steel, *Archaeology*, Vol. 6.

Lang, J. and Williams, A.R. 1975, The Hardening of Iron Swords, *Journal of Archaeological Science*, Vol. 2.

Smith, C.S., 1957, A Metallographic Examination of some Japanese sword blades, *Quaderno II del Centro per la Storia della Metallurgia, A.I.M., Milano*, 1957, p.46:

Muhley, J.D., Wheeler, T.S. and Maddin; R. 1977 An Iron Adze of the 5th-4th Centuries B.C. from Al Mina", *Levant*, Vol. 9 (1977) p. 153.

Lang J. and Williams, A.R. 1975, The Hardening of *Iron Swords, Journal of Archaeological* Vol. 2 (1975) pp. 199-200.

Moss, A.A. 1975, Meteorites A Consise Account, (London, 1975) p. 11.

Herding as the Backdrop to the Growth of Agriculture in West Asia and South Asia

S.P. GUPTA &
ARUN KESARWANI

On conceptual level, two inter-related models for the Neolithic have dominated the archaeological thinking till recently—the one presented by Childe (1952), known generally by the term 'Neolithic Revolution' (of the late Holocene), and the other presented by Braidwood (1953), known generally by the term 'Incipient Agriculture' (of the Early Holocene). However, both of them were based upon two common postulates: one, that the change from 'hunting and gathering' economy to 'food production' economy occurred first in the 'Fertile Crescent', and second, that this mode of life 'diffused' from here to different parts of the world, although there may have been a few other secondary and independent centres. To these authors, this change took place between 8000 and 4000 B.C. They visualized this change in terms of domestication of animals and agriculture. The basic difference between their approaches was simple: while Childe looked at it as 'revolution', Braidwood took it as slow 'evolution'. In South Asia, particularly in north-western Indo-Pakistan subcontinent, according to them, this change occurred not earlier than the fourth millennium B.C., as a result of diffusion from West Asia (Subbarao 1958). For eastern India, on the other hand, Krishnaswami (1962) visualized diffusion from south-east Asia and southern China (Fig. 1).

Of late, we find these postulates inadequate. For example, the term 'Fertile Crescent' emphasizes two things: first that the region called

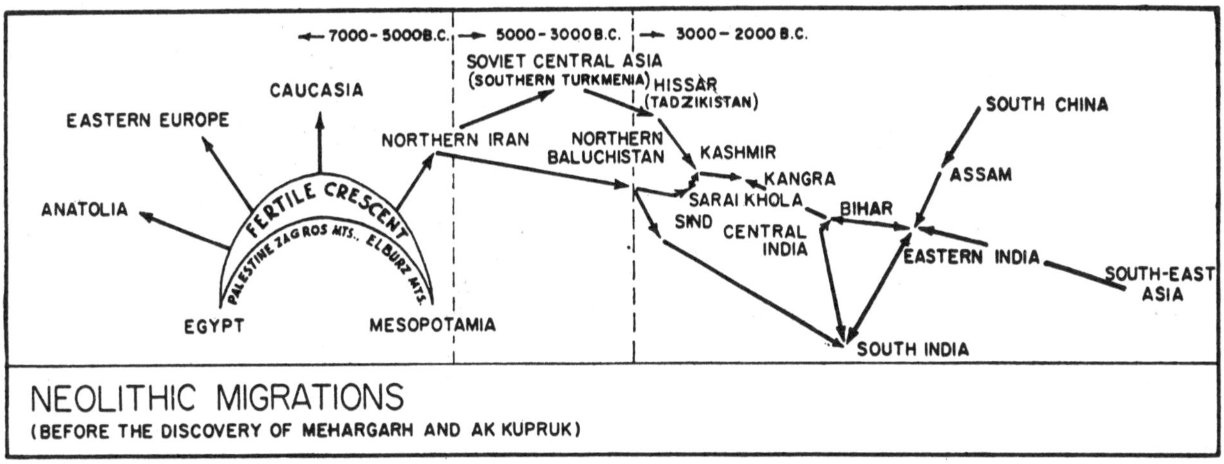

Fig. 1

'Crescent' was fertile—'fertility' stood for agriculture. In other words, for early Neolithicism agriculture was supposed to have been more important than the domestication of animals. Secondly, outside the 'crescent' even if nature had provided conditions for the growth of domesticable wild cereals, as Vavilov had said about Afghanistan and India in 1929, man did not exploit them. We now know that at a number of sedentary sites in the Orient, 'domestication' of animals preceded 'domestication of cereals' (Gupta 1979). It has also been found that by no means the neolithic sites in the Fertile Crescent are the oldest; in Asia Minor and in South Asia, even in parts of South East Asia, (Indonesia, Thailand and Burma, for example), the Early Neolithic sites are as old as the sites in the Fertile Crescent (Glover 1982). Therefore, the concept of priority of West Asia over South and South East Asia in matters of food producing economy has collapsed.

In 1969, Flannery came out with a new model, called 'Broad Spectrum Revolution' which has been summarized by Moore (1982) as follows:

> "About 20000 B.C. a shift occurred in the hunting and gathering economy of the peoples of the Near East, away from a pattern of almost exclusively ungulate hunting to exploitation of a greater variety of plant and animal resources. These included both large and small game birds, fish and invertebrates as well as for the first time, significant quantities of wild fruits, nuts and cereals. Such wild resources were sufficiently abundant in some areas to permit the formation of sedentary villages. *This hunting and gathering pattern was typical of the Epi-palaeolithic Pleistocene (Kebaran Natufian) and the Zarzian of the Zagros. Farming began quite abruptly early in the Neolithic in both (Khuzistan and Palestine*). The evidence from aceramic Hacilar (Helbaek 1970: 198) suggested that a similar transition occurred about the same time in Anatolia, at least among some groups. Long after agriculture was known, some communities continued to maintain a sedentary existence by exploiting wild resources."

Moore (1982:232) goes a step further, calls the development of agriculture and herding 'no more than the systematic practice of exploitation techniques on occasion for much of the Pleistocene. He then observes:

> "The evidence from Levant suggests that towards the end of the Pleistocene, traditional hunting and gathering was intensified and new methods of obtaining food were developed. Thus herds of gazelle and oats were exploited in a manner that conserved their numbers. This was achieved by selective hunting and perhaps in certain instances by capturing and confining some animals. Among the plants einkorn and perhaps other cereals and legumes were deliberately cultivated. These changes accompanied the formation of the earliest settlements. *Thus most of the changes hitherto regarded as characteristic of the earlier stages of the Neolithic took place during the Epi-palaeolithic.* The best evidence for this comes from the Levant but there are indications that the pattern was similar in Mesopotamia, the Zagros and Anatolia."

We have, however, our own difficulties in accepting this fresh model. That the process of selection of plants and animals through trials may have been initiated during the late Pleistocene period, but to us the beginning of Neolithicism in the sense of production economy can hardly be placed at this stage; we would rather look for the bones of animals, and if possible associated plant products which exhibit some morphological changes which take place due to man's conscious interference in their 'wild' style of life, such as herding and sowing.

It has been pointed out (Higgs and Jerman 1969) that *the process of selection of certain species of animals for food* out of a large number of animal species intimately known to the hunters was initiated far back in time in the Middle Palaeolithic Europe. But to us, that many have been only a matter of preference or choice for one reason or the other, such as 'easy to hunt' or 'readily available' or 'its meat is more tasty. In any case the Upper Palaeolithic deposits have clearly shown a systematic preference for certain range of animals as Moore (1982) has shown. At Ksar Akil in the Near East fallow deer bones were found in largest numbers, followed closely by the bones of the Caprines (Hooijer 1961). Concentration on hunting the goats and red deer has been well established in the Zagros also, at Yafteh cave and some other sites in the Khorramabad Valley (Hole and Flannery 1967:161, 165). At Shanidar, Perkins (1964:1566) has noted that in the Upper Palaeolithic deposits goats and sheep bones dominated (Chart I). Whichever may be the predominant animal species killed at a particular site, the fact remains that in the Upper Palaeolithic times the 'field of choice' in the process of selection had narrowed down to four or five animals. And this is of most vital importance since this very process culminated in what we call the 'domestication of goat, sheep and cattle' in the Early Neolithic times, which may be kept in the time bracket of 8000 B.C.-6000 B.C. It is to be clearly noted that in this process of selection, the plant world was perhaps only marginally involved, if at all; at least we have no clear evidence of the 'selected cereals' from the Upper Palaeolithic deposits.

The process of 'selective hunting' of the Upper Palaeolithic times of Epipalaeolithic-1 (18000-10000 B.C.) did not directly lead to the 'domestication of animals'; there was still a stage in between, and this was, in fact, the most crucial stage. It is called 'herding'. Why 'herding' was crucial and not 'selective hunting' is easy to understand. Selective hunting, whatever its dimensions, shall never bring about those morphological changes in the animals without which 'domestication' in our sense is meaningless.

During the period between 10000 and 8000 B.C., called Epipalaeolithic-2, the process of selection of one species of animals continued but with a very important difference: in age group, *the animals killed were now largely immature*, as Moore (182) has shown. Legge (1977:54-59), on this basis, postulates that Nahal Oren, Hayonian and Mugharet el wad, the inhabitants practised gazelle husbandry. At Abu Hureyra along with gazelles, onagers were herded, while at Beidha the goats were put to the same kind of herding or incipient domestication. The argument is quite convincing since immature animals are likely to have been found in controlled herds more commonly than in the wild groups. In this context, it is equally important to note that at sites like Abu Hureyra and Ain Mallaha the settlements were more or less of the sedentary or semi-sedentary type. Levant, therefore, provides the best evidence for the herding stage, although at Zawi Chemi Shanidar in Iraq also similar evidence in favour of sheep is available.

A point which had not been generally noted in this context is the nature of the species selected for herding in the Epipaleolithic times: practically all of them—sheep, goat and cattle—are herbivorous. Consequently, these animals were less ferocious than the carnivorous animals like the tiger and lion. The same applies to the pigs, horses, and asses which were domesticated slightly later.

In the herding stage one more vital phenomenon seems to have occurred: morphological changes in bones and decrease in the overall height of the herded species of animals. The process must have been very slow. In fact, it took about two thousand years, 10000 B.C.-8000 B.C. (this is the overall bracket, for individual sites the continuous period must have been very small) since in the 8000-6000 B.C. levels of Jericho, Tepe Asiab, Ali Kosh-B, Ak Kupruk, Mehargarh etc. the goats and sheep had already shed their wild morphology and their bone characteristics had acquired what are called 'characteristics of the domesticated species'. The sub-stages of change which must have occurred during the process of herding have, however, not been worked out so far but we hopefully look forward for this kind of study. It is significant to note that morphological changes take place when some kind of control on the behavioural patterns of the animals is exercised. This control is effected through taming. Herding, therefore, tames the animals and they start responding to the dictates of the human masters. In return they get security of life and fodder for food. The two processes move simultaneously in inter-twined fashion. Each new generation gets more and more dependant on human protection. The degree of this dependence determines the degree of change in the behavioural pattern of the herded animals. It is common knowledge that the behavioural pattern determines the body structure—monkeys have long hands because they often move from one branch of the tree to the other by hanging and swinging but human beings have comparatively short hands because they do not live on trees and move like monkeys. Meadow (1979:160) feels that 30 to 100 generations (in 200 years) for sheep and goat and 20 to 67 generations (in 200 years) for cattle were enough for physiological changes in the herded species at Mehargarh.

The herding stage, however, does fall in the direct line of selective hunting since it is based on the economically most viable animals whose eventual domestication was least cumbersome. Since 'hunting' seems to have dominated over 'gathering' in Palaeolithic times, as the field data shows everywhere, 'herding' of animals appears to have preceded 'incipient agriculture'. However, the gap between the two at any given site, may not have been substantial; Meadow (1979) has put it to 200 years for Mehargarh. The archaeological evidence gathered so far proves that agriculture, even in its most rudimentary form, appears in 8000-7000 B.C. levels, only slightly later than the first real domesticated animal starts appearing around 9000-8000 B.C. bracket.

We, therefore, hypothesize that there was a direct causal relationship between the 'domestication of animals' through herding and the 'beginning of agriculture through reaping' during the Epipalaeolithic—2 times (10000-8000 B.C.), since the former prepares the conditions conducive to a kind of settled life which is essential to wait, watch and reap a field rich in wild cereals, such as the einkorn. It is common knowledge that nomadism was the consequence of hunting although in certain quarters it continued even with the domestication of animals since habit dies hard, particularly in the hilly regions where the plant world is not rich enough. But 'herding' inevitably led to a certain degree of sedentary life, which increased immensely with the final 'domestication' of animals. With agriculture, sedentarism, permanent or seasonal, became inevitable; the reason is not far to seek—domestication of animals provides a stable source of food and clothing,the two basic requirements of human life.

True, men never lived by meat alone, the plant world also supplied good items. In the herding stage, it is logical to think that the collection of domesticable cereals was also initiated, although its exact nature is not known to us. It is in 8000-7000 B.C. levels that we in fact start getting real domesticated cereals like emmer and barley, as well as pulses, at Jericho, for example, albeit in a very small quantity; cereals of the earlier dates are still completely wild (Chart II). With the domestication of animals, the basic requirement of men and animals became the same —secure food. Since the domesticated animals were not carnivorous, stocks of fodder in dry season, when the pasture lands did not provide sufficient natural food, was essential. The search was made for such cereals which fed both—man and animal. Wheat, barley, rice, etc. provided cereals for man and a large amount of fodder for animals at one and the same time. Thus, while in the herding stage, when semi-sedentarism was the life style, only some kind of harvesting of wild cereals may have been there, in the 'domesticated animals' stage, when sedentary life played the major role, agriculture became the most dominant occupation in the every day life of human beings; of course, in those areas where land and environment were ideal for this occupation, conditions which are hardly applicable to 'domestication of animals'. The trouble is not with the history of domestication of plants—it was a process which developed slowly and gradually from the stage of 'harvesting' or 'reaping' to the stage of 'cultivation'; the trouble is with us, the scholars, who, as Moore points out, like to fix a date and place for its FIRST occurrence, as if it was an event of history which it was certainly not. Therefore, truly speaking, we can only give a rough time bracket for the process of change and visualize, roughly again on the basis of meagre archaeological evidence, three to four major stages in this process.

With these equations in mind, when we try to visualize the history of mankind, it at once becomes clear that the road to Neolithicism was a matter of Man's reaction to nomadism as a way of life—insecure, troublesome, and short, constantly faced with the problems of food, clothing and shelter. (Let us, however, be clear of one thing on this issue—nomadism of pre-Neolithic period is not the same as that of the post-Neolithic periods since in the nomadism of the second variety nomadic people largely interacted with the settled people both for the food items and manufactured goods, which was not the case with the pre-Neolithic nomads). This reaction must have been present in some people all the time but nature does not appear to have favoured them with 'domesticable' flora and fauna and technological ability to exploit nature in this direction.

When in the beginning of the Holocene nature brought about significant changes in the biosphere, man's reaction to largely unsettled life of the past resulted in the positive action of domestication of animals and cereals and establishment of villages. From now onwards a new phenomenon appeared in human life—formation of society. All later developments in human life emerged out of social behavioural patterns—ideational, material and moral, also called 'cultural patterns' in history.

Thus, if at the base of Neolithicism lies man's basic reaction towards his unsettled Palaeolithic life, then how could it arise in the minds of just a few humans, due to whose grace, as if, the rest of the humanity was civilized? The theory of fertile crescent in effect brings about the superiority of the land and people of this region over the rest of the world. More and more evidence is now getting accumulated to prove the fact that the Early Neolithicism took place not only in the Fertile Crescent but also at various places in the world; but since the environment all over the world was not the same its form, based on its preferences for certain animals and plants, was also not the same. Where opportunity for agriculture was extremely limited, in mountainous region, for example, Early Neolithicism was largely reflected in animal husbandry and not in agriculture but where nature offered wild cereals in plenty, agriculture soon predominated. In between, there were obviously several other shades of Neolithicism but that does not concern us here.

Since the theory of diffusion of Neolithicism from Fertile Crescent to various parts of the world stands completely discredited and has been replaced by the theory of independent origin at various places and in various forms, we will consider the case of South Asia. In South Asia the best evidence comes from Afghanistan and Baluchistan. It is as follows.

In the foothills of the Hindukush mountains in northern Afghanistan there are a number of caves with open-air terraces, ranging from Middle Palaeolithic through Upper Palaeolithic, Mesolithic and Neolithic (Dupree 1973). In the Middle Palaeolithic (29,050 b.c.) it may be noted, there are skeletal remains of wild unidentified sheep/goat as well as cattle *(Bos primingenius)* at Dara-i-kur. In times to come man selected these very species for herding, and finally for domestication. In the Upper Palaeolithic, called Kuprukian A & B (14,665∓215 b.c.), there are the skeletal remains, at Ghar-i-Mar and Ghar-i-Asp, of wild sheep (*Ovis orientalia cycloceros*). goat *(Capra hircus aegagrus),* unidentified sheep/goat *(Ovis/Capra),* horse*(Equus spp.),* red deer *(Cervus elaphus),* cattle/deer *(Ovis/Capra),* dog *(Canis aureus sp.)* and fox (*Vulpes sp.*). Clearly, along with several species of animals killed for food, sheep, goat, and cattle continued to be the most favourite ones. In fact, sheep and goat bones counted for 89% of the total bones (Perkins 1972).

The Mesolithic or the Epipalaeolithic at Kara Kamar (10,000 B.C.-8000 B.C.) was the most crucial one since herding seems to be an important occupation of the people. Unfortunately, no other site of this period has been properly excavated in Afghanistan. Still, the wild animals found here included sheep, gazelle and mole vole. Although so far goat and cattle bones have not come from the excavated trenches yet it is impossible that these animals were not herded since in periods earlier to it and succeeding it these were the choicest items with men in this part of the world. In the Aceramic Neolithic their domesticated forms are found in abundance. Obviously, unless these animals were present in the earlier periods in close proximity to human settlements, how could these be domesticated?

The Aceramic Neolithic, both levels A & B, respectively older and younger, at Ak Kupruk (Ghar-i-Mar) which has yielded two radiocarbon dates, 8566 b.c. and 6960 b.c., has also given for the first time a small quantity of bones of domesticated sheep (*Ovis sp.*) goat *(Capra hircus);* cattle (*Bos. sp.*) has been included in the category of possibly 'domesticated'. These species were represented along with a large number of bones of wild animals, like gazelle, red deer, horse and unidentified sheep/goat, all of which were hunted during the Upper Palaeolithic times, as mentioned earlier. What does this evidence show? Let me quote three observations:

The excavator (Dupree 1973:263) writes,

> ".....the foothills of the Hindu Kush mountains in north Afghanistan must be considered one of the early centres for the domestication of plants (though carbonized plant remains have as yet not been identified, at least not published) and animals, the Neolithic Revolution (Childe 1946). Probably the wheat/barley—sheep/goat complex developed in a general latitudinal (34°-40°N) altitudinal (500-750 above sea from north-Central Afghanistan to Anatolia and possibly to Aegean area. Most early Asian Neolithic sites of 9 to 11,000 years ago fall within this latitudian altitudinal ecological zone."

Dupree, therefore, proposes the origin of Neolithicism in Afghanistan from where it travelled towards the West Asia along the 34°-40°N latitude. But then it again becomes an event in the diffusionary model of history which is not acceptable to us.

R.S. Davis (1978:69) on the other hand observes:

> "The Epi-Palaeolithic (same as Mesolithic) is known from several sites, the most notable being Ak Kupruk II and III. The indications are that there was a heavy dependence on sheep and goat hunting within the northern folds of Hindu Kush. In more open locales, as in the Haibak area, gazelle was also an important species. As yet, none of the Epi-Paleolithic sites give any indication of a high degree of sendentarization. The occupations levels are all thin and the areal extent of the sites is limited....A complex of interaction between human population and wild sheep and goat in the late Palaeolithic eventually led to their domestication, and northern Afghanistan was assuredly part of this process."

Davis talks of 'complex of interactions' but does not visualize the actual process involved in it. He ruled out population pressure in an earlier passage but this is stating the obvious.

Jim G. Shaffer (1978:73-74) is more clear on the point. He starts with an observation made by Fairservis (1971:105):

> "In other words, wild wheat may be native to Afghanistan, for example; thus mesolithic society could have domesticated it there independent of the West, but when a cultivated wheat is found in an early site in Afghanistan associated with domesticated barley and goats (both not native to Afghanistan) it is probable, but by no means certain, that the whole complex was diffused from Western Asia, where all are found in domesticated forms, presumably at an earlier date."

However, the fact of the matter is that scholars have been so busy in West Asia that we have very little data on Afghanistan in the field of domesticable flora and fauna, still Fairservis is incorrect in respect of goat which was present in its wild form in the Upper Palaeolithic levels. In any case, the limited amount of data implicitly suggests the possibility of domestication having occurred in areas outside the Near East. Indeed, the recent realization that domestication represents a process, a change in man/animal/plant relationships, rather than a specific event in time and space increases possibilities that this imoprtant transition was occurring in more than one place. In fact, it was as early as 1929, that Vavilov and Bukinini suggested from their field data that Afghanistan may have domesticated the domesticable wild plants and animals independent of any previous knowledge flowing from West Asia, although about barley we have as yet no clear idea since the carbonized grains have as yet not been identified. However, selective hunting and herding of sheep, goat and perhaps cattle, was a phenomenon present in Soviet Central Asia during these periods (Masson and Sarianidi 1972:14-32) and, therefore, one need not go all the way to the Fertile Crescent for its borrowal. Shaffer makes the pertinent remarks:

> "Until more accurate data is available concerning the presence or absence of domesticable plants, similar assumptions about their diffusionary origins are unacceptable. The present data, strongly pleads for an expansion of the conceptual frameworks explaining technological and sociological changes which may have innovated within Afghanistan itself."

Here we will add that it is not only a question of domesticated plants and technological and sociological changes for which an independent origin in Afghanistan has to be visualized, but also of the process by which certain non-carnivorous animals, sheep and goat in particular, were selected over a period of over 2000 years, first by selective hunting, then by herding, and finally by what is called domestication. At Ak Kupruk the evidence of this process of changing relationships between certain animals, such as goat and sheep, as well as cattle and man. right from the Middle Palaeolithic times, through the Neolithic, all independent of West Asia, which eventually led to the formation of a very important limb of 'food production', called animal husbandry, is almost conclusive.

With this background from the Middle Palaeolithic to the Epipalaeolithic in Afghanistan, let us move to the next stage of culture change—the Aceramic Neolithic, the most vivid picture of which we are getting at Mehargarh in Baluchistan. The site is located in the Kachhi piedmont plains, spanning the borders of the Suleiman ranges and the Indus river. The Bolan river presently cuts across the ancient site, exposing the entire section of the Neolithic deposit.

The location of the site is very significant—since it is situated on the river, the availability of water, one of the major sources of life to the people was perennial. Since it was located on a fertile plain, it had all the advantages required for agriculture. Since it was placed on the mouth of the river where it debouches into the plains, the people had easy access to the natural resources of the hills, particularly of the Quetta region. In fact, the site of Kile Gul Mohammad in this region was also occupied during this period and it is most likely that the two settlements had close culture-interaction. In fact, they appear to be the two centres of one and the same nuclear zone of the aceramic neolithic of northern Baluchistan. Further, since it was near the Indus river also it had the easy opening to the advantages of the vast plains on the east. In fact, on the Gomal river, we have another aceramic neolithic site at Gumla. in the piedmont plains. All these four sites of the aceramic neolithic, known so far in South Asia, make a very good triangle, comparable with that located in West Asia.

As we have pleaded so far. before agriculture becomes a permanent feature of everyday life of the people. animals were herded, which in effect is the incipient domestication. At Mehragarh, we have clear evidence of the transition from the 'wild' to the 'incipient domestication of animals' or from the hunting to herding. The analysis of the faunal remains from areas MR. 3 and MR4 show the following.

> "In the lower Period I deposits, the remains of gazelles (*gazella dorcas*) wild goats *(Capra aegagrus)*, wild sheep *(Ovis orientalis)* and wild cattle, probably *(Bos namadicus)* are the most abundant. The category of mixed wild includes relatively rare food animals, such as wild pigs, onagers, Indian spotted deer, black-bucks, and water buffaloes. Two other wild species, the large antelope, called the nilagi *(Boslaphus tragocamelus)* and the swamp deer, or barasingha *(Cervus duvauculi)* together account for 14 percent of the animal remains in the lower deposits. Neither species is represented in the upper deposits of Period I (middle) and the reduced size of the cattle/sheep and goat bones indicates that by then all three of those animals were domesticated. By period II, after the Neolithic as Mehargarh, game does not contribute significantly to the remains, domesticated cattle are dominant." (Jarrige & Meadow 1979).

The date of lower strata of Period I goes back to the 8th millennium B.C. while of the upper strata to the 6th millennium B.C. Period II is placed in the 5th millennium B.C.

The above details, we are sure, will make it amply clear that the herding process of the 8th and pre-8th millennium B.C. in Afghanistan Baluchistan was not at all initiated by either the people of West Asia or the 'idea' coming from that direction. The entire course of the Neolithic in Indian borderlands flowed from within its own framework of man/environment interaction. to begin with, man/ animal relationship. closely followed by man/cereal relationship—the directional changes were towards domestication of both even though the evidence of animal domestication is more definit.

We, therefore, present the following model for understanding the beginning of agriculture in West Asia and South Asia.

We visualize two rough herding triangles—one in West Asia and the other in South Asia

(Fig. 2). We have some dfinite evidence of 'herding' in the 10000-8000 B.C. levels at sites in both the triangles, even through the evidence in the South Asian triangle is much less but it is compensated by the evidence of Mehargarh (8th millennium B.C. Aceramic level) where a small percentage of bones of fully domestimated animals has been found—this is the indirect evidence since this evidence pre-supposes the herding stage in the preceding period. In a personal communication Jarrige informs me that in some of the graves of the lowest Aceramic Neolithic levels, infant goats were buried. Obviously, the situation is the same as in West Asia where also immature sheep and goat show herding. We feel that *herding was both a technique and a cultural process which started effecting morphological changes in animals from about 10,000 B.C.* By the time (8th millennium B.C.) we start getting the bones of morphologically changed animals, called 'domesticated', we also see remains of domesticated cereals like wheat and barley. Thus, some kind of selection and harvesting of cereal crops may have taken place during 10,000-8000 B.C. but the nature of man's behaviour towards them is not as clear as we have in the case of animals. We feel that, unless man really reached the stage of herding, when some kind of sedentary life style ushered in, man could not go for any kind of incipient agriculture. We do not think that animal's and plant's reactions towards man's behaviour were the same. Animals' reaction to 'selection' 'taming', 'herding' etc. is quickly observed and methods to tackle problems which came in their way can be suitably changed and adjusted but the same is not possible when man dealt with the plant life—it must have taken a little more time to domesticate them. We are comparing the two triangles for one more reason: these triangles provide the first opportunity to the peoples of the two regions for long distance incipient trade, by chanin-exchanges or otherwise ,since the sites located in these triangles have a limited number of objects, the raw materials for which came from far off places. And above all, the climate—temperature, rainfall, humidity—of Mehargarh and other such piedmont sites for the first time made the people realise that it was far better a place to live in than elsewhere.

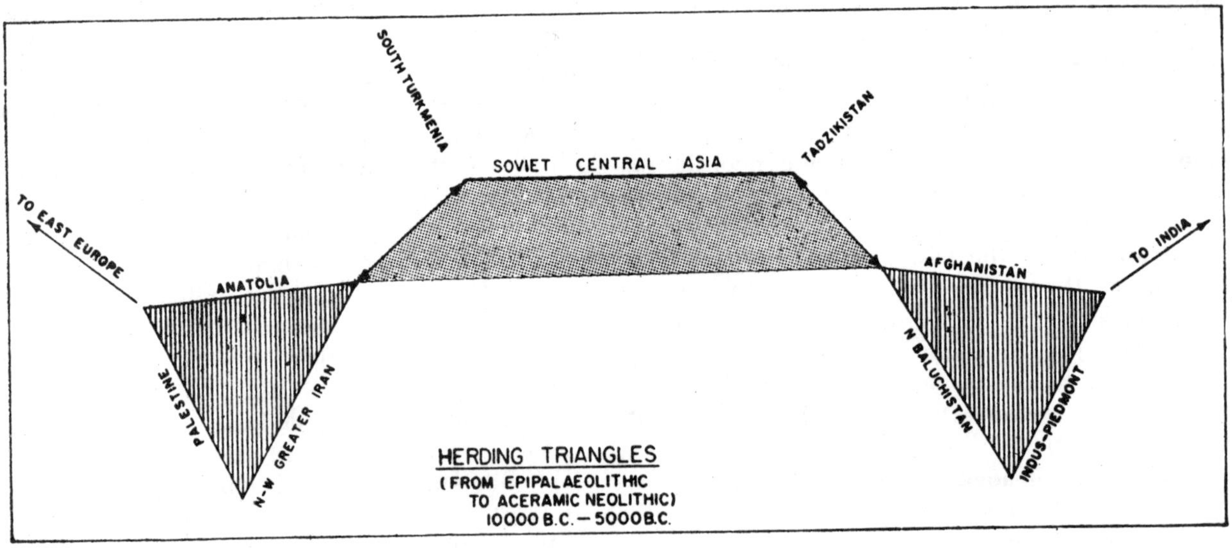

Fig. 2

TABLE I (Animals)

WEST ASIAN UPPER PALAEOLITHIC (Pre-18000 B.C.)

Sites	*Hunted Animals*	*Notes*
Ksar Akil	Fallow deer; Caprines (goat/sheep)	It is to be noted that the pattern of selection of animals was not the same in the Upper Palaeolithic and the Epipalaeolithic I times—in the former caprines dominated while in the latter gazelle dominated.
Yafteh Cave	Red deer; goat/sheep	
Shanidar	Goat/sheep	

EPIPALAEOLITHIC I (18000-10,000 B.C.)

Sites	*Hunted Animals*	*Notes*
En Geve I	Gazelle	It would mean that we cannot treat the terms agriculture and herding of animals simply in the sense of 'exploitation techniques' since techniques may have remained the same but their consequences changed.
Nahal Oren	Gazelle, high proportion of immature ones.	
Kehara	Gazelle, high proportion of immature ones.	
Wadi Madamagh	Goats	
Ksar Ali	Goats	

EPIPALAEOLITHIC II (10000-8500 B.C.)

Sites	*Hunted Animals*	*Notes*
Nahal Oren	Gazelle, immature ones dominated the scene of butchery	This will show that gazelle and Onager were the first choice before the Neolithic, although goats also was selected at some places. It is common knowledge that eventually, in the Neolithic, goats and sheep were selected for full domestication and not the gazelle and onager.
Mugharet el Wad	Gazelle	
Hayonium	Gazelle	
Beidha	Goats, immature ones dominated the scene of butcheery	
Abu Hureya	Gazelle, Onager	
Ain Mallaha	Gazelle, Onager	
	Goats	

NEOLITHIC (8000-7000 B.C.)

Sites	*Hunted Animals*	*Notes*
Pre-Pottery Jericho	Goats and sheep, Domesticated species	
Tepe Asiab	"	

TABLE II (Plants)
WEST ASIAN EPIPALAEOLITHIC (18000-10000 B.C.)

Sites	*Archaeological materials*	*Notes*
	Gringding stones, some. Their number increased during Epipalaeolithic II. The plant remains are not known. Natufian sites excavated by Garrod (1957:216, 226) had grinding stones, etc. which made her think that agriculture was there during this Mesolithic times.	As may be noted, the process of domestication of plants does not appear to have been initiated on the same scale as the domestication of animals. Moore (1982) feels that Einkorn was perhaps cultivated, but it is doubtful; in any case, it is the wild variety of wheat. About the rest also we can at best say that some kind of selection was made in matters of 'gathering' from the plant world.
Abu Hureyra	People lived here from spring till late autumns, no winter occupation. *wild varieties* Einkorn (was perhaps sown deliberately), some barley and rye, lentils, vetches, edible fruits, nuts, seeds,	There is no proof, morphological or otherwise, that these were sown. But it is true that first steps towards 'selection' were taken during this period and if 'selection' is the first stage of domestication then we can say that in one sense Neolithicism had started in Epipalaeolithic times. However, 'selection' was a process it was not the 'final selection' about which we have clear indications not before 8000 B.C. 'Final selection' in this sense is the same as the 'incipient agriculture'. At Tell Aswad (phase Ia 7800 B.C.) there are the domesticated variety of cereals.
Al Nahal	Oren (Noy *et al* 1973) (Table 6) also similar items are found	
NEOLITHIC (8000-6000 B.C.)		
Tell Aswad	Peas, emmer, lentils, probably barley.	

REFERENCES

Braidwood, R.J. and L. 1953, The Earliest Village Communities of South Western Asia, *Jr. World History*, I, 278-310.

Childe, V.G. 1952, *New Light on the Most Ancient East* (4th Ed.) London.

Davis, R.S. 1973, *The Archaeology of Afghanistan* (Ed. F.R. Allchin and N. Hammond) London, 37-50.

Fairservis, W.A. 1971, *The Roots of Ancient India New* York.

Dupree, L. 1973, *Afghanistan*, Princeton.

Flannery, K.V. 1969, Origins and Ecological effects of early domestication in Iran and the Near East. In *The Domestication and Explotation of Plants and Animals* (ed. P.J. Ucko, G.W. Dimbleby) London 73-100.

Glover, I.C. 1982, Prehistoric Plant Remains from Southeast Asia with special reference to rice *South Asian Archaeology 1977* (Naples 1979) ed. M. Teddei, 7-38.

Gupta, S.P. 1979, *Archaeology of Soviet Central Asia and the Indian Borderlands* Vol.II

Helbaek, H. 1970, The plant husbandry of Hacilar In *Excavations at Hacilar* by J. Millart, Edinburg.

Higgs, E.S. & Jarman M.R. 1969, The Origins of agriculture: a reconsideration, *Antiquity* vol.43, 31-41.

Hole, F. and Flannery, K.V. 1967, The Prehistory of Southwestern Iran: a preliminary report: *Proceedings of the Prehistoric Society*, vol. 33, 147-206.

Hooijer, D.A. 1961, The fossil vertebrates of Ksar Akil, a Palaeolithic rock shelter in the Lebanon, Zoologische Verhandelingen, Leiden, No. 49, 1-67.

Jarrige, J.F. and Meadow, R. 1980, Antecedents of Civilization in the Indus Valley, *Scientific American,,* vol. 2431, No. 2.

Krishnaswami, V.D. 1962, The Neolithic Pattern of India *Ancient India*, No. 16, 25-64.

Legge, A.J. 1977, The Origins of agriculture in the Near East. In *Hunters, Gatherers and First Farmers Beyond Europe*, ed. J.V.S. Megow, Leicester, 51-67.

Masson, V.M., Sarianidi, 1972; *Central Asia;* London.

Meadow, R. 1979, Early Animal Domestication in South Asia. In *South Asian Archaeology 1979*, Berlin, ed. H. Hartel, 143-80.

Moore, A.M.T. 1982, Agricultural Origins in the Near East: A model for the 1980s. *World Archaeology*, Vol. 14,2, 224-236.

Perkins, D. 1964, Prehistoric fauna from Shanidar, Iraq; *Science*, Vol. 144, 1565-66.

Shaffer, J.G. 1978, *The Archaeology of Afghanistan* (ed. F.R. Allchin and N. Hammond), London, 71-185.

Subbarao, B. 1958, *The Personality of India* (2nd Ed.) Baroda/Poona.

Vavilov, N and Bukinich, D. 1929, *Zemledel cheskiy Afghanistan*, Supplement 33 of *Bell. of Applied Botany, Genetics and Plant Breeding* Leningrad.

NOTES AND NEWS

Typological Differences Between Indian and European Upper Palaeolithic Assemblages

The existence of the Upper palaeolithic in India is still controversial. We try to find out the exact prototypes of the European tools which we rarely get.

Here I have examined only one artifact type viz., '*end scraper*' which is very common in European Upper Palaeolithic.

European prehistorians have defined end scrapers differently, e.g., F. Bordes (1961 : 22) definition is based on the shape or contour of the working edge (which should be rounded and seldom straight) i.e., ogival, or pointed, fanshaped, thick nosed, shouldered or flat nosed. H.L. Movius (1968:9) definition is based on the retouching technique (i.e., convergent, semi-convergent and non-convergent) as well as on the contour of the working edge (i.e., asymmetrical, flattened, pointed or irregular). Whereas R.J. Braidwood (1957 : 77-8) defines it according to its shapes (arc-shaped) and function, etc.

The common features of these definit'ons are as follows:

(1) Convex working edge with steep lammellar retouching (convergent and semi-convergent) on distal end.

(2) The retouching on working edge from dorsal surface.

I have personally examined the assemblages of some important Upper Palaeolithic sites e.g., Renigunta, Shorapur Doab Collections from Cudappah district, from Bhimbetka, Banda and from southern U.P. (in the museum of the Department of Ancient History).

After examining the assemblages from the above sites my general observation is that the common factors in the Indian 'end scrapers' and the European 'end scrapers' are as follows.

(1) Working edge on distal end.

(2) Retouching has been done by removing minute flakes with centrally driected flake scars.

(3) In some cases the working edge is convex and the retouching is steep.

The typical 'End Scrapers', as described by the European Prehistorians are very rare in Indian context. In Indian collections, I observed some specimens with straight (flat) distal end with ordinary regular retouching without convergent or semi-convergent scars and some have ventrally retouched working edge.

Now the question arises as to whether such artifacts should be classified as 'End Scrapers' or not. If we follow the typology described by European prehistorians then such artifacts cannot be categorized as 'end scrapers', but can more correctly be classified as scrapers with (flat or straight or convex) distal end retouched.

If the typology has to be determined on the basis of the scraping edge, then, since the artifacts having side retouching are classified as side sorapers, those having retouch at their end should be correctly classified as 'end scrapers', irrespective of the fact that they have convergent, semi convergent or ordinary retouching.

Allahabad University, Allahabad.

TULIKA BANERJEE

REFERENCES

Bordes, F. 1961, Typologie du Palaeolithique Ancien et Moyen' Translation; Boredeaux.

Bordes, D.S. 1963 'Upper Palaeolithic Culture in W. Europe' *Science* Vol. 142.

Braidwood, R.J. 1957 '*Prehistoric Man*', Chicago.

Movius, H.L. 1966 'The Analysis of Certain major classes of Upper Palaeolithic Tools". *Peabody Museum Bulletin* No. 26.

Prehistoric Archaeological Studies in Manipur

In Manipur, the esatern most state of India and inhabited by the people of different ethnic groups, the knowledge of archaeology is very scanty. In fact, excavations are lacking. However, in the field of archaeological research in Manipur, it may be stated that the work had begun as early as 1929 when W. Yumjao Singh, an amateur archaeologist, carried out excavations at two places in the valley: one at *Sangaithen*, once a capital of Manipur, around the middle of the 18th century A.D., and the Second at *Kameng* where the so-called Chinese invaders were settled in the 17th Century A.D., in the years 1929 and 1932 respectively (W. Yumjao Singh 1935: 52, 61). From these excavations he collected various articles which were despatched to the Indian Museum, Calcutta, for examination by experts; but, unfortunately, they are not traceble so far (Singh 1980 : 148).

It is only in October, 1967, that we have heard of archaeology in Manipur for the second time after a long gap of 32 years, when Okram Kumar Singh had started stray collection of the neolithic stone tools from *Phunan* hill situated at a distance of about 22 Km. from Imphal towards south-east. The collection includes a number of potsherds such as plain wares, stamped wares, incised wares, cord marked wares, wares with circular spots and applique wares (O.K. Singh 1980 : 149). This work of stray collection was followed by exploration of the prehistoric cave site *Khangkui* in 1969 on his own initiative. The *Khangkhui* caves and rock-shelters in East district of Manipur are located at about eleven Km. towards south-east of Ukhrul. I has the elevation of 1967 metres above mean sea level. The stream flowing near the western foothill of *Khangkhui* made the area suitable for habitation. The cave situated on the western slope is called cave No. 1, the cave on the northern side of the first Cave No. 2 and the cave at a little higher elevation, towards the south of the second as Cave No. 3. In the third cave which is the biggest of the three, O.K. Singh had conducted an exploratory excavation in 1969 and 1972. This revealed that the cave was inhabited by Stone Age people as evident from the number of stone and bone tools found in their stratified context. In addition to these, there were charcoal and animal bones. Limestone was the chief material for making tools in the cave. A few tools include handaxe, scrapers, points blades, burins, borers and flakes (O.K. Singh 1972 : 1-3). But the work in the cave is still incomplete.

Besides the archaeological remains found at Khangkhui, a good number of neolithic stone tools from the Central District in the valley, East, South, North and Tengnoupal districts in the hills have been collected. The most common tool types are the hoe-blade, shouldered celt, quadrangular axes and adzes and triangular axes (O.K. Singh 1980 : 152).

In addition to the cave site at Khangkuhi given above, another significant exploration, in December 1979 by the State Archaeology of Manipur, is the Tharon Cave site. The cave site is located at a distance of about two Km. to the north of *Tharon* village in the West District of Manipur.

The villagers call the cave *Kalemki*, 'the house of bats'. The altitude of the cave site is 3200 ft. above mean seal level. The rock type of the area is sandstone of Bariel Series. A stream called Kalemkimagu is flowing on the southern side in front of the caves. The caves, probably formed owing to the weathering of the rock, are five in number. One cave is very long and looks like a channel. While exploring the cave, one flake tool and five pebble tools of Haobinhian character were discovered which were widely distributed in the regions of south-east Asia during 7000-6000 B.C. (Singh November/December, 1981 : 24). Again, in January, 1981, an archaeological survey was conducted under the directorship of Okram Kumar Singh, Superintendent of Archaeology, Govt. of Manipur, by 'The Committee on Writing Regional Composite History of Manipur'. As before, more edge ground pebble tools were collected.

Another intersesting work was the exploration of the megalithic culture at Mao-Maram area in 1978, the report of which had been presented in the 10th I.C.A.I.S., Post Plenary Symposium on 'Recent Advances in the Indo-Pacific Prehistory' held at the Department of Archaeology, University of Poona, during December, 1978. In this report, an attempt was made to trace its affinity to the neighbouring tribes and South-East Asia as far as Indonesia (Singh 1978).

In the year 1979, a team of experts under the leadership of R.V. Joshi of Deccan Collage, Post-Graduate and Research Institute, Poona, had conducted a geo-archaeology exploration in the Imphal valley. The exploration did not yield anything on the Stone Age artifacts, but the appreciable work of the team was the discovery of three river terraces in the Imphal valley and projection of a probable fluctuation of climate during the quarteanary (IAR, 1978-79 : 29-30).

The latest discovery, in the year 1981, of a prehistoric site is located at *Wangu* in the Imphal valley. It revealed pebble choppers, flakes with traces of grinding to make cutting edge, etc. and a number of potsherds including handmade tripod vessels ranging in thickness from 7 mm to 2 mm. Most of the wares are decorated with cord-mard (Singh December, 1981).

Now, it may be concluded that although the prevalence of prehistoric culture in this hilly State of Manipur is evident from the discovery of the palaeolithic, neolithic and megalithic remains but our knowledge about the cultures is still scanty. The reconstruction of the evolution and the development of prehistoric culture of this part of India is not possible now for the simple reason that the sites are not yet fully excavated and studied.

Department of History, Manipur University
Canchipur, Imphal.

M. JITENDRA SINGH

REFERENCES

Indian Archaeology A Review, 1978-79.

Singh, O.K. 1972, *'The Antiquities in Manipur'*, Bulletin, Manipur State Museum.

——————,1978, *Live Megalethic Culture in Manipur*, a report read in the 10th I.C.A.I.S. Post Plenary Symposium on Recent Advances in the Indo-Pacific Prehistory held in the University of Poona, December, 1978.

——————, 1980, *'Archaeological Research in Manipur'* Eastern Himalaya (Ed) T.C. Sharma & D.N. Majumdar, New Delhi.

——————, December, 30, 1980; *'Tool Gazing at Tharon-Did Austroloids once inhabit Manipur,'* Resistance, Imphal.

——————, Nov./Dec., 1981, *'Manipurgee Meihourol'*, Yeningtha, No. 4. Imphal.

——————, Dec., 1981, Discovery of Pre-historic Site at Wangu', Resistance, Vol. VI; No. 5.

Singh, W. Yumjao, 1935, *'Report on Archaeological Studies in Manipur'*, Imphal.

Nageshwar, an Industrial Centre of Chalcolithic Period

Location

Nageshwar village (22° 17' noth latitude and 69° 10' east longitude) is about 17 km. north of Dwarka, the Taluka headquarters of Okhamandal Taluka of Jamnagar district on the north-western tip of the western peninsula of the Gujarat State. It is approachable by State transport bus service and is on Dwarka-Gopi Talav bus route. The village is famous for Nageshwar Mahadeva temple as it is locally believed to have one of the twelve *Jyotirlingas* in India.

Archaeological Site

In the jurisdiction of this village, a Chalcolithic

site was located nearly less than 0.5 km east of Nageshwar Mahadeva temple, on a low lying area near a pond locally known as Bhimagaja talao. The site measures about 250×300 m approximately and has archaeological debris of nearly one meter height. Unfortunately, the site is damaged considerably, due to digging of number of pits, for removing earth, for the construction of dam of the tank. This dam is located on the southern side of the site and seems to have occupied some portions of the ancient site. The excavated pits reveal at several places some plinth like constructions of local stone.

Hydrology and Vegetation

Whole of the Okhamandal taluka has scant vegetation and saline water. Potable water is very much scarce. The present site is mostly covered with acacia and throny Cactus (Thur) plants. Some aquatic plants also grow along the banks of the Bhimagoja talao. The presence of fresh water and nearness of the site to the sea seems to be the main attraction for chalcolithic people, who settled there.

Exploration

During surface exploration of the site a large variety of antiquities were collected which includes ceramics, bones, microlithic blades and vast quantity of shell manufacturing waste.

Ceramics

The ceramic assemblage of the site consists of plain, painted and incised Red were, Buff ware, Gray Ware and Coarse Red ware. (Fig. 2 and 3).

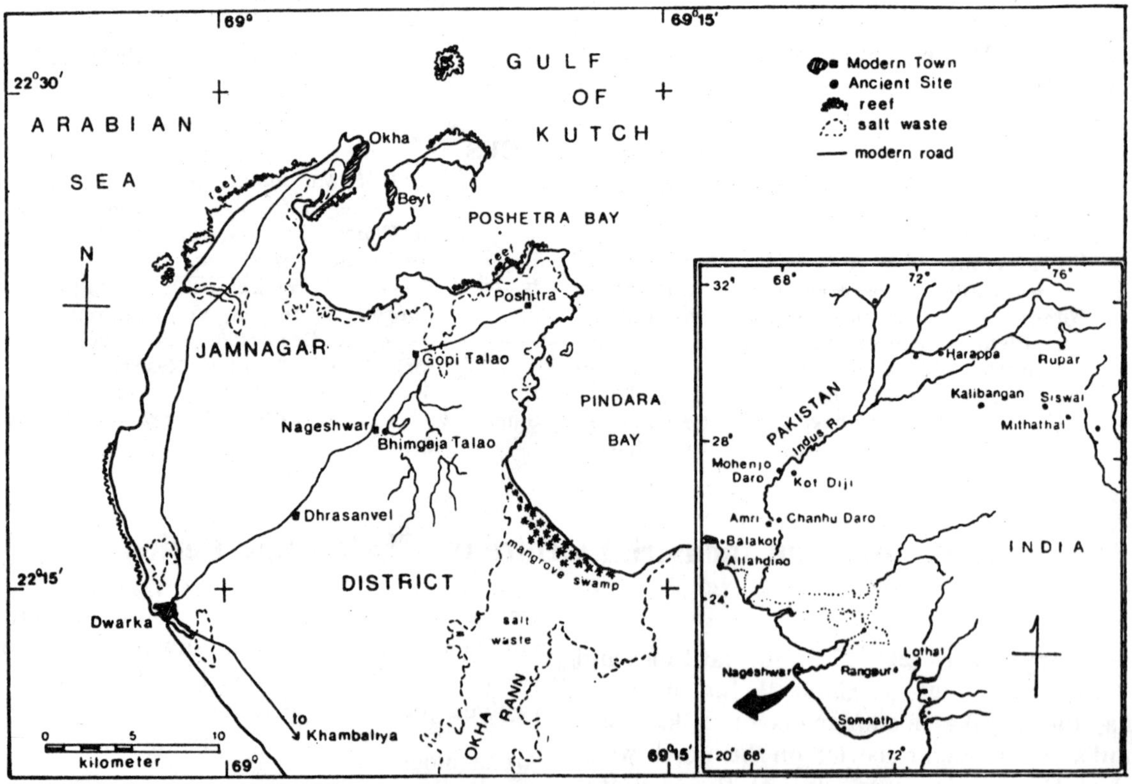

Fig. 1 : Nageshwar and other important Harappan sites.

The Red ware is represented by various parts of dish-on-stand, perforated Jars, Convex bowls, stud-handled bowl, basins, storage Jars, globular pots, lids and a terracota lamp, Dish-on-stand with dishes having projected rim and sharp carrination at lower part and the dish slightly with beaded rim (Fig. 2; 1.2), Jar with bulbous body and projecting rim (Fig. 2; 3) basin wtih projecting rim (Fig. 2; a) storage jars with heavy rim and rim (Fig. 3; 12, 13), can favourably companed with the pottery reported from Rangpur II A' and II B (Rao, 1962-63, pp. 68-109). Still another variety was represented by obtusely incised pattern on the inside on basins or flat dish (?), (Fig. 3; 19). This type of incised ware has been reported from Mohenjodaro and Kalibangan, (Mackey 1963 : 291; Sankalia, 1974 : 345).

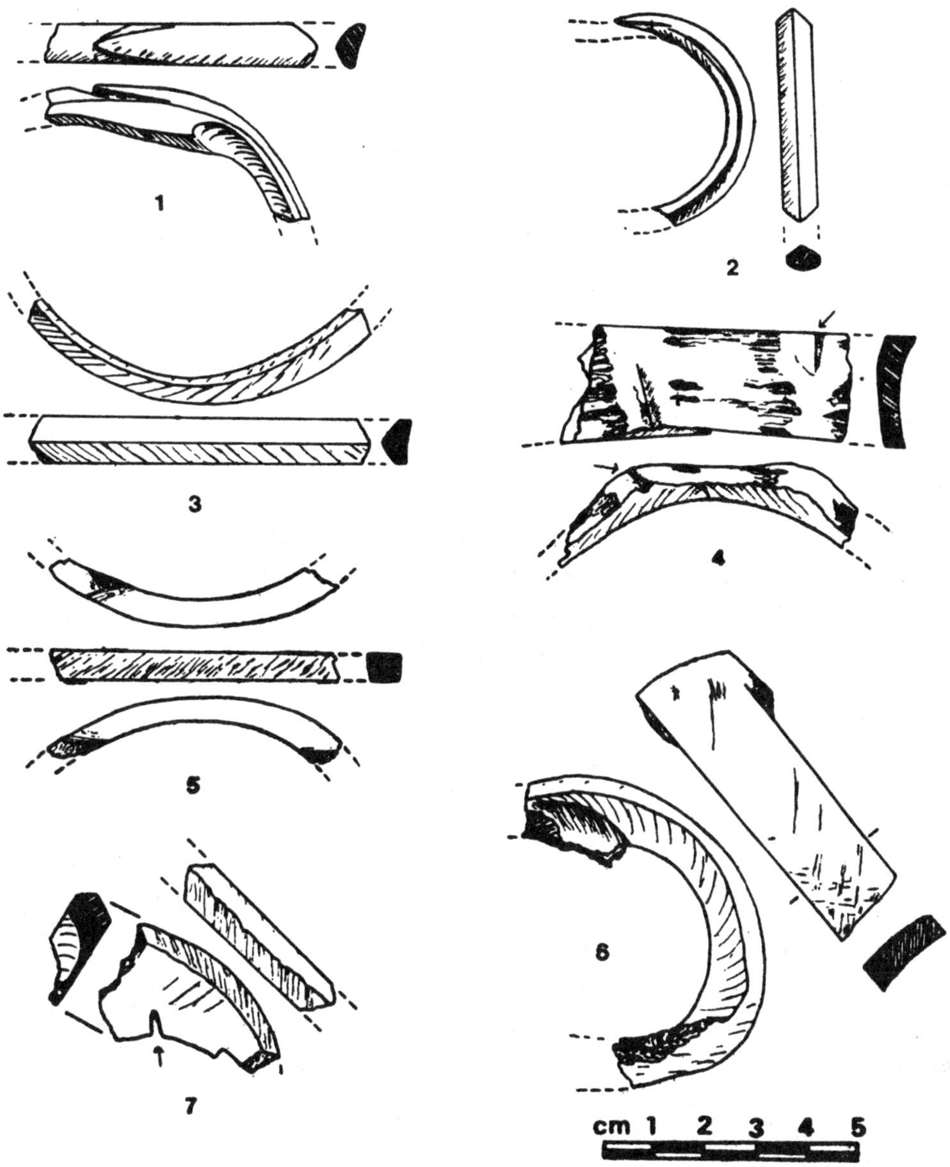

Fig. 2: Shell bangles: finished (1-3), unfinished (4-7)

They Grey ware is represented by convex bowl, pedestal base of a pot (Fig. 3; 22, 23) and few non-descriptive sherds. The Grey ware has also been reported from Mohenjodaro (Mackey 1953): 269). While the Buff ware was represented by various non-descriptive sherds only.

Coarse red ware was found in small quantity possibly used for rough use. This type of pottery includes plain as well incised ware (Fig. 3; 25). The clay used for this type of pottery is not levigated and gritty with clay, sand, grass and broken potsherds, (Fig. 3 : 26). This type of pottery has been reported from Mitathal II B and Siswal I, in Haryana (Chaudhary 1972), Jokha, Dhatva and Kanewal (Mehta 1971; 1975; 1980), Rangpur (Rao 1962-63), Somnath (Nanavati and Mehta 1956: 35) in Gujarat, A few over-baked pottery specimens were also recorded from the site which indicated local manufacture of pottery.

The ceramic assemblage suggests that the site might have been active during Harappan period, comparable to Rangpur II A and II B Periods.

Antiquities

Besides above ceramic assemblage, two broken blades and some bones in semi-fossilised condition were recovered from the site. They have been identified by Mrs. D.R. Shah as those of goat, cow and fish. They thus indicate the presence of cattle farming and activities of fishnig.

Shell Industry

The presence of vast quantities of shell manufacturing waste as the site suggests that it was an important centre for the manufacturing of shell artifacts during Harappan period. We find only wo species of shell being used as raw materials: *Turbinella pyrum* (Lam.) or the Sacred Sankha and *Chicoreus ramosus* (Linn.) or the Great Murex. Both of these are marine species commonly found in the Gulf of Kutch near the site. The major collection area for the *T. pyrum* at the present is in Poshetra Bay which is only 8 to 10 kilometres north of the site (see map Fig. 1).

Before discussing the shell industry itself, it is important to look more closely at the raw materials used, and how accessible they were to the ancient fisherman. The *Turbinella pyrum* is a very thick, sturdy gastropod without any exterior protruberances. The central columella is solid, complicated and is suitable for manufacture of various heavy, solid objects. The shell prefers to live on sandy bottoms or sandy areas between coral reefs or rocky areas. The depth at which they occur ranges from the intertidal zone to the shallow littoral zone, 3 to 10 fathoms. Mr. S.I. Patel (Research Officer, Gujarat Fisheries Research Station, Sikka) has observed that the *T. pyrum* in these waters roll up with the current from the deeper waters during the warm months and then disperse back to the deeper waters during the winter months. The present fishing season begins in Apr.l and ends in June and then after the monsoon season continues from October till January. The *T. pyrum* found in the shallow zones near the coral reefs are often interlaced with bore holes from the boring *Cliona* sponges or other boring organisms. *Hornell* (1914; 26-27) stated that the bore holes are not found on the shells collected from deeper waters or from beds which are regularly fished. In other words, each new influx of shells to be collected before they are exposed to the predations of the various boring organisms living in the coral reefs. The *Chicoreus ramosus* on the other hand live primarily in rocky areas or coral reefs, consequently these shells are generally found to be perforated by numerous holes, especially at the apex and the anterior portions.

The fragments of *T. pyrum* collected from Nageshwar indicate that the shells were selected for the absence of worm holes and were therefore most probably collected regularly from the deeper beds. This is suggested by the fact that only 4 out of 30 fragments examined, show bore holes. The *C. ramosus* fragments however, show 15 to 18 having bore holes, and the 3 fragments without holes come from the interior parts of the shell which would not normally exhibit such features even if the exterior were laced with holes. On the basis of these data one can suggest that the ancient fisherman were using boats and were diving in the deeper waters to collect the *T. pyrum,* while they were wading and collecting the *C. ramosus* from the rocky areas and coral reefs during low tides.

The preliminary survey of the shell fragments indicates that *T. pyrum* was more commonly used than *C. ramosus,* but it must be noted that the *C. ramosus* fragments are much more plentiful than has been recorded from any other Harappan site. Both species of shell were used for the manufacture of bangles, while the *C. ramosus* was also used to make the ladle or dipper which is found at most Harappan sites. The manufacturing waste from the *T. pyrum* is identical with that found at all the major Harappan sites and indicates that the same manufacturing technique was used here. At Nagaeswar a complete range of manufacturing waste was obtained so that it is possible it understand the process of manufacture. It is interesting to note that the processes used for manufacture of objects of *C. ramosus* and that used on *T. pyrum* are different. The main difference is that the apex of the shell was not perforated and that the columella was freed from the shell whorls by breaking the septa from the anterior end, through the shell orifice. This process does not affect the fiinished product at all but it does exemplify the ingenuity and technical skill of the Harappan artisans.

A detailed study of the shell waste from the major Harappan sites has provided some new insights as to the size and form of saw used in cutting the shells. The data from Nageshwar serves to further substantiate these findings. The saw appears to have been heavy, with a long convex cuttng edge. The edge was denticulated and the thickness of the cutting edge might have been between .5 to .75 mm and between 60 to 180 mm wide. From other Harappan sites we have examples which have been shown to the depth of 250 mm, so we can suggest that the width of the cutting edge was between 200 and 300 mm. The saw was undoubtedly made of copper-brozne, as this was the only metal known to the Harappan, and it was certainly within the technical capabilities of the Harappan metalsmiths to produce a saw which could easily cut through the shell, since the hardness of the fresh. *T. pyrum* shell is between 5 and 6 on the Moh's scale of hardness.

The bangle fragments which were collected from Nageshwar basically represent the same major styles found from other Harappan sites. The thinner type of bangles have a single ridge and a rough triangular section. (Fig. 4: 1-3); while the wide bangles have a slightly convex or rectangular section, (Fig. 4: 4-6). The incised chevron motif is identical with that found at other Harappan sites and is invariably located at the suture point of the shell circlet, (Fig. 4: 1-2). The *T. pyrum* bangles range in width from 4 mm to 22 mm and the *C. ramosus* bangles range from 9 mm to 22 mm.

Table 1 : Bangle Fragments

Species	Unworked	Partly Ground	Finished	Not Determinable	Total
T. pyrum	5	1	6	1	13
C. ramosus	1	1	—	—	2
Total :	6	2	6	1	15

No fragments of finished ladles were found in the surface survey, but several fragments of unfinished laddles were found, as well as the manufacturing waste (plate I). Besides bangles and ladles, a large, variety of shell artifacts such as inlay pieces, beads, etc. were used by the Harappans at other sites. Further surveys or excavations at Nageshwar will probably reveal the presence of these objects, especially since these are produced from the waste pieces left from bangle manufacture. The large quantities of shell waste preclude the assumption that the industry at the site was not solely for the personal use of the inhabitants. The suggestion is that the site was a centre of production which was established near the source of the raw shells, and that this site supplied raw shells, bangles and other finished artifacts to the other towns and villages in the adjacent regions and seems to have imported stone blades, which possibly were to manufactured at the site.*

* Explorations of Jamnagar district conducted by first author has revealed several huge Chalcolithic blade industries, with typical 'crested ridge' cores. The absence of any 'crested ridge' core from the Nageshwar possibly indicate that they imported blades in exchange.

Economy

It appears that shell industry, cattle breeding, agriculture, pottery manufacture and fishing were important integral component of their economy. This area is bereft of wood needed for boats. But the reeds like Berdi or Typha Angasta are present. It will provide excellent raw material for boats. The vast amount of shell manufacturing waste suggest that this village settlement was mostly inhabited by craftsman class and seems to have occupied an important place in the society and undertook laborious work of manufacturing shell objects, which in words of Hornell, "needs highly trained eye, perfect sturdiness of arm and iron-like capacity to sit for long period in position of great discomfort".

It is interesting to note that according to Indian sources like Bhagavata and Harivamsa and Buddhist literature, the Yaduvas under Krishna migrated from Mathura to Dwarka. This place was known as Kusasthali then (Sankalia 1970: 54). The Kasa also is a reed which idicates the presence of fresh-water areas, where the Typha Angusta also occurs as natural reed. The present discovery of Nageshwar pushes the antiquity of Kushasthali area further back to *circa* 2100-2000 B.C., if the present cliam of Kushasthali is accepted, and its industry helps in understanding the place name also. From all these evidences it is clearly evident that the area around present Dwarka was regularly habited by the farmers, cattle-breeders and craftsmen of shell industry. This industry was based on the expertise of navigation and deep diving capacity of the collectors of raw materials.

ACKNOWLEDGEMENTS

The authors are very much indebted to Prof. R.N. Mehta for having initiated us to write this paper and for his constant guidance. Prof. K.T. M. Hedge and Dr. S.N. Chowdhary share our acknowledgements for their constructive criticism which helped us to improve this paper a lot. Finally authors would like to thank Dr. (Mrs.) D.R. Shah, for studying the bone specimens of the site and Shri R.J. Khatri, who prepared the drawings.

KULDEEP K. BHAN and J.M. KENOYER

REFERENCES

Chowdhary Suraj Bhan 1972, *Prehistoric Archaeology of the Sarasvati And the Drisadvate Valleys* (Haryana) Baroda, (Unpublished thesis)

Hornell James, 1910-1914, *Memoirs of Asiatic Society* Vol. III 1910-1914, Bengal

Mehta, R.N. 1971,*Excavation at Jokha;* Baroda

——————, 1975, Excavation at Dhatwa; Baroda

——————, 1980, *Excavation at Kanewal;* Baroda

Mackey, E. 1953, *Mohenjodaro and Indus Valley Civilization;* (ed.) Sir Johan Marshall, Vol. I and II, London

Nanavati, J.M. and R.N: Mehta, 1956; *Somnath;* Baroda

Rao, S.R. 1962-63 *Excavation at Rangpur and other explorations* in Gujarat, Ancient India, Nos. 18 and 19; New Delhi

Sankalia, H.D. 1970, *Gazetteer of Jamnagar District;* Ch. II, 1970, Ahmedabad

——————, 1974, *Pre and Proto-History of India* and Pakistan, Poona

Excavation at Zekhada

The excavation at Zekhada was conducted by the Department of Archaeology and Ancient History, M.S. University of Baroda, during 1977-78, under the direction of Prof. R.N. Mehta.

Zekhada (23° 40′ N. and 71° 20′ E.) is situated at a distance of about 7 K.M. to the north of Varahi, the headquarter of Santalpur taluka of Banas Kantha district of Gujarat State in Western India. In the vicinity of this village about three kilometres in the south-west direction, there is a sandstone out-crop. On this mound, once some Harappan remains were discovered (Parikh, 1972). This mound is variously known as *Harmasri*, *Harpasri* or *Amasri no Tekro.* It is about 600 metres east-west and about 200 metres north-south. The mound has four high grounds showing deposits varynig from 50 cms to 1.5 m The total hight of the mound is 3m to 4m from the surrounding plain.

On the west of the mound is a pond and on its eastern side it ends near a 'Vangha', a seasonal water passage which goes in north-west towards the river Khari which is about 3 Km from the site. This river remains dry except during monsoon. The little Runn of Kutch is 10 Km to the west of site.

The surrounding area of the site is a sandy plain and almost treeless. There are bushes of Cactus. Babul and Pilu trees. The area has scanty agriculture.

Apparently it was felt that the archaeological deposit was more at four different points on the mound and probably the settlement divided into small groups. With this view the settlement was named as locality I, II, III and IV. Out of these only one locality (II), which occupied the central portion of the mound, detailed work was done.

In all, seven layers were recognised in the deposit (Fig. 1). From all the layers Harappan, Post-Harappan and non-Harappan pottery was obtained. The physical characteristics and contents of the layers were as follows:

Layer 1: This humus layer was of compact brownish clay with Kankar and pottery. It was of 5 cms. to 10 cms. thickness.

Layer 2: This layer was 5-12 cms thick. It was ashy, loose layer with ash and debris of huts with wattle and daub. The other contents were objects of terracotta, stone, chank, copper and variety of beads. Three circular huts No. 10, 11, 12 wer encountered. This layer represented Phase IE.

Layer 3: This was 10-20 cms. thick. It was ashy loose, with ash, wattle and daub and patches of brown clay. The cultural material was same as layer (2). A sherd with painted bull head was obtained. At this level there were two huts No. 8 and 9. This layer was named as Phase ID.

Layer 4: This was 5-18 cms thick. It was ashy but more compact than layer (3). The antiquities and pottery were similar to the upper layers. In this layer also two huts No. 6 and 7 were traced. From the floor of one of these huts a small pot filled with micro beads of steatite and two gold beads was obtained. The other antiquities were the same as encountered in upper layers. This layer represented Phase IC.

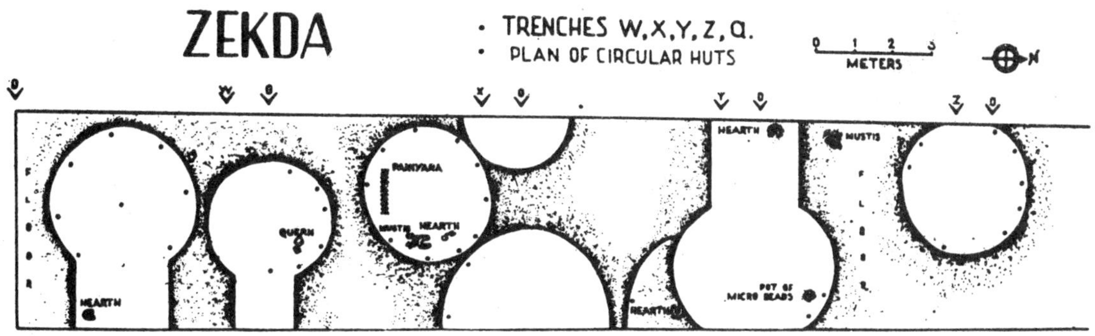

Fig. 1

Layer 5: This was 7-20 cms thick and ashy with brown patches of clay. This layer represented less antiquities and pottery. At this level three huts No. 3, 4, 5 were destroyed by fire. This belonged to Phase IB.

Layer 6: This was 5-12 cms thick and had brownish black compact mud, earth, ash and wattle and duub. This also revealed less antiquities. Two floors of huts raised on natural earth were traced. This was the first Phase IA.

Layer 7: This was black natural soil developed on disintergrated sand rock.

Structures:

The excavation was concentrated more on locality II where floorings of 12 circular huts (Fig. 2) were encountered in five different phases. In localities I, III and IV limited excavations were conducted. In locality I, the floor of a hut was encountered in the first Phase IA only.

The twelve huts discovered in locality II were of two types: (i) circular, (ii) circular with a porch on one side. The diameter of the huts vary from 2.60 metres to 3.60 metres. The floor were 10 cms to 20 cms thick. made of rammed yellow earth mixed with kankar and sand. Somet'mes they were plastered with cow dung. The debris on the floor indicated that the walls were made of wattle and daub and plastered with mud mixed with cow dung.

The wall was supported by posts erected alongwith the circle at a distance 60 cms. to 80 cms. In a big hut there was a central pole to support the roof. In some of the huts there were lobbies measured about 2.30 metres long and 1.50 metres broad.

The huts were furnished with a fire place either in the centre of the hut or in the lobby. In one of the huts a raised pot-rest was traced.

From the huts came pottery, saddle querns, mullers, terracotta lamp, triangular and oblong cakes (musties). From the floor of one of the huts, a miniature pot filled with micro beads of steatite and two gold beads were recovered. All the evidence indicated that huts were used for

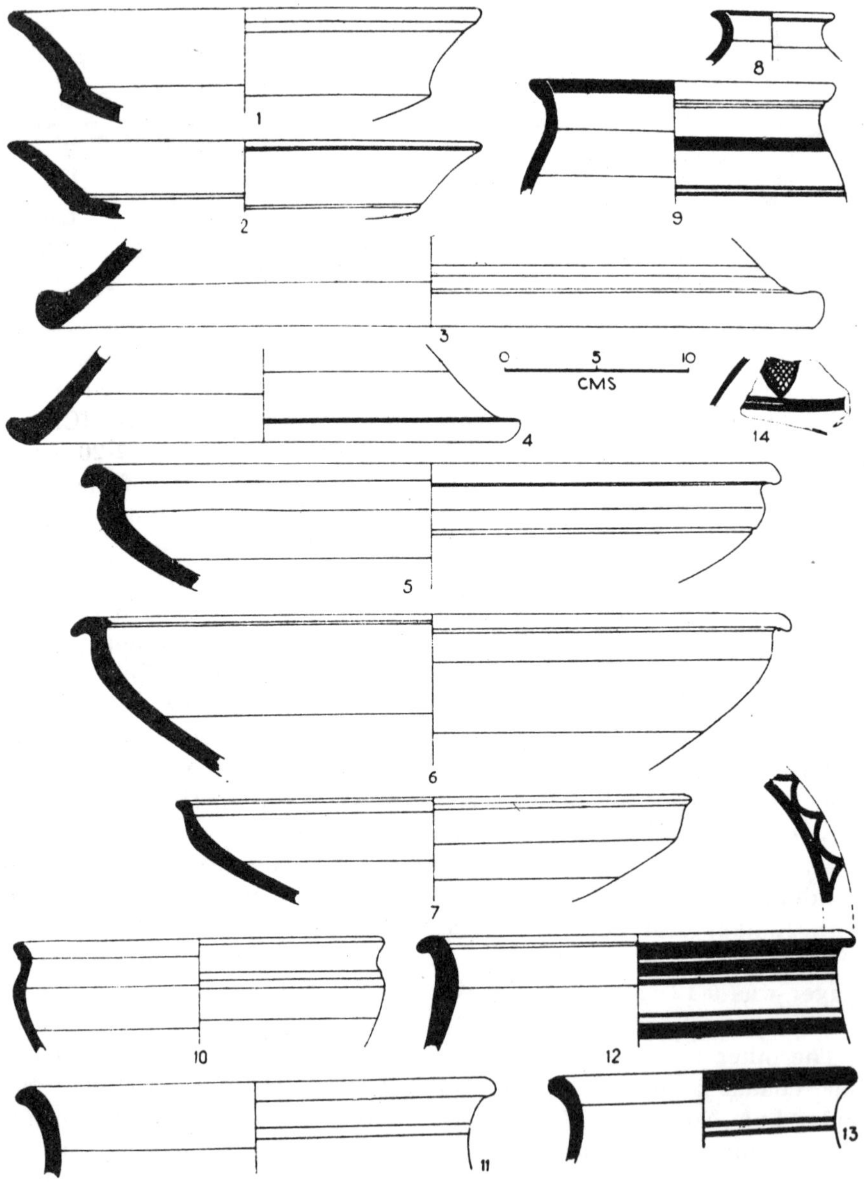

Fig. 2

living and there was no change in the construction of huts in different phases of their occupation. Similar huts have been reported from Kanewal (Mehta, Momin and Shah, 1980) Nesdi at Valabhipur and Vaged (Momin, 1981: 1982).

Antiquities:

In the excavations a variety of antiquities were encountered. They were made of terracotta stone, copper, chank, etc. The terracotta objects included triangular and circular cakes, musties, toys-like fish, cart frame, wheels, hopskotch, pallets, spindle whorls, net sinkers, a finger ring and a pendent. No figure of bull was found except the figure of a bull painted on a pot sherd from Phase ID.

The copper objects included an arrow head,

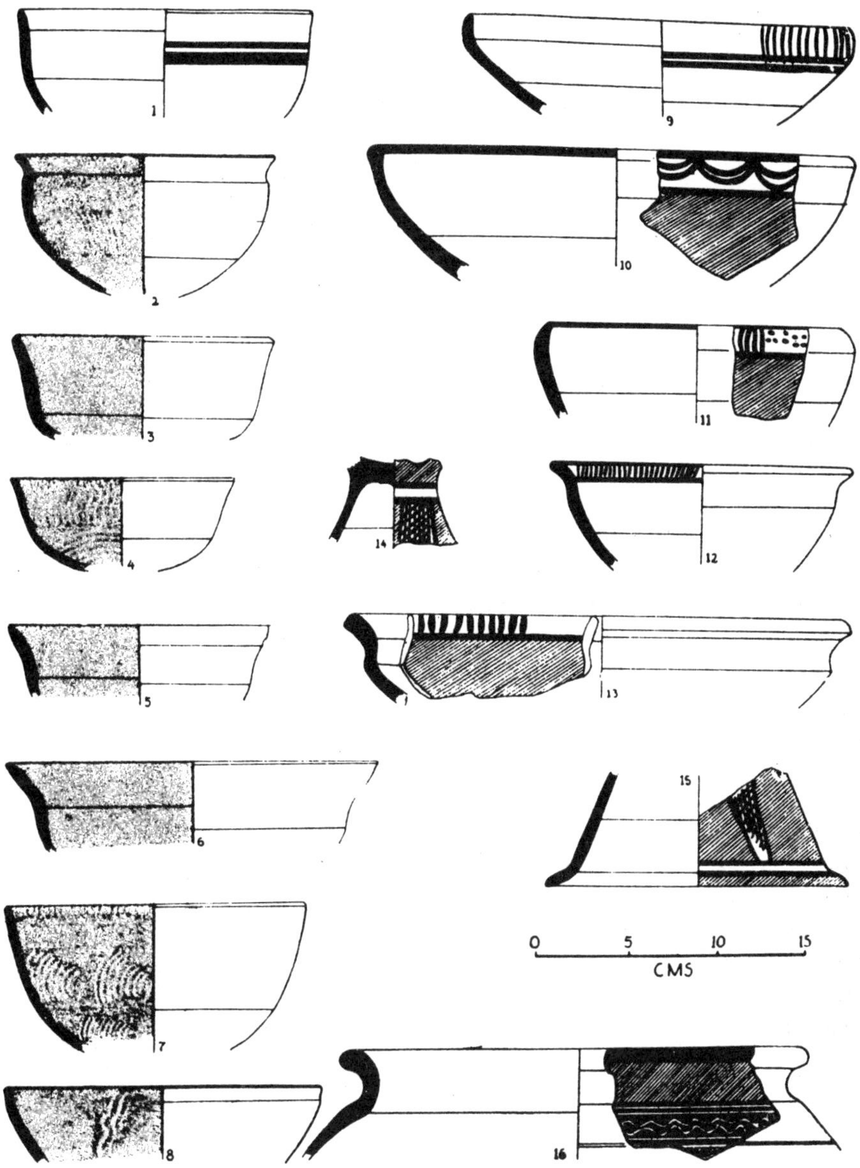

Fig. 3

strips, wires and fragments of copper and a pendent like object.

From the huts and their habitational levels saddle querns, mullers and pestles were encountered. Broad chert blades and small chalcedony blades and cores were rather limited in number.

A variety of beads made from different materials, like carnelian, jasper, lapis lazuli, agale, steatite and faience, were encountered. They were of tubular, spherical, drum and disc shaped. The terracotta beads were of arecanut and biconical shape. Numerous microbeads of steatite furnish the evidence of high perfection in the art of lapidary.

A number of chank bangles, chank slices and stems were encountered. The finished chank bangles and waste material indicated local manufacture of chank articles.

All the above discussed antiquities have strong affinities with those reported from other Harappan sites.

Pottery:

The excavations revealed, Harappan, Post-Harappan and non-Harappan creamics from all the phases. The Harappan pottery is distinguished by thick sturdy vessels with thin texture. Though this pottery is comparatively less in amount but it represents black painted red ware (Fig. 3), chocolate ware and perforated ware. Buff ware was represented with a few sherds (Fig. 3). Different shapes, like beakers, bowls, basins, dished, dishes-on-stand, globular pots, pots with funnel mouth and high necked pots were recovered. This pottery has affinity with Lothal B (Rao, 1956) and Surkotada IC (Joshi, 1972).

The Post-Harappan pottery included plain and painted black-and rod ware, coarse gritty ware, plain and incised crude ware and Lustrous Red Ware (Fig. 4). These types of pottery have affinity with Rangpur IIC, and III, (Rao, 1962-63) Surkotada IC (Joshi, 1972) and Ahar IC (Surkotada, Deo & Ansari, 1969). The bulk, however, was of non-Harappan pottery. It included different varieties, like red slipped polychrome ware, polchrome cream slipped ware, and reserved slip ware (Fig.4).

Polychrome ware was inconsiderable quantity. tI is in various froms, fabric, shapes and colour. In addition to this, surface treatment also differ from shape to shape and fabric to fabric. Various colours, such as red, deep red and violet red have been used as wash, and black and violet are used for making bands, and white for various other designs. The shapes included dish-on-stand and globular pots. The reserved slip ware is represented by a few sherds only. This pottery has affinity with Surkotada IC, (Joshi, 1972).

Conclusion:

The first settlers at Zekhada built their circular huts on primary black soil formed on out-crop of standstone.The mound shows a typical settlement pattern. It was occupied at four different places which shows that there were clusters of hamlets. It seems that in this chalcolithic village, different families lived in separate clusters at various places. This feature indicates a nucleated village with plenty of space between each group of hamlets. At present also this type of huts are found in Saurashtra and parts of Gujarat, where they are known as *Danga* and *Kuba*, respectively.

The pottery evidences shows that there is no change in pottery in different habitation levels. It shows that the Harappan merged with the post-Harappan culture without any clear break. The ceramics present at Zekhada include Harappan ware and post-Harappan wares like black-and-red ware and Lustrous Red Ware, which has affinity with Surkotada IC, Ahar IC and Rangpur IIC and III periods. From Surkotada Lustrous red ware is not reporte' but it has been reported from Ahar. This shows that Lustrous Red Ware from Rangpur must have penetrated in Rajasthan through Zekhada. The white painted black-and-red ware has been reported from earliest levels at Lothal whereas at Surkotada it dominates in Period IC, along with Harappan pottery. The same situation has been observed at Zekhada in all the levels. This shows that probably after the decay of the Harappans in Saurashtra, in about 1700 B.C., the Harappans moved in parts of Kutch (Joshi, 1972, 40) and north Gujarat. In the same way painted black-and-red ware of Rajasthan penetrated in north Gujarat and Kutch through Zekhada. Thus Zekhada became the meeting place of cultures like late Harappan with black-and-red ware of Ahar and Lustrous Red Ware of

Rangpur.

The contact of Zekhada and Surkotada could be established by the other non-Harppan ceramics like Red slipped ware, Reserved slip ware, polychrome ware which has been encountered in abudance fom both the sites.

The evidence of Harappan culture at Zekhada shows that the Harappans moved not only in Saurashtra, Kutch and some parts of Gujarat but also penetrated in north Gujarat through Zekhada.

K.N. MOHIM

REFERENCES

Hedge, K.T.M. Karanth, R.V. Sychanthavong, S.P. 1982, On the composition and Technology of Harappan Microbeads Harappan civilization. p. 2243

Joshi, J.P. 1972, Exploration in Kutch and Excavation at Surkotada and new lights on Harappan migration. Journal of Oriental Institute M.S. University of Baroda. Nos. 1-2 Baroda.

Joshi, J.P. 1972, Transformation of Harappan culture in Kutch. Examination of evidence from Surkotada, Kurukshetra. p. 40

Mehta, R.N. Momin, K.N. Shah D.R 1980, Excavations at Kanewal Vadodara. pp. 15-17

Momin, K.N. 1981, Personal observations during the excavation at Nesdi at Valabhipur and 1932 at Vagad in Ahmedabad District.

Parikh, R.T. 1972, "Zekhda" An important newly discovered Harappan sites in Banaskantha district, North Gujarat, Archaeological Congress and seminar. pp. 46-50.

Rao, S.R. 1956-57, Excavations at Lothal Lalitkala. No. 3-4

Rao, S.R. 1962-63, Excavation at Rangpur Ancient India. Vol 18-19

Sankalia, H.D. Deo, S.B. Ansari; 1969; Excavation at Ahar: p: 138

Excavation at Rohira

Rohira (tehsil Malerkotla, district Sangrur) is situated on Ludhiana-Malerkotla Road, about 36 Km. from Ludhiana and 12 km from Malerkotla. Sikh historians connect this place with the massacre of about 32,000 men, women and children by the forces of Ahmed Shah Abdali in 1762. The mound which is about 6 m high from the surrounding fields lies about 300 m to north west of the village and covers an area of 300x300 m. The western portion of the mound is occupied by modern grave-yard. The excavations were taken up during the field season 1982-83 by the Department of Cultural Affairs, Archaeology & Museums, Govt of Punjab with a view to establish the sequence of cultures and also to know the pattern of Harappan and Pre-Harappan settlements. Keeping in view the above objectives thirty-nine trenches, measuring 6x6 m, were taken up for horizontal excavation in the north-east portion of the mound. They were named as A, B, C, D, E, & F. Two trenches named P-31 and P-34 were taken up on the western fringe of the mound. Two more trenches A-22 and B-22 were taken up in the middle of the mound.

The sequence of cultures (Fig. 1) is as under:

Period	I-A	Pre-Harappan
	I-B	Mature Harappan
	I-C	Late Harappan (Bara)
Period	II.	Painted Grey Ware, Grey Ware, and Black-slipped Ware.
Period	III.	Sunga-Kushan
Period	IV.	Medieval.

Period IA The earliest habitation of about 0.60 metre divisible into four layers started on the yellow compact nature soil. The earliest inhabitants selected an elevated spot for their dwelling. On the basis of pottery and other antiquities these people represent the Pre-Harappan culture (Kalibangan-I and Banawali-I). The pottery recovered which is basically thin represented all the fabrics of Kalibangan. Due to restricted excavation only limited structures and steatite beads were noticed. The main pottery types were dish-on-stand, cup-on-stand, vases with black bands, storage jars, troughs with incisions on the interior.

Period IB:—

The complex of IA continued but mature Harappan also made its appearance. This period witnessed the arrival of new elements represented by pottery and antiquites such as, sealing, graffiti marks, objects of copper, chert blades and brick structural activity and a defence complex represented by mud fortification. The mud fortification has been denuded upto the length of 72 metres. The orientation of the wall was north-south. (Pl. 1) It was 1.60 m wide at the top. However, it was strengthened at different stages by fillings and width went upto 3.40m at the base. The wall which was straight took a curve on south-western side. It was built up of different

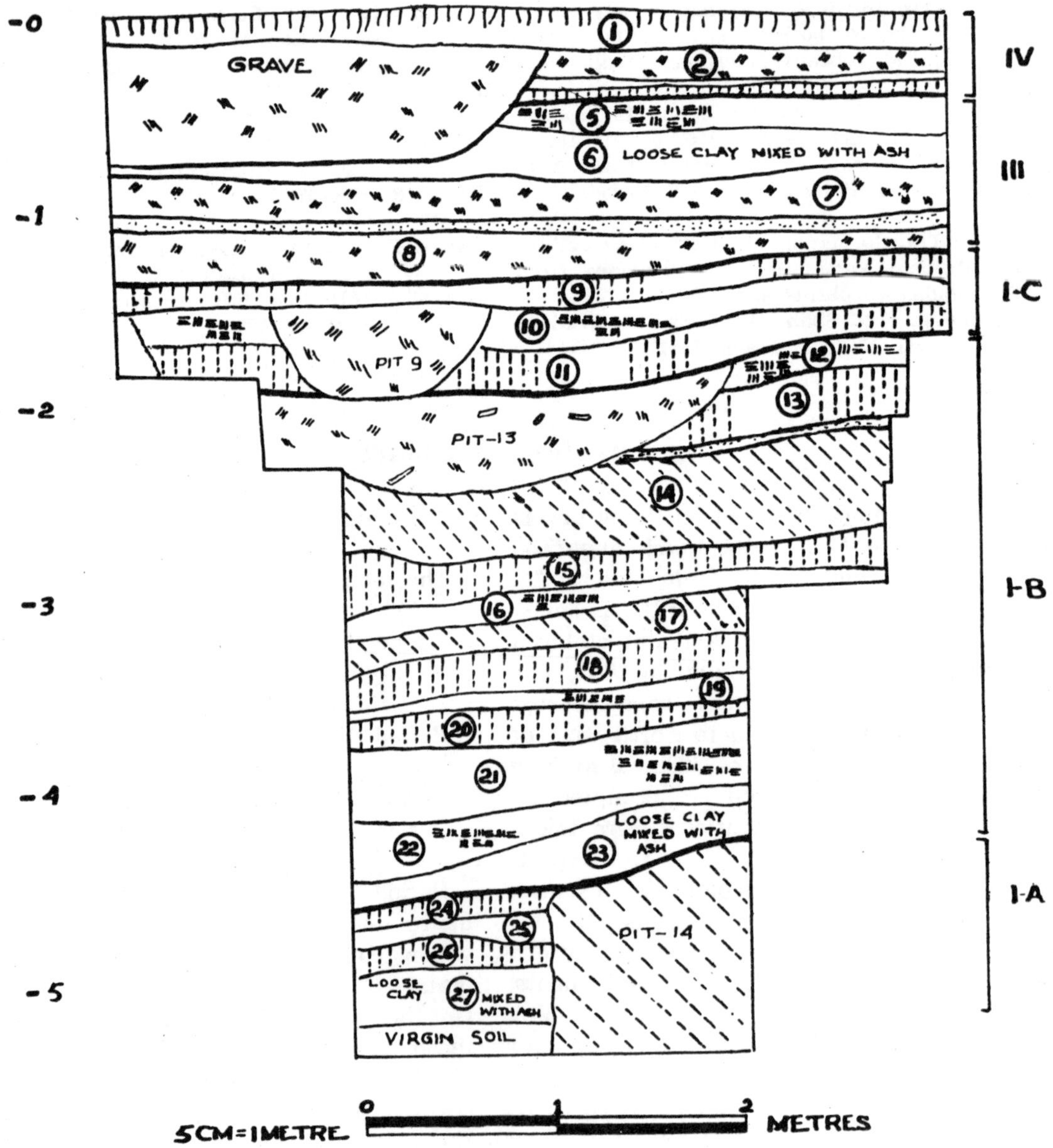

Fig. 1 : Section

sizes of bricks. The maximum height available was 1.40 m and 12 courses of bricks were seen clearly. Brick sizes were 42x28x14 cm, 36x24x12 cm and 39x26x13 cm. Another wall also met this wall on the east-west side.

The orientation of houses was east-west and north-south and were constructed against a defence wall. There were five structural phases of the mature Harappan but orientation of the houses did not change. Only sun-dried bricks were used. Harappan size bricks in the ratio of 1:2:4 were used (8.5x17x34 cm and 10x20x40 cm). There was no gap between the Pre-Harappan and Harappan settlement, as long with mature Harappan pottery, the Pre-Harappan pottery also continued throughout.

The Harappan pottery was mainly thick, and sturdy as compared to thin Pre-Harappan type. The main types were dish-on-stand, storage jars, vases, perforated jars, miniature vases. Graffiti marks were seen on several potsherds. The main antiquities were two terracotta sealings, (i) One peculiar octagonal sealing has impressions on all sides representing a human figure with a bow and arrow in hand and an effigy of a monster (?) standing in front and on top right there is a symbol of rising sun (Pl. 2) (ii) Other is a beautiful square button of steatite depicting *Swastika* symbol. A copper chisel, a borer, and arrow head were also recovered. Amongst the other antiquities were numerous beads of steatite, carnelian, a few micro beads of gold; terracotta bangles; toy cart wheels and frames; terracotta bulls; terracotta cakes of various types such as, triangular, circular and dumb-bell shaped, terracotta sling balls and terracotta gamesmen and parallel sided chert blades (Pl. 3).

A well of wedge-shaped baked bricks with 97 cm internal dia. and 1.60 m external diameter was unearthed (Pl. 4). This was dug probably during the last phase of mature Harappan period. The size of bricks in the well was 31x16 cms at the broader end and 11cm at the smaller end and width of 7 cm. Inside the well mature Harappan pottery was discovered. The site was deserted.

Period I-C:

The newcomers at the site were late Harappans, who occupied the site after some period. The gap was clear in tench M-14. Three layers 9, 10 and 11 represented Bara settlement with a total deposit of 50 cm.

There was evidence of settlemet of these people over a fairly large area. Their settlement lay over mature Harappan house complex. Some of their corn-bins were built up right on the top of defence wall and they cut their pits over earlier Harappan layers. The pottery represented thick well baked pots with characteristic incised designs on cooking vessels and water jars. Faience bangles and beads and beads of agate were recovered in this period.

PERIOD II

This period was represented by Painted Grey Ware, black-slipped, grey ware and associated red wares. The maximum occupational deposit was 0.52 m as represented by layers (9), (10) and (11). Terracotta balls, and vase shaped beads were antiquities recovered from this level.

PERIOD III

This period was represented by layers (5) to (8). It was confined to north-east and western portions of the mound. Terracotta beads, stamped pottery, bone styli, spindle whorls, terracotta figurine of mother goddess, human figurines, and bone objects were also recovered. One coin of Indo-Parthian King Gondopharnese (Ist cent. AD) and a few late Kushan coins which were collected from the surface belonged to this level. Kushana bricks with three finger marks were found in exploration, but a structure of baked brick was also noticed in the excavation.

PERIOD IV

This period is represented by layers 1 to 4. Knife-edged bowls and other associated pottery were discovered in this period.

The excavation has brought forth for the first time an independent horizon of Pre-Harappan in Punjab. Earlier excavations never revealed any such phase. However, furher work is needed in this direction.

G. B. SHARMA and
MENMOHAND KUMAR

The Unearthed Copper Antennae Sword of Tamil Nadu

Recently for the first time in Tamil Nadu, a rare treasure trove object, believed to be a copper antennae sword was brought to the notice of the authorities of the Madras Government Museum for examination, by the Collector of Ramanathapuram District. It was an accidental find from Shavinipatti village, by the local workers, while laying a road towards Minnalkudi village in Tirupattur taluk. It is a long double edged sword (length : 28½ inches; width : 1½ inches; weight: 685 grams) with a strong medial rib, the hilt bifurcating like the antennae of an insect.

On superficial examination, the sword seems to have an antique appearance and it is covered uniformly with reddish brown earthy deposit leaving bluish-green spots here and there. Wherever scratches are made, the original metal surface is visible and the metal is in good condition.

For identification of the constituents of this sword, the electrographic sampling technique was adapted for collecting the samples, non destructively, in the Chemical Conservation Laboratory of the Madras Government Museum and accordingly, the reddish-brown earthy material consists of iron, copper and nickel. The second layer of bluish-green patches were found to have copper. iron, tin, nickel and chlorides and carbonates. The metal portion seems to have major amounts of copper and less amounts of gold, tin and lead.

Yet outside India, occurrences of the antennae swords are recorded in the past, especially at Koban region of Upper Iran—comparable in shape to Indian types—but the hilt and the handle portions are in separate pieces and have been joined later and the blade has plain cross section with a hole, these characteristics being quite contrary to Indian antennae swords. It is ascertained that these Iran antennae swords are made of copper with in India but outside the Ganga plains, probably from Andhra Pradesh.

Summing up the similarities and other notable features of the copper antennae sword found at Tamilnadu, it is considered that in shape, structure and chemical composition, this antennae sword is in line with other Gangetic antennae swords yet it has got traces of gold and lead which are wanting in Gangetic antennae swords. Secondly, the antennae portion of the hit of the Tamil Nadu sword is not tapering at the distal end; instead it becomes thickened and ends bluntly. Thirdly, the blade of the Tamil Nadu antennae sword is not so tapering at the distal end as in other Gangetic specimens. Fourthly, no associated find was un-earthed along with the Tamil Nadu antennae sword as compared with the copper hoards containing eight items found in the Gangetic plains. Fifthly, this is the first time that this type of copper antennae sword which was recorded in the whole of Tamilnadu as a treasure trove object. Since there are traces of copper antennae swords recorded in Andhra Pradesh, which was once a part of the composite Madras Presidency before the reorganisation of the States, it is conjectured that there may be ample possibilities of this type of culture of the antennae swords of the copper hoard, having penetrated into the neighbouring districts, such as Ramanathapuram, Tirunelvely etc. of Tamilnadu from Andhra Pradesh, in early times. In that case, it may to some extent confirm the predictions of B.B. Lal, that there may be possible southward extensions of the copper hoard culture from Gangetic basin across the Vidhyas and Kaimur ranges. Therefore judging from its antique nature, the Tamilnadu antennae sword may roughly be dated back to 4000 years old, preceeding the advent of the Iron Age in South India.

N. DEVASAHAYAM

REFERENCES

Extracts from the letter from the Collector, Ramanathapuram District-No. 93948/82 dated 28-6-82 addressed to the Director of Museum, Government Museum, Madras-8.

Extracts from the report of the Electrographic sampling technique carried out by Thiru V. Jeyaraj, Curator at the Chemical Conservation Laboratory, Govt. Museum, Madras-8. The

Banerjee, N.R., *Iron Age in India;* (1965);
Lal; B.B., "Further Copper hoard from Ganetic basin a review of the problems", *ANCIENT INDIA* No. 7 (Jan. 1951), pp. 20-40.

The author is thankful to Thiru N. Harinarayana, Director of Museums, Government Museum, Madras, for encouragment in preparation of this article.

Distribution of Painted Grey Ware Sites in District Bharatpur (Rajasthan)

Bharatpur, a North-eastern district in Rajasthan, lies between 26° 43′ and 27° 50″ N 76° 53′ and 77°46′ E. It is bounded in the north by the Gurgaon district of Haryana, in the west by Alwar, in the south by Jaipur and Dholpur districts (Rajasthan) and in the east by the Agra and Mathura districts (Uttar Pradesh).

The present paper covers the exploration of five tehsils: Bharatpur, Nodbai, Dig, Kaman and Nagar of Bharatpur district of Rajasthan. This is in addition to the work already done by the State Department of Archaeology and Museums, Govt. of Rajasthan.

A brief description of the sites is given below:

1. CHAKAJAN (Lat. 27°7′ N Long 77°29′30″ E)

12 Kms. away from Noh, in the east. It is oval shape and measures 200 x 200 m., with a height of 10m. It yielded PGW, Black-and-Red Ware and Kushan red ware sherds.

2. SINPINI (Lat. 27°10′ N and Long 77° 25′ E)

3 Km. away in the west of sewar on National Highway it lies in the west and measures 50x50x 50m. It yielded medium fabric of PGW and Kushan red ware.

3. TATAMAR (Lat. 27°11′ N Long 77°27′ E)

It is about 4 Km. away from Sewar, and measures 50 x 50m, with a height of 5m. It yielded PGW, and Kushan red ware.

4. BHAMDOR (Lat. 27°16′30″ N Long 77°27′30″ E)

Bhandor measures 500 x 500 m. with a height of 6 m. It consists of PGW Sherds, Kushan Red Ware.

5. KASODA (Lat. 27°14″ N and Long. 77°25″E)

It is close to the Bharatpur Nadbai railway line. It yielded PGW and Kushan red ware.

6. JHEELRA (Lat. 27°12″ N and 77°28″ E)

Jheelra is an extensive mound and measures 600 x 400 m. with a height of 1½ m. It consists of black-and-red ware, Painted Grey Ware, black slipped ware and Sunga Kushan red ware.

7. BORAI (Lat. 27°17″ N and Long. 77°26″ E)

Borai is located close to the Homes canal. It measures 40 x 40 m. with a height of 3 m. and consists of PGW, Kushan red ware and brick structures.

8. SANTROOKA (Lat. 27°20′ N and Long. 77°28′ E)

Santrooka is a border village of tehsil Bharatpur. It measures 400 x 400 m. with a height of 8m. close to the Goverdhan drain. The ceramics recovered are PGW, Kushan red ware, and a few medieval pot-sherds.

9. NAGLA MAITHENA (Lat. 27°20′ N and Long. 77°22′ E)

It measures about 50 x 50 m and lies in the north west of Kumher town. The pottery yielded is mainly early historic period.

10. PALA (Lat. 27°18′ N and Long. 77°20′ E)

Village Pala is located close to the Kumher Dig road. The mound is capped by a late medival temple. It is oval in shape and measures 100 x 50 m. with a height of 10 m. The habitation deposit is around 3 m. The early historic ceramics like

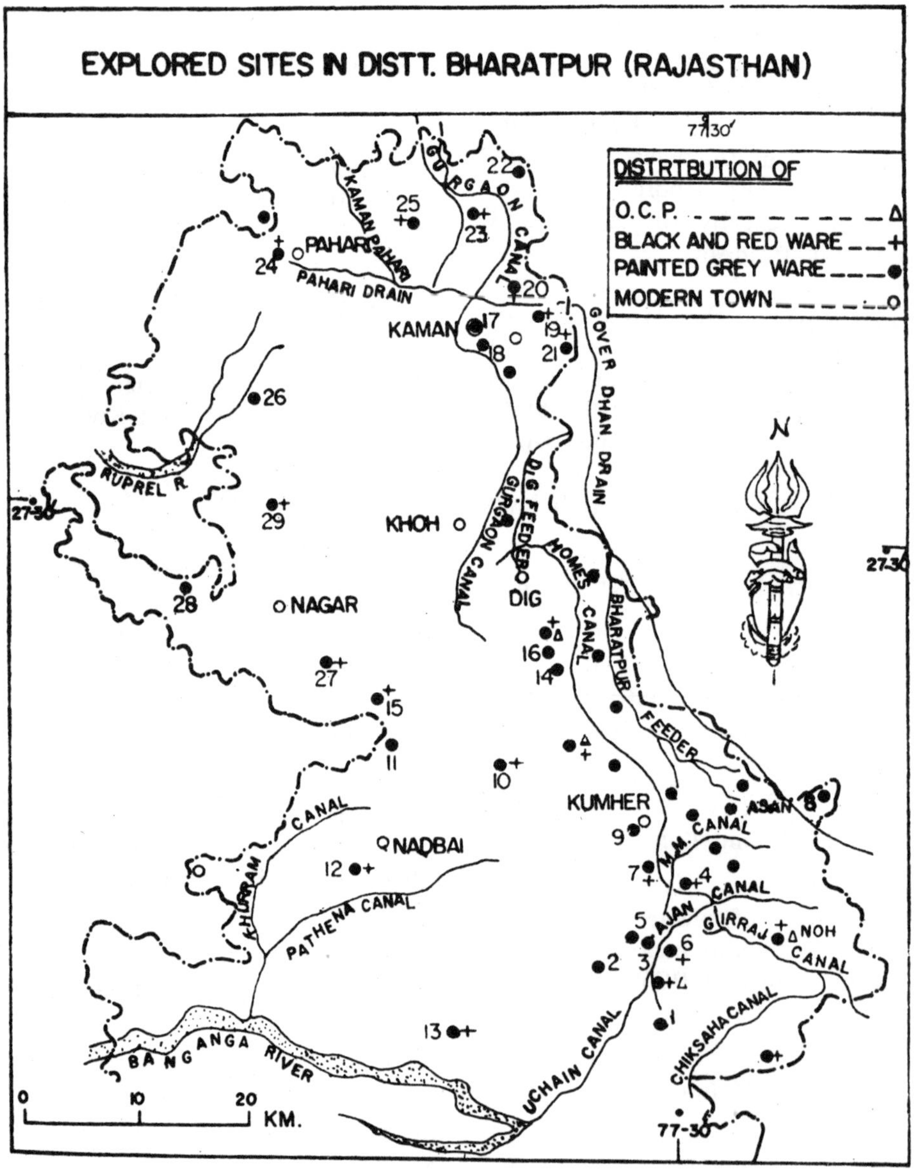

Fig. 1

Painted Grey ware, comprising typical dish and bowl of fine faric were picked up.

11. UNAYA (Lat. 27°14′ and Long. 77°18″ E)

Unaya is 15 km. away from Nadbai town. It is an extensive mound divided in two parts east and west. The measurement of the eastern part is 150x100 m. and western part is 150x150. m. with a height of 1 m. of both. The ceramics recovered are PGW and Kushan red ware including some medieval pottery.

12. KARON (Lat. 27°13′ N and Long. 77°14′ E)

Karon yielded an important ancient mound of tehsil Nadbai, located near Nadbai Jaipur railway line, close to the Pathena canal. It is level with ground, measuring 500 x 500 m. The ceramics recovered are Painted Grey ware, Black-and-Red ware, Black slipped ware, all in fine fabric and Sunga Kushan red ware sherds.

13. KOTHEN-KALAN (Lat. 27°5′ N and Long. 77°20′ E)

It is located south of the Karon on Jaipur National Highway and measures 800 x 400 m. with a height of 15 m The ceramics recovered are Black-and-Red ware (coarse fabric), Painted Grey ware, Black slipped and Kushan red ware.

14. SONGAON (Lat. 27°20′ N and Long 77°20′ E)

Songaon is 3 km. away from Aau village towards west. The mound measures 500 x50 m. with a height of 15 m. The ceramics recovered are PGW, Grey ware and Sunga Kushan red ware.

15. JATOLITHUN (Lat. 27°12′ N and Long 77° 22′ E)

Jatolithun yielded an ancient extensive mound of tehsil Dig, measuring 900 x 600 m. with a height of 10 m. from the ground level. The ceramics recovered are: Black-and-Red ware, Painted Grey ware, Sunga Kushan red ware, Muslim Glazed ware and structural remains of 18th Century.

16. GAHNAWALI (Lat. 27°20′ N and Long. 77°21′ E)

It is 4 km. away in the west of the Aau village on Dig Kumher Road. It measures 500 x 500 with a height of 5 m. The ceramics recovered are PGW, Grey ware, Kushan red ware and Medieval pottery.

17. KAMAN (Lat. 27°23′30″ N Long. 77°17′30″ E)

Kaman is a small town of Bharatpur district. An ancient mound lies 3 km. away from the town on Kaman-Kosi road, locally known Bhagalpur. It measures 250 x 250 m. with a height of 3m. Painted Grey ware and its associated grey ware and Kushan red ware sherds picked up from the mound.

18. AGMA (Lat. 27°36′ N and Long 77°17′ E)

Agma mound lies in the south of the Kaman town at a distance of 3 km., close to the Goverdhan canal. It measures 500 x 150 m. with a height of 10 m. The ceramics recovered are painted Grey ware, Grey ware and Sunga Kushan red ware.

19. VAJHERA (Lat. 27°41′ N Long. 77°20′ E)

Vajhera is an extensive mound in the east of the Kaman town. The mound is measuring 800x300 m. with a height of 20 m., The ceramics recovered are Painted Grey ware, Sunga Kushan Red ware and Medieval Pottery. A few fragmentary pieces of Kushan sculpture including Punchmukha Shiva linga of spotted red sand stone was found scattered over the site.

20. NANDERA (Lat. 27°40′ N and Long. 77°17′ E)

Village Nandera is 10 km. away from Kaman town towards north east. It measures 600x6 m. and is close to the Gurgaon Canal. The ceramics recovered are Black-and-Red ware, PGW, Black slipped ware, Sunga Kushan red ware and Muslim glazed ware sherds.

21. SAHERA (Lat. 27°44′ N and Long. 77°17′ E)

Sahera is located 2 km. away from Naunera, It is measuring 800x800x20 m.. It yielded Painted Grey ware, Grey ware, Sunga Kushan red ware and Muslim ware sherds.

22. NAUNERA (Lat. 27°47′ N and Long. 77°17′ E)

Naunera is close to the Gurgaon canal and measures 800 x 300 x 15 m. The pottery consists of the Painted Grey ware, Black-and-Red ware, Kushan red ware and late medieval pottery.

23. PAI (Lat. 27°46′ N and Long 77°14′ E)

Village Pai lies close to the Kaman Jurhera road. The mound measures 500 x 50 m. with a height of 15 m. The ceramics recovered are Painted Grey ware and Sunga Kushan red ware.

24. PAHARI (Lat. 27°42′30″ N and Long 75°5′ 30″ E)

Pahari is a small town of Kaman tehsil. The mound is located about 1 km. away from the town on Pahari Ferozepur Jhirka road. It is measuring 800 x 800 x 10 m. The potteries yielded Painted Grey ware and Kushan red ware including a few sherds of medieval pottery.

25. SAHESAN (Lat. 27°46′ N and Long 77°4′ E)

It is situated on Kaman Jurhera road. The ceramics found are Painted Grey Ware and its associated grey ware, Kushan Red ware and Medieval pottery.

26. DANIYALPUR KHERA (Lat. 27°35′ N and Long. 77°1′30″ E)

It is 8 km. away from Seekri town. It measures 800 x 800 x 5 m. The surface collection of the finds are Painted Grey ware and its associated grey ware, black slipped ware and coarse black-and-red ware sherds.

27. GANGAWAK (Lat. 27°23′ 30″ N and Long. 77°10′ E)

Gangawak is an ancient mound of tehsil Nagar. The mound measure 800 x 800 x 10 m. The pottery yielded is mainly early historic period but in addition to it coarse Black-and-Red ware, Black and grey ware, Sunga Kushan red ware was also picked up. The Painted Grey ware comprising typical bowl and dish with painted rim was also found.

28. RANOTA (Lat. 27°26′ N and 70°1′ E)

This is a small village of tehsil Nagar, it measures 25 x 25 m. The pottery consists of Painted Grey ware and its associated Grey ware.

29. BERU (Lat. 27°30′30″ N and Long. 77°10′ E)

It measures 800 x 800 x 15 m. It consists of the Painted Grey ware comprising typical bowl and dish with design formed by vertical lines and black band rim. Black-and-Red ware, black slipped ware, Rang Mahal ware sherds are other significant finds.

The exploration revealed that during the Painted Grey Ware times the area was densely populated. For knowing the settlement pattern of the PGW uses, the excavation of one of these sites is a desideratum.

Archaeological Survey of India. **B.S. NEGI**

REFERENCES

Gupta, S.P. 1977, Painted Grey ware sites in relation to old river beds in Rajasthan in Ecology and Archaeology in Western India, (ed.)Agarwal, D.P. and Pande, B.M., New Delhi.

Tripathi, V. 1976; The Painted Grey ware An Iron Age Culture of Northern India, Delhi.

The Aryans—A Fresh Appraisal

The identification of any material culture with the early Aryans has been an enigma. Therefore, whenever a protohistoric cultural complex came to light in and around the land of *sapta-Sindhava* (the land of seven rivers), referred to in the Rigveda, an attempt was made to associate it with the Aryans.

Though no attempt was ever to equate the pre-Harappan/OCP people with any wave of the Aryans, a claim can now be raised on their behalf in the light of new evidences. Their cultural context and the habitational zone appear to strengthen their case (Gaur, 1973). Thus the Pre-Harappan/OCP people seem to belong to the first wave of the Aryans whose eastern settlements were extensively washed away by a great deluge. The *Satapatha Brahmana* perhaps makes a reference to this flood in which the Manu is said to have been the only survivor.

In this context the following facts are vital and worth considering:

1. OCP Complex originally belonged to the stock of the pre-Harappans of the Indus valley and the former is an eastern extension of the latter. The pottery complex of Lal Quila (upper Doab), Sothi (Rajasthan), Saraikhola and several other a similar sites in Pakistan remarkably resemble with each other. The principal forms of pottery at these places are squat globular vessels of medium size with short everted or beaded rims, usually bearing a wide painted band around the neck—varying in thickness, on a cream or dull red slipped surface. Other painted motifs include circular loops or triangles joining horizontal line round the neck, hatched and solid triangles, floral and animal motifs etc. Though these motifs are generally in black, a few in white pigment are also present. However on OCP pots they are occasionally or rarely noticed. Besides these, various types of bowls, basins, lids, etc. are also found. Some of these pots are also painted and quite a few of them bear incised decorations of graffiti marks. A great deal of other cultural remains including copper, bone terracotta and stone objects found at these sites show common affinity.
2. The thermoluminiscent dates of twelve sherds from Atranjikhera, Lal Quila, Jhinjhina and Nasirpur reveal that OCP was not only contemporary with the pre-Harappan and Harappan cultures but continued to survive for a few centuries even after their end. The earliest date of each site is 2280 B.C., 2030 B.C., 2650 B.C. and 1500 B.C. respectively.
3. The pre-Harappan/OCP Culture belonged to the land of *'Sapta Sindhava'*, often referred to in the Rigveda. The early Aryans were familiar with river Ganga, obviously with its surroundings too, commonly known as upper Doab, which was the eastern limit of their habitation.
4. Saraswati was the most popular river during the *Rigvedic* times and several hymns of the *Rigveda*, particularly those of X mandala were composed on its banks. We also know that decline of mature Harappan Culture, as is indicated by the site of Kalibangan, was mainly due to drying up of the Saraswati. The Saraswati valley has yielded primarily material remains of three protohistoric cultures: pre-Harappan, Harappan and PGW. The sites of the last culture are of much later date and sometimes are found in the dry bed of Saraswati itself. It appears that by that time this river had disappeared and thus the PGW Culture had no link whatsoever with it. So far the Harappan Culture is concerned, its cultural milieu is different and does not tally with the habitational pattern of the Aryans as discribed in the *Rigveda*. *Thus, the co called pre-Harppans of the Sapta Sindhava region appear to be the early Aryans.* With the emergence of the Harappans in the region, an era of war began. The two fought for their supremacy in the region. In their fight other living in the region joined sides. As there were at least five-Aryan tribes so there would have been several non-Aryan tribes too. The *Rigvedic* hymns often refer to these wars. Most probablly the Aryans wer defeated initially. At Amri (Casal, 1964) and Kot Diji (Khan), there are clear traces of burning which brought general destruction coinciding with the emergence of the Harappans. Perhaps this was the time when the battle on the bank of the Ravi at a place called Hariyupiya, probbably Harappa, took place. Under those circumstances, it appears that a sizeable population of the Aryans left their settlements and moved eastward to resettle at safer

places beyond the Indus Valley and even as far as the Upper Ganga-Yamuna basin. Since without iron the dense forests of the upper Doab could not be cleared, their settlements in that region naturally were small and scattered along the banks of the rivers.

5. *Rigveda* attests that the horse and the bull were favourite animals of the Aryans. Terracotta bull figurines have been found from several pre-Harappan sites as well as from Lal Quila. Representation of bull painted on a globular pot at Lal Quila seems to have affinity with the bulls painted on pre-Harappan pottery.

However, of great significance is the presence of a horse (Equus cabalus; Linn). bone at Lal Quila which has been found for the first time along with the bones of other animals, including the cow, buffalo, goat, sheep, dear, pig, nilgai, and dog, during the course of excavation. Though no horse bone has been reproted so far form any pre-Harappan/OCP sites, it may be hoped that a careful study of bones found at other sites will prove the presence of horse during the pre-Harappan period. Earlier equine teeth were reported from Ranaghundai, though some doubts about it were raised by Zeuner who took it as onager. However, a definite evidence of domesticated horse came from Surkotda, (Sharma, 1974) a Harappan site in district Kutch. In this context the earlier reports (Swell & Guha, 1931) about the existence of bones of Equus cabalus (Linn.) from Mohenjodaro, Harappa, Ropar and Lothal may also be recalled (Nath, 1968; Prasad, 1936). All this evidence proves that the domesticated horse became known first to pre-Harappans and then to the Harappans, or to both almost simultaneously.

So far the knowledge of spoked wheel chariot, generally associated with the early Indo-Aryans, is concerned, it may be stated here that the pre-Harappan level at Banawali (Bisht). has yielded a canopied cart with spoked wheel. Earlier Rao had drawn our attention to somewhat similar type of evidence in Harappan context at Lothal, (Rao, 1973). On a hubbed erracotta wheel, the diagonally painted lines were perhaps indicative of spokes. Sali later on found a bull chariot made of copper at Diamabad.

6. Another interesting evidence is related with agriculture and forestry. Among the crops recovered from Atranjikhera, an OCP site in district Etah (U.P.), are paddy *(Oryza sativa)*, barley (*Hordeum vulgare*), gram (*Cicer arietinum*) and khesari (*Lathyrus sativus).* The wood remains of the site include chir (*Pinus roxburghii*), sissoo *(Dalbergia sissoo)*. sal *(Shorea robusta)* and babul (*Acacia nilotia*). Among these finds barley, gram and chir have their link in north -wesern region, including parts of Iran, Afghanistan and Pakistan. Since there is nothing common between the OCP deposit of the Ganga valley and Harappa of the Indus valley, except barley, it will be rash to presume that the barley in the Ganga valley came from Harappa. During the last three decades evidence of early wheat and barley cultivation have come to light from Central Asia (Agrawal, 1982), Iran (Baienitsky, 1968), and Afghan's-tan (Chowdhury, 1977). It is possible that the carriers of the barley seeds passed through the Khyber Pass and collected the chir wood on their way to India. The tall coniferous tree of chir grows mainly on the hills and mountains of the Indo-Pakistan region and spreads north-west into Afgianistan. As far as gram is concerned its cultivation might have spread to southern Turkmenia along with that of wheat and barley and from there it reached India upto Doab region via Iran Afghanistan. The *chir* most probably was used for certain rituals in which the practice to burn incense was prevalent for burnt chir wood gives fragrance, specially the pieces with high resin content. The above crops indicate that these people had started grownig two crops a year, paddy in summer and barely, gram and khesari in winter. The rotation of crop was useful in maintaining soil fertility and crop productivity. Among these crops rice has no link whatsoever with Indo-Pakistan region. It originated somewhere in south-east-Asia and from there reached India. It seems possible that the OCP people came in contact with the people of the eastern region when they came to settle in the upper Doab. From them they learnt the technique of growing paddy. During this contact the Copper Hoards were also associated with them. These two are local elements with which Aryans became familiar when they reached the upper Ganga basin.

While they were still living in Punjab and Haryana, the Aryans of the second wave arrived with a new ceramic known as PGW. This is evident from the fact that the earlier red ware tradition not only preceded in this region but got interlocked with the PGW as has been confirmed through the excavations at Dadheri, Nagar and Kathpalon all in Punjab and Bhagwanpura in Haryana (Joshi, 1977). By this time the Harappan Culture had come to an end. This is why the PGW Complex is found nowhere overlapping with the Harappan Complex.

As soon as they became familiar with iron, once again they marched ahead towards the east with their horse driven chariots and the iron weapons to colonise the eastern region beyond Drisadwati in the Upper Doab, around 1200 B.C. The sites of Noh, Hastinapura and Atranjikhera belong to this period. At this time cultivation of wheat started and once again *Chir* wood appeared in their cultural complex. During the course of this settlement the war of the *Mahabharata* was fought sometime around 1000 B.C. It is in this region that the PGW using people came in contact with the Black-and-Red Ware and Black Slipped ware using people. Their traits survived throughout with the PGW Complex. Here it would be worthwhile to recall what Gordon Childe had said in 1926 that the Aryans had no really common characterisic pottery but remarkably adopted whatever local technique suited their needs.

According to Puranic traditions Nichakshu, the fifth in the line of Parikshita, was forced to shift his capital from Hastinapura to Kausambi when a great flood in Ganga destroyed a considerable portion of Hastinapura (Lal, 1954). The eastern movement of the PGW perhaps synchronizes with the last phase of the later Vedic time. With the emergence of the NBP Ware Culture the Later vedic period ends.

R.C. GAUR

REFERENCES

Gaur R.C. 1974, of. 'The Ochre Coloured Pottery: A Reassesment of the Evidence', *South Asian* Archaeology, 1973, ed. J.E. Van Lohuizen-de-Leeuw and J.M.M. Ubaghs:

Satpatha Brahmana, 1.8. 1., 1.6; also see *Matsya Purana*, 1, 11-32.

Rigveda VI. 45.31., X: 75:5.

Casal J.M. 1964, Fouilles at Amri, *Fouilles de Pakistan.*

Khan, F.A. Excavations at Kot Diji, *Pakistan Archaeology* No. 2.

Recently Dr. (Mrs.) D.R. Shah, Reader in Zoology Department of Ancient Indian History & Archaeology, M.S. University, Baroda, has informed the writer that she has identified a bone of the horse in the bone collections of Lal Qila Excavations sent to her for analysis.

Stuart Piggot, 1961, *Prehistoric India;* Penguin Books.

Sharma, A.K. 1974 'Evidence of Horse frm the Harappan Settlement at Surkotda', *Puratattva*, No. 7.

Swell, R.B.S. & B:S: Guha, 1931; 'Zoological Remains' in Sir John Marshall, *Mohenjo-daro and the Indus* Civilization, vol. II.

Bhola Nath. 1963, 'Advances in the Study of Prehistoric and Ancient Animals in India A Review', *Records of the Zoological Survey of India*, vol. 61,

Prasad, B. 1936, 'Animal Remains from Harappa', *Memoirs of the Archaeological Survey of Indai.* No. 51.

Bridget & Raymond Allchin; 1968; *The birth of Indian Civilization*, Penguin Books.

Bisht, B.S. *The Glory that Haryana was-Banawali-1.*

Rao, S.R. 1973, *Lothal and the Indus Civilization* (1973).

Agrawal, D.P. 1982, *The Archaeology of India;*

Baienitsky. A. 1968, *Central Asia;* translated by J. Hogarth.

Chowdhury, K.A. 1977; 'Plant Remains from Tepe Yahya, South Iran', unpublished paper; cf. *Ancient Agriculture & Forestry in Northern India*,

Chowdhury, K.A. 1963, 'Plant Remains from Deh Morasi Ghundai, Afghanistan'; *Anthropological Paper, American Mus. Nat. History*, 50 part; New York.

Chowdhury, K.A. 1977, *op. cit.*

Jagat Pati Joshi, 1977, 'Overlap of Late Harappan Culture and Painted Grey Ware Culture in the Light of Recent Excavations in Haryana, Punjab and Jammu', Paper read at the Seminar on *The Indus Civilization: Problems and Issues*, held at Indian Institute of Advanced Study, Simla, Nov. 1977.

Gordon Childe, V. 1926, *The Aryans* .

Lal, B.B. 1954, Excavations at Hastinapura and other explorations 1950-52, *Ancient India*, Nos. 10, 11.

Urbanisation of Vaisali

Vaisali is one of those Indian places which were, in the days of yore, towns or cities and have, in course of time, ceased to possess an urban character. Needless to say that evidences, recorded in the ancient Indian Literature and revealed by the archaeological discoveries, bear witness to the fact in detail.

On the basis of the available evidence, whether literary or archaeological, efforts have been made, in this treatise, to trace how and when the place in question, was urbanised.

Although the earliest reference to the Vaisali-Videha region is traceable in the Satapatha Brahmana (1.4.1.10-19) in the story of Videgha Mathava in connection with the spread of the Vedic culture in the land, but Vaisali by name does not appear in any form here or in any other Vedic text. Vaisali figures as a city in the Epic-Puranic literature. The Ramayana of Valmiki (Balakanda) mentions that the city of Vaisali was founded by king Visala, a son of Iksvaku and the heavenly nymph Alambusa, after whose name the city was called as Visala. The *Visnu Purana* (Chap. 47) records that Trinabindu, a descendant from Iksvaku, had by Alambusa a son named Visala who founded the city of Vaisali. According to the Ramayana, Rama, Laksmana and Visvamitra had a view of the city of Vaisali from the northern shore of the Ganga. Since the Epic does not clarify that the city of Vaisali was exactly on the bank of the Ganga and since it clearly records that while seated on the northern shore of the river, the above-mentioned travellers viewed the city, it may be inferred that towers or the pinnacles of temples, if any, of the city were probably seen by them when they had cast their glance towards north. The travellers, referred to above, had been to the city as royal guests. This city has been described in the Epic as excellent, charming and heavenly.

The Jataka I refers to the three ramparts, at a regular distance of a gavuta (or a quarter yojana) from one another, surrounding the city of Vesali (Vaisali) which had gates with watch-towers and buildings at those three places. The Vinaya texts acquaint us with the fact that this celebrated city possessed numerous storeyed buildings. pinnacled houses, pleasure-gardens and lotus ponds. The later Buddhist texts also bear witness to the existence of high buildings and towers of Vaisali. The *Lalitavistara* mentions that the city of Vaisali was "adorned with buildings of every description, storeyed mansions, buildings with towers and palaces, noble gateways and charming with beds of flowers in her numerous gardens and groves." In accordance with Buddhaghosa, the Mahavana of Vaisali had a Kutagarasala, a storeyed building (pasada), built on pillars and putting a pinnacle above, resembling a chariot of gods *(devavimana).*

As early as the 5th century A.D. Fahien, a Chinese Buddhist traveller in India, also saw the Kutagarasala (double-gallaried vihara) along with many other buildings including the monastery built by Amrapali and a few topes. The records of Yuan Chwang, a seventh century Chinese traveller in India, refer to the double-storied Preaching Hall in connection with a wonder-working tope which was built on its old foundations. Besides, the Chinese pilgrim presents a dilapidated picture of the city as he came across dilapidated viharas and the topes built on the corporeal relics of Buddha and Ananda. We find in the Tibetan Dulva (III, f. 80) that the city of Vaisali was divided into three districts; the first district had seven thousand houses with golden towers, the second possessed fourteen thousand houses with silver towers and in the third district there were twenty-one thousand houses with copper towers. The Tibetan works have described the city of Vaisali as earthly paradise with its handsome buildings, parks etc.

The archaeological evidence, as revealed by the scientific excavations, showed that Vaisali was once a great city but there was no brick structure in the region of Vaisali before the time of the Mauryas. In the pre-Mauryan strata only mud structures were met with. Even the Lichchhavis had no brick buildings; the stupa erected on the corporeal relics of Buddha by the Lichchhavis

[1] Vaisali, modern village of Basadha and its neighbourings in the district of Vaisali and Muzaffarpur of Bihar.

was a mud structure as revealed by the recent archaeological operations in 1958. The earlier rampart around the Raja Visala Ka Garh was also made of earth. But these evidences of architectures do not minimise the early urban character of Vaisali, rather they take it to the hoary antiquity. Vaisali, like many other early towns and cities of north India, traces its urban origin to the beginning of the Northern Black Polished Ware, if not earlier. From the fineness, unparallel polish, superb glaze in different colours and excellent durable character of the N.B.P. Ware, one can easily distinguish its specimens from those of contemporary associated common wares and classify them in such a deluxe group of antiquities as were the representative of the rich, residing in the then towns or cities. The examples from Vaisali were, undoubtedly, very fine; they were made of well-levigated clay, and were fired in a very high temperature under reducing condition, possibly in a sagger ,as is evidenced by the uniform firing of the ware. The discovered examples possessed brilliantly burnished slip of the quality of glaze in varied colours, such as, golden, silvery, jet-black, metallic steel-blue and sometimes with reddish brown patches. With the advent of the N.B.P. Ware, Vaisali seems to have built up its urban personality; during that period it not only constructed its defences, but it also made other architectural edifices, whether religious or secular. The early religious structures, made of earth, included mostly stupas and the secular ones, which were both Mauryan and post-Mauryan, were represented by residential and other administrative buildings. The stupas, built of bricks during the Mauryan and later periods, were also encountered in course of archaeological excavations. The ceramics, associated with these structural remains, also included the N.B.P. Ware, which not only reflected a deluxe character but also clearly represented an urban life of the region concerned. It would not be out of place to mention that the hitherto discovered find-spots of the deluxe N.B.P. Ware in India represented only urban settlements. Needless to say that the Painted Grey Ware, discovered from the pre-N.B.P. levels at many sites in north India, mostly in U.P., Haryana and Punjab, is the representative pottery of the early urban settlements, but the examples of the P.G. Ware, unearthed from Vaisali, were very few and found in association with the N.B.P. Ware. The ceramic specimens, picked up from the pre-N.B.P. level of Vaisali, represented by a few sherds of the black-and-red, grey and red wares, were negligible showing simply the evidences of human settlements on the site.

The other associated antiquities from the N.B.P. Ware level of Vaisali, undoubtedly, added a lot to the early urban character of the site. The discovery of terracotta seals and sealings, beads of different semi-precious stones, such as, jasper, carnelian, crystal, agate, amethyst, coral etc., in numerous shapes and contemporary copper cast and punch-marked coins, both in silver and copper ,bore witness to the fact that the site, in question, was completely urbanised during the N.B.P. Ware period. The terracotta seals and sealings from Vaisali, a few of which belonging to traders, bankers and guilds or corporations, discovered from one single spot, namely, Raja Visala Ka Garh, in as many numbers as seven hundred and twenty in 1903-4, in an encouraging quantity in 1913-14 and further in dozens in the succeeding operations of 1950 and 1958-59 well reflected the commercial status of Vaisali continuously for centuries together from the beginning of the Mauryan period, if not earlier. Similarly beads of semi-precious stones traceable in numbers from the site ,under review, with the appearance of the N.B.P. Ware certified to the contemporary wealthy urban aspect of the Vasalians, Hitherto no sites in India have singly yielded as many of these objects as have been unearthed from Vaisali. The excavations of 1958-62 alone have yielded as many as one thousand four hundred and twelve specimens. The numerous quantities of cast and punch-marked coins, found in association with the NBP Ware from the site, in question, undoubtedly, bear witness to the fact that Vaisali was well urbanised by the beginning of the NBP Ware. As many as sixty-eight copper cast coins and fifteen punch-marked specimens were picked up as a result of archaeological excavation in 1958-62 and a hoard of more than fifty-two silver punch-marked coins was found in course of digging a foundation trench of a wall of a building by a local individual. Numismatists think that different symbols on these coins represented the marks of different trade-guilds or corporations. It is worth-noting that no rural sites have yet been reported to have yielded such antiquities in numbers. The discovery of terracotta figurines and other objects, used as toys or for decorative purposes in urban houses, from the NBP Ware level, showed clearly an urban way of life of the Vaisalian society. Lastly the archaeological examination of the Kharauna tank, one of the earliest tanks of the locality, revealed that such tanks were dug by the 6th century B.C.

From the above study one can conclude that Vaisali was urbanised with the appearance of the NBP Ware, i.e., by the beginning of the 6th century B.C. Early urban evidences, revealed by the archaeological researches, that people of the city of Vaisali in its early stage of urbanisation lived in mud houses, combined with other perishable materials, such as, wood, thatch etc. They had brick-buildings during the time of the Mauryas. They wore ornaments of beads of semi-precious stones and decorated their houses with terracotta toys which represented the local contemporary society. They were industrialists, traders and bankers as are suggested by the numerous seals, seal ings and early numismatic evidences. The existence of old tanks bear witness to the fact that the city of Vaisali had many big tanks within its boundary in its early stage of urbanisation.

Department of Archaeology and Museums, Bihar, Patna.

SITA RAM ROY

REFERENCES

Sat. Br., 1.4.1. 10-19.
Visnu Purana, chap. 47, vv. 11-2.
Ramayana, Balakanda, Chap. 45, v. 9.
"उत्तरं तीरमासाद्य सम्पूज्यर्षिगणं ततः गंगाकूले निविष्टास्ते
विशालां दिदृसुः पुरीम् ।"
'*ibid.* VV. 10-11.
'विशाला नगरीं रम्यां दिव्यां स्वर्गोपमां तदा"
Jataka, (Fausboll); I; p. 504.
"वेसालिनगरं गावुतन्तरे तीहि पाकारेहि परिक्खित, तीसु ठाने
गोपुरट्टालौक्युत्तं ।"
Vinaya texts, II; SBE p. 171.
Lalitavistara (Lefmann), chap. 111; p. 30:
"इयं वैशाली महानगरी रिद्धा च स्फीता च खेमा च सुभिक्खा च
रमनीया चाकीर्णबहुजनमनुस्सा च बितदिनियुंह तोरणगवाक्ष
–हमकूटागारप्रासादतलसमलङ्कृता च पुष्पवाटिका-वनरा-
जिसं कुसुमिता च भ्रमरभवन पुरप्रकाम्या साप्रतिरूपास्य..."
Sumangalavilasini, I; p. 109.
Legge; *Travels of Fahien*, p. 72.,
Watters, On Yuan chwang; II; p. 71.
Rockhill, *Life of the Buddha*, p. 62.
Indian Archaeology A Review, 1957-58; Vaisali Excavations 1958-62.
ASI (1903-4).
ASI (1913-14).
A Guide to Vaisali and the Vaisali Museum (1964),

Excavation at Taradih

A trial excavation at Taradih mound just to the south west of the Mahabodhi temple, Bodh Gaya was taken up by the Directorate of Archaeology and Museums, Government of Bihar with a view to ascertaining the cultural sequence and the potentiality of the site. The excavation revealed five cultural periods as detailed below:

Period—I was marked by the appearance of a celt, a carnelian blade, a quern, four pestles, four balls, and a few fish-hooks which were quite significant, as it not only qualified the site for its chalcolithic character but also hinted at its fishing economy during the period under reference. Among the bone objects, mention may be made of socketed, tanged and barbed arrow-heads, points and a chisel. The terracotta beads and conical objects from this period were no less important. A few disc shaped beads of white colour with perforation at the centre were also noteworthy.

The present excavation revealed a developed rural economy during the period in which agriculture, hunting and fishing played an important role. The remains of huts and earth-rammed floors indicate the structural activities. Ovens of different sizes, met with during this period, were most probably meant for melting copper besides cooking purposes.

The ceramic industry although dominated by red ware, is also represented by black-and-red ware and black ware. The pottery had usually fine and thick slip from chocolate through crimson red, light red, orange to ochre in colour on the sherds of red ware as well as on the red portion of the black-and-red ware.

The main pottery types included dish-on-stand, bowl with pedestal base, bowl with globular or ovaid body and outcurved or featureless rim, ring-based bowl, perforated bowl, lipped bowl, spouted vessel, shallow and deep dish, small vase, small to medium size jars with sharp carination at the neck and flared out rim etc. Pots were also decorated by applique designs. The vessels were also found decorated by post firing scratched designs.

A fairly good number of painted Black-and-red ware along with painted black ware and red ware were also found. Both interior as wall exterior of the pots were painted. Potsherds bore white or creamish white painting on the red and the black surfaces. The painted designs included wavy lines, straight and oblique strokes and dots.

Period—II was characterised by the appearance of iron and Nothern Black Polished Ware along with its associated fine and thin black slipped ware. A few pieces of black slipped ware painted with creamy white design representing loop and group of intersecting circles alongwith graffito marks were also noticed. Some specimens of red ware bor black paintings on their profile. A terracotta ring well was encountered. A few iron implements, such as nails, a leafshaped spear head were also discovered. Besides, a punch marked rectangular copper coin alongwith crucibles was also recovered. Other antiquities of the period were beads of terracotta and semi-precious stones, bangles of copper, bone and terracotta, rings of different materials, arrowheals and points of bone etc. Some neolithic celts of different sizes, unearthed from this level, showed their undoubtable survival.

Period—III was represented by the antiquities of the Kushan period. Important finds included beads of semi-precious stones, conical objects, dabbers and disc.

Period—IV revealed the evidence of Gupta and late Gupta Periods. Out of important finds a terracotta seal depicting three stupas and the Buddhist creed below, is noteworthy and a round terracotta sealing depicting Buddha in *dhyanamudra* in the niche of a *stupa,* flying figures represented above the stupa on both the sides, two male figures shown standing in the *tribhanga* pose and the Buddhist creed in two lines below the *stupa,* are remarkable.

Other important finds were beads of semi-precious stones, bangles of bone, terracotta and glass; stone image of Buddha, Avalokiteshwar, broken stellas, votive *stupa,* a replica of temple, *chhatravalis* and a beautiful die of bone etc.

Period—V revealed the remains of Pala structures made of reused bricks in five phases. The floors of the building were also made of reused bricks and brick bats. The ruins of the above mentioned structures seemed to have been the monastic in character. Important finds were a stone image of seated Buddha, in *varada* mudra; back portion of the image showing a part of the Buddhist creed and the name of the donor in the contemporary script; a headless figure of Buddha in *Bhumiasparsa mudra* and an unfinished and broken image of Goddess *Tara* indicating that it was locally manufactured. Other discovery was inscribed beads of stone and plain beads of stone and terracotta.

The excavations have pushed back the antiquity of the site before the time of Buddha.

Department of Archaeology & Museum, Bihar, Patna

AJIT KUMAR PRASAD,

Archaeology of Early Medieval Towns in Bengal

The study of urbanisation as a district institutional formation has become of late an established fact of Indian historiography. Thus, urbanisation is decidely an indicator of the socio-economic and cultural levels of a civilisation, a point which needs better appreciation in the early medival Indian context. The present paper makes an attempt to analyse the early medieval urban scene of Bengal with distnct archaeological perspective.

Some recent studies have tried to show that from the post-Kusana period, India entered a phase of deurbanisation. It has been sought to establish that the new socio-economic formation which became explicit roughly towards the close of the Gupta period, marked a departure from the early historic pattern. From the archaeological point considerable support comes from a survey of the early north Indian urban centre. In the context of urbanisation it can be, however, pointed out that not all urban centres of northern India declined though a majority of them had certainly disappeared by the end of the Gupta period.

At the outset it should be clarified, however, that the emergence of new urban centres or the continuation of the older ones, in no way seriously challenges the hypothesis of the emerging feudal pattern of the Gupta and post-Gupta times. In the context of Bengal, we have shown elsewhere, that the beginnings of feudalism synchronises with the end of the Gupta period. It is universally accepted that the self-sufficient economic units are the hallmark of a feudal society but at the same time this development should not be equated with a complete abandonment of the urban tradition.

I

On the basis of archaeological excavations we can refer to at least four sites of Bengal that remained in occupation even after the Gupta period. The first of these sites is Khana-Mihirer Dhipi at Chandraketugarh (district 24-Parganas), situated at a distance of 37, Kms. to the north-east of Calcutta. The site revealed remains of a fortified township whose period ranged possibly from pre-Mauryan to Post-Gupta times. It is interesting to note that the remains of pre-Gupta levels indicate that the structures had been of mud, bamboo and timber with tiles for the roof; it was the Gupta phase of occupation which witnessed the introduction of burnt bricks. The most important structure brought to light was the remains of a stupendous polygonal brick structure belonging to the Gupta period. On the basis of the fully exposed build.ng complex and the re-entrant angles the excavator concludes that it had been a temple. Other structure of this period also revealed, and it is obvious, that unlike the occupational pattern of the sites of other parts of the country, the Gupta phase marked the beginnings of meaningful structural activities at this site.

The structural acitivities at Chandraketugarh continued during he succeeding phase of occupation. Thus, the Pala period has abundant signs of prosperous habitation. The upper part of the massive western wall of the polygonal temple built during the earlier period was repaired and renovated wih bricks of different sizes, decorative bricks being sometimes used in place of ordinary ones, the latter being an obvious improvement upon the previous period. The costruction of a rough and massive brick structure covering a building of the earlier period, with its foundation starting at a lower level, was also exposed. Another important structural discovery was a small brick temple 5.94 metres square, with a central pit showing descending offsets to a paved floor, .40 centimetre, square in area. Other Pala relics discovered from the site make it certain that it was an urban centre during the Pala period. In fact, remains of the post-pala structures have also been noticed but they are too few to suggest any large scale habitation, but these are meaningful in nature. These post-Pala structures, though very few, suggest that the site was not at all abandoned even after the pala period.

The Chandraketugarh occupational pattern is further repeated at Rajabadidanga (district Murshidabad). Excavations at this site suggest that at the time when urban centres in other parts of the country were decaying Rajababadidanga was shaping itself into an urban centre. Structural remains belonging to six distinct phases were discovered. It has been suggested that while the two earlier phases belonged to the period from *circa* second to the fifth century A.D. and phase III to the sixth-seventh century A.D. other subsequent phases extended upto the twelfth-thirteenth century A.D. Surprisingly the first two phases are structurally very poor and in the case of phase I even these structural activities are limited only to certain areas of the site. The only noteworthy structure of phase II is the construction of a wall designed to protect the inhabited area against inundation.

It is interesting to note that while the pre-Gupta and Gupta layers are structurally not so impressive, the post-Gupta phases are strikingly rich in terms of these remains. Besides a granary, the most imposing structure of Phase III is a *Panchayatana* temple-complex consisting of a rectangular enclosure wall, four square shrines at the four corners, main temple of *triratha* plan, the rectangular *mandapa* on the north, *Surkhi*-rammed platform, etc. This temple was in successive use duirng phases III and IV. In Phase V, all these structures were covered by a *Surkhi* rammed platform. In the deep diggings on the southern and northern sides of the compound wall and on the eastern, southern and western side of the main temple structure, building remains consisting of walls, platforms, etc., were encountered. On the southern and eastern sides of the main temple-structure were exposed *surkhi* floors of different occupat:onal periods, the earliest occupational evidence not going before phase II.[5] Besides other structures, one part of the site exposed walls, floors, ovens, corridors, rooms, etc., belonging to phases II, III and IV. Phases IV and V revealed an oblong temple-complex with the *ardhachandra* entrance-platform, walls, brickbat platforms covered with *surkhi*-ramming, lime plaster etc. A similar structure was also encountered at the site but it has not been properly dated. Phase V also exposed an enclosure wall with four square structures, while phase VI yielded enough evidence of structural activity including walls, floors, brick-bat platforms, a circular *stupa* basment and a platform with post-holes.

The site is very rich in antiquity. Terracotta sealings and figurines, beautiful stucco mouldings, pottery, bronze images, stone seals, etc., have been discovered in substantial numbers but except for pottery these finds are generally posterior to phase III. On paleographical grounds the seals and sealings were assigned to a period between the sixth and the tenth century A.D. This implies that the most developed period of the site was the post-Gupta phase, and it remained in occupation till the twelfth-thirteenth century A.D.

At Goswamikhanda (district Burdwan) too the occupational pattern indicates distinct signs of Gupta and post-Gupta habitation. The site revealed a massive structure of laterite blocks, showing different phases of repair. Initially the platform, measuring 8.40 metres X 6.25 metres, was built on a hard bed of cemented laterite nodules. Another contemporaneous structure exposed was an extensive floor of beaten pellety laterite with signs of large post-holes Thereafter, a smaller, platform was added in the east and a group of four square pillars with slightly tapering bases were found lying between the two platforms. To this period of second structural phase belonged conical cups and moulded bricks with opposite stepped merlons. The last structural phase witnessed the addition of another drak-grey laterite nodules exactly above the earlier floor. The upper-most construction showed here and there iron dowels beneath the debris of laterite rubbles mixed up with fragments of Brahmanical images and pottery assignable to about 10th century A.D.

Though it is difficult to focus on the urban nature of the site (mainly because of the very limited nature of the excavation), it is beyond doubt that this place was a religious centre during the Pala period and it was only after the Palas that size was abondoned.

The site of Banagarh (district Dinajpur) too presents a some what similar pattern of habitation. Altogether five structural phases were identified, dating from the Maurya to the "early medieval" period. Period III covering the Kusana and Gupta times, yielded various impressed decorative designs. During this period and period IV, when the Palas had appeared on the scene, the rampart-wall was raised higher indicating distinct structural improvements as well as the increasing importance of the site. A small but unique lotus shaped tank, originally covered with a pillared canopy and belonging to Period IV, was also exposed. With the tank at the centre, the primary plan of the buildings to which it pertained was cruciform, a chamber on each corner communicating with the tank. Other relics of this period included stone sculptures and carved bricks. The post-Pala period represented by Period V, was rather poor in material content, for no structure was encountered in this period. Thus, it appears that the most prosperous phase of the site was the Pala period, after which decline set in.

But this pattern of post-Gupta habitation is hardly universal in the context of Bengal. It is interesting to note than an important site of this region, Tamralipti, conforms to the general pattern of decline and desertion during post-Gupta times noticed in other parts of the country. Period IV of this site, covering the Kusana and Gupta times, revealed better signs of habitation than the post-Gupta times, represented by Period V. While typical Gupta terraccottas along with other relics were discovered from Period IV, only pieces of sculptures were forthcoming from the Pala and Sena times. That Tamralipti, which was earlier a very famous urban centre, completely lost its importance after the seventh century A.D. is also indicated by the absence of any reference to this place in contemporary sources for about five hundred years.

II

Khana-Mihirer Dhipi, Rajabadidanga, Goswamikhanda and Banagarh are important instances more so because of t heir chronology of the continuity of urbanisation in medieval period, but by themselves they can hardly provide any meaningful answer to the problems related with the gradual crystallisation of fedual pattern during this period. The type of information that one necessarily needs for such analyses is not forthcoming from the limited nature of excavations carried out at these siets. Thus, the major problem with Bengal region is to deduce some sense out of the seemingly contradictory sets of evidence—evidence of deurbanisation as well as evidence of urban continuity. The problem becomes more baffling when viewed from the perspective of the general framework of early medieval feudal pattern. Ote is at once faced with an important question: (1) Was the Bengal region unaffected by the general developments taking place in other parts of the country in early medieval India? But in a recent study of early medieval Bengal it has been demonstrated that this region, like other parts of India, witnessed a thorough feudalisation of the society, leading to a stagnant economic situation. Thus, the material factors responsible for the decline of towns in other parts of the country were already present in the Bengal region, yet a majority of urban centres of this area continued to thrive; only Tamralipti declined and conformed to the general pattern. The reason for this development may provide a vital clue in the context of the survival of other towns of this area. It is well known that Tamralipti was a port town which derived its rationale for existence from the commercial and maritime activities of the area. That the emerging feudal pattern led to the stagnation of economy and decline of Tamralipti is fairly clear. This development will seem logical from the theoretical point also.

A number of recent studies are trying their best to show that the economic basis of the early urban centres of northern India, including Bengal, was an agricultural surplus generated by the introduction of iron technology and by the gradual crystallisation of a power structure which ensured the production of surplus as well as its appropriation.

From the above discussion it follows that even in a feudal milieu urban centres having no commercial or mercantile association can flourish more so in the case of early medieval Bengal.

At Khana-Mihirer Dhipi the most dominating structure was the remains of a stupendous polygonal temple originally built during the Gupta period. During the Pala period not only this temple was renovated but other ecclesiastical structures were also built. These structures are sufficient indication of the religious significance of this place. Some of the important finds also bear out this aspect. Besides a serpent deity[4] and a bronze image of a female deity with a mirror in her left hand and an indistinct animal indicated on the pedestal as her vehicle, numerous other cult objects have been discovered. Thus, a stone Visnu plaque, belonging to the early eighth century A.D., was recovered from the debris covering ambulatory passage of the main temple. A lotus-medallion made of caved brick with a semi-precious stone bead placed in the centre, was found at the bottom of the square *Kunda* at the centre of the miniature shrine of the main temple at the north-east corner. A miniature bronze image of a standing Maitreya, a rare iconographic type, was also picked up. The importance of the temple complex can be gauged from the discovery of two furnaces, used for burning shells for making lime together with troughs packed with burnt shells. It is a peculiarly significant complex and it was in the service of the temple. The lime thus produced was used as mortar and for moulding decorative stucco panels for the niches, mutilated or . The conclusion about Khana-Mihirer-Dhipi's close association with religion is unassailable; it was a religious town with distinct Brahmanical manifestations.

The Rajabadidanga evidence projects a similar nature of the site as far as its broad association with religion was concerned. The most imposing structure of the site, belonging to the late Gupta and post-Gupta times, was a *panchayatana* temple-complex which was in successive use during the succeeding period. The antiquities forthcoming from this site make the picture more clear. Besides other funds the site has yielded a copper *chakra* of *circa* eighth century A.D., terracotta figurines of votive nature' together with substantial quantity of seals and sealings from deposits posterior to the Gupta period. Except for a few, legends on them are illegible. The commonest type consists of a small circular disc containing inscriptions .Besides, spherical sealings with impressions were also available. Amongst them the most important one was a circular flat sealing with the usual *dharma-chakra* flanked by two deer and two lines of inscription below. A stone seal containing a beautiful representation of *dharma-chakra* with a legend was also discovered. Four bronze images, three Buddhist[40] and one of Ganesa were also picked up. On stylistic grounds, all the four images have been ascribed to eighth-ninth century A.D. Thus, the Rajabadidanga evidence is very clear about the religious nature of the site. It was primarily a Buddhist site with clear Brahmanical associations.

The exact identification of Rajabadidanga has been facilitated, however, by the discovery and decipherment of some of the available seals. Many of the decipherable ones bear the legend *Raktamrittika-mahavihara* and refer to its *acharya-bhiksu*. One of the seals contains clearly the legend: *Sri Raktamrittika Mahaviharakaryabhiksu Samghasya*. On the basis of the combined evidence of structures, antiquities and inscriptions it has been reasonably suggested that the site of Rajabadidanga was the locale of the famous Buddhist monastery *Raktamrittika-vihara* of Hsuan-Tsang's accounts, which stood in the neighbourhood of Karnasuvarna, the metropolis of the Gauda kingdom of the seventh century A.D. That the site had certain Brahmanical associations too is clear from the discovery of a bronze Ganesa as well as from seals bearing impressed sun-symbol and representation of bull-the latter being significant for the inscription reading *Atyugrakkasya,* i.e., belonging to the sect of Atyugra (Siva). It is interesting to note, however, that the Brahmanical seals have beet attributed generally to the period ranging from *circa* fifth-sixth to seventh-eighth century A.D. This will imply the gradual decline of Bramanical influence over that area after seventh-eighth century A.D.

The Goswamikhanda evidence is equally explicit about the nature of the site. The massive structure of laterite exposed at the site seems to have been a temple structure. The addition of a smaller platform to the original structure together with a group of four square pillars with slightly tapering bases in the later phase of construction is quite meaningful in this context. Though the site is not very rich in antiquities, it has yielded a few important pieces of Brahmanical images, This certainly indicates the religious nature of the site-more so because the images are amongst the very few available objects.

The Banagarh evidence is similar in nature. The most important structure of the Pala period was a small but unique lotus-shaped tank, covered with a pillared canopy. With the tank at the centre, the primary plan of the buildings to which it pertained was a cruciform, having a chamber on each corner communicating with the tank. Although it can not be asserted but it can be suggested that the structure seems to be quite similar to a shrine, a suggestion which is strengthened by the discovery of sculptures of Brahmanical deities and carved bricks from the site.

Thus, the most striking feature of Khana-Mihirer Dhipi, Rajabadidanga, Goswamikhanda and Banagarh is their explicit religious association and significance. The natural deduction following from this situation is the obvious religious basis of the survival of these towns. Here it may be to noted that a few seals of Rajabadidanga bear legends connected with merchants. Thus, we have two seals bearing the legends *Vani(?)Kasya* and *Sri Vanika Varendrasya* respectively. This will indicate that even purely religious centres were engaged in limited economic activities.

It is significant that the exit of the Guptas from the scene did not mean political dismemberment of Bengal for any substantial period. The Palas who subsequently appeared on the scene might have provided the basic sustenance to such towns which were not purely economic or commercial in nature. Interestingly one of the towns, Rajabadidanga, which survived the Guptas, was probably the capital of an intermediary king of Bengal, Sasanka. Much cannot be made of this evidence but the fact that the most prosperous phase of all the four sites correspond with the Pala rule over Bengal hints at the role of political organism in the sustenance of towns. Thus, Khana-Mihirer-Dhipi, Rajabadidanga, Goswamikhana and Banagarh are all examples of non-commercial townships surviving under the aegis of a political authority; but they have the obvious limitations of a non-commercial urban centre.

Department of History, Patna University

VIJAY KUMAR THAKUR.

REFERENCES

V.K. Thakur, *Urbanisation in Ancient India* (New Delhi, 1981); A Ghosh, *The City in Early Historical India* (Simla, 1973).

R.S. Sharma, "Decay of Gangetic Towns in Gupta and post-Gupta Times", *Proceedings of the Indian History Congress*, 33rd Session Muzaffarpur, 1972); pp. 92-104; V.K. Thakur, *Urban Life in Ancient India (c. 600 B.C.-A.D. 500)* (Unpublished Ph.D. Thesis, Bhagalpur University; 1980); pp. 332-419.

V.K. Thakur, "Beginnings of Feudalism in Bengal", *Social Scientist*, Nos. 66-67, pp. 68-82.

IAR, 1956-57, p. 30.

IAR, 1957-58, pp. 51-52.

IAR, 1960-61, p. 40.

IAR, 1957-58, p. 52.

IAR, 1960-61, p. 40

IAR; 1961-62, p. 63.

IAR; 1957-58, p. 53

IAR, 1963-64, p. 63.

Ibid.

Ibid.

IAR, 1964-65, p. 49.

Ibid.

Ibid., p. 50.

Ibid., p. 49.

Ibid.; pp. 49-50.

IAR, 1963-64, p. 63.

IAR; 1964-65, p. 49.

IAR, 1963-64, p. 63.

CF. IAR. 1962-62 p. 46; 1963-64; p: 62; 1964-65; pp: 49-51; 1968-69 p. 43; 1971-72, pp. 50-51; 1972-73; pp. 37-38.

IAR, 1963-64, p. 63.

Ibid.; pp: 60-61.

Y.D. Sharma, "Remains of Early Historical Cities", *Archaeological Remains, Monuments and Museums*, Pt. I (New Delhi, 1964); p. 79.

Ibid.; p: 78; IAR, 1954-55, p. 19. A recent excavation of the site fails to notice any antiquity of post-Gupta times (*IAR, 1973-74*, p. 33).

S. Beal, Buddhist Records of the Western World, Vol. II (London, 1906), pp. 200-201.

N.R. Ray, *Bangalir Itihasa (Adi Parva)* (Calcutta, 1948), p. 199.

R.S. Sharma; *op. cit.*, pp. 92-104, V:K. Thakur, *Urban Life in Ancient India (C. 600 B.C.-A.D. 500)*, pp. 332-375.

V.K. Thakur, "Beginnings of Feudalism in Bengal". *Social Scientist*, Nos. 66-67, pp. 68-72.

R.S. Sharma, *Light on Early Indian Society and Economy* (Bombay, 1966), pp. 57-59.

A. Ghosh, *op. cit.*, pp. 20-21.

IAR, 1957-58, p. 51.

IAR, 1961-62, p. 63.

IAR, 1964-65, pp. 52-53.

IAR, 1962-63; p. 46.

For the seals and sealings unearthed at this site, see *IAR, 1962-63*, p. 46; *1963-64;* p. 63; *1964-65;* p: 50; *1968-69;* p: 13; *1972-73;* pp: 37-38:

IAR, 1964-65, p. 50.

IAR, 1963-64, p. 63; 1964-65, p. 51.

IAR, 1964-65, p. 51.

IAR, 1962-63, p. 46.

IAR, 1963-64, p. 63.
IAR, 1972-73; p. 36.
IAR, 1968-69, p. 43.
IAR, 1972-73, p. 37.
Ibid.; p. 38:
Y.D. Sharma, *op. cit.;* p. 79.
IAR; 1968-69; p. 43.

Kashmir—Where the Roots of Western Tibetan Art lie

Kashmir enjoys a unique position in the Indian history because of its situation on the northern border post of India and absorbed all the living cultural strands of India and her northern neighbours since remote past, besides being instrumental in disseminating the Indian culture and religion to Central Asia, China, Tibet and Western Tibet.

It's geographical position resulted into the development of an eclectic art tradition which achieved a highly accomplished nature and aesthetic merit in the history of Indian art. The history of the origin and development of Kashmiri art is perhaps most intriguing but at the same time fluid as it extended far beyond its frontiers. Discussions on the Kashmir art tends to be an unmanageable task due to paucity of archaeological remains. Besides a few Buddhist and Brahmanical stone sculptures and terracotta found in proper Kashmir valley, mostly obtained from ancient Buddhist temples and monasteries of Western Tibet built during the period of re-establishment of Buddhism from tenth to twelfth century.

The aim of the present paper is to show that at the beginning stage the art of Western Tibet was largely based on the medieval art tradition of Kashmir and how this region acted formative scource in the growth of Western Tibetan art. And yet without a brief historical introduction any discussion on the topic would be meaningless.

The remote and inaccessible Western Himalayan region, in former times, known as Western Tibet comprised Ladakh, Baltistan, Zanskar, Lahaul-Spiti, Kinnaur, Guge, Shang-shung, Purig, Demchok, Rudak and Purang (Francke, II, 1914: 94-95). At present Ladakh, Zanskar, Baltistan, Lahaul-Spiti and Kinnaur are parts of India and rest are under Chinese occupation. The history of Western Tibet prior to the tenth century is not known. Only Ladakh as a border post has figured in peripheral manner in the history of India, for we find the references of the Buddhist missionary activities in Ladakh in the period of Mauryan Emperor Asoka (Waddell 1895 : 43) and Kushan King Kanishka (Cunningham 1970 : 317-57). These references indicate that Buddhism was introduced to Ladakh in much early age. Unfortunately, we do not know much about the state of Buddhism in the region prior to the tenth century. Similarly, no particular indigenous art tradition seems to have existed in Western Tibet prior to second spread of Buddhism. The earliest relics of religious art, the colossal relief sculptures of Buddhist deities are found at Mulbek and Parkatse in Ladakh region, they date from the seventh century and reflect distinct features of Kashmiri tradition.

With the emergence of Western Tibetan empire in the tenth century its kings felt an urgent need to reform and re-establish the Buddhism in the region, to reach this aim they established close cultural contacts with the most developed and living centre of Buddhism of those days Kashmir. One can notice an influence of Kashmiri art on the western Tibetan art tradition.

The period of Buddhist resurgence from tenth to twelfth century can be attributed as renaissance in Western Tibet when under the royal patronage of king Yesheod (950 - 1040) of Guge in Western Tibet and spiritual guidance of Rinchenzangpo (958 - 1050) a vital movement of temple building and translation of the Sanskrit texts into Tibetan language started (Frncke 1 1914 : 50 ff; Tucci I 1949 : 272). Tibetan chronicles record that novices from Western Tibet used to go to Kashmir for education in Buddhist theology. The great scholar Rinchanzango was educated in Kashmir and when he returned to Western Tibet he brought with him a group of seventy-five gifted Kashmiri craftsmen including painters, sculptors and carpenters for construction and decoration of the temples (Tucci I 1949 : 272). It is said that Rinchanzangpo constructed about one hunderd and eight temples and decorated them with beautiful art objects, for this he obtained the services of the Kashmiri craftsmen who introduced the art of painting, sculpting, casting and carving of their own Kashmiri tradition of the period in Western Tibet (Tucci and Ghersi 1935 : VIII).

Hence, the actual credit to start art activities significantly in the inner Himalayas would go to Rinchenzangpo. The growth of Buddhism in Western Tibet offered better prospects and opportunities to the Kashmiri artists when in their own homeland needed patronage declined day by day. The early temples in Western Tibet yield Kashmiri prototypes in abundance. This attests the tremendous demand of the Kashmiri artists particularly between tenth to twelft century to fulfil the vaccum of ritual art objects as by then no ready local artists were available.

Tucci's discovery of Mangnang wall paintings in the fourth decade of this century, is an outstanding achievement which opens up new vistas of the Kashmiri paintings of bygone centuries, about which we almost know nothing (1936-41). These paintings are attributed to have been created in the tenth-eleventh century by Kashmiri painters (Tucci, 1949 : I, 272). The date assigned to paintings seems very reasonable as the paintings show further development in continuation of the Kashmir tradition that was characterized in the paintings on the book covers of Gilgit manuscripts dated to the ninth century (Banerjee, 1968 : 117). Stylistic study of the Kashmiri art objects dating from 9th to 11th-12th century represents a commingling of late Gupta tradition of Eastern and Western India with the indigenous local elements largely based on Gandharan tradition.

The parallel examples of the Mangnang paintings are found in the temples of Alchi and Mangyu in Ladakh, Sumda Chhun in Zanskar, Tabo and Lhalung in Spiti and Nako in Kinnaur. In general all the examples belong to one and the same tradition and period with slight variation of execution. Most possibly, it is due to various hands employed at works.

The miniature wall paintings in the old temples of Alchi resonate with the same mediaeval Kashmiri tradition that is characterized in the paintings of Mangnang. Two examples of Alchi paintings clipped up in this paper show Prajnaparmita (Plate-I) and Bodhisattava Padmapani (Plate-2). Both the examples characteristically show a striking use of chiaroscuro and naturalistic modelling by deepening of body hues to produce impression of volume—which is fairly rare in Indian paintings. The figures are shown characterized by a peculiar Kashmiri penchant for slim, well proportionate but sensuous bodily forms with illuminating the contours—some times through the tight fitting and translucent costumes. This feature is very well demonstrated in the female figures as can be seen in the figure of Prajnaparmita (Plate-1). Another important typical Kashmiri feature lies in the delineation of abdominal muscle and slightly corpulent belly by skilled modelling with naturalism which is distinct in the examples under discussion. The facial type in this period is marked as ovaloid and slightly plump with chubby cheeks, slightly exaggerated double chin, high arched eyebrows, summarized but full lips and prominent nose.

In the paintings we observe the project on of one eye from the profile of half turned faces. This appears to be a characteristic featur of the mediaeval Kashmiri paintings like elsewhere in Indian paintings. The eyes, in the Kashmiri art of post Karkota period are depicted always narrow and slanting. Apart from anatomical details meticulous rendering of very fine and naturalistic details of costumes and ornaments observed in the Kashmiri art examples of tenth and eleventh century is perhaps matchless.

The focus of the present paper is mainly set upon hitherto unpublished material which I have discovered by carrying out several exploration tours in the inaccessible valleys of the Western Himalayas.

One of the examples of wall paintings from the temple of Nako in Kinnaurs (formerly a province of Western Tibetan empire) in Himachal Pradesh, is being produced for the first time. The painted figure represents Bodhisattava Manjushree. Stylistically, this figure belong to the same tradition discussed above. The painting suffers a severe damage, yet it presents a beautiful examples of immense modelling of body with fair naturalism. Th painting may be dated to the eleventh century.

The wall paintings in the temple of Vairochana in Sumda Chhun village of Zanskar appear to be painted by the same group of artists who painted at Alchi. Local tradition asserts that the temples of Sumda Chunn were built contemporary with Alchi. The general style of the painting at Sumda Chhun presents a very close affinity with that of Alchi. Although, Sumda Chhun is not as grand as Alchi and paintings are in poorer state of preservation. The figure of flying Apsara bears a distinct relationship with the same figures of Alchi in her stylistic delineation.

Besides the wall paintings, the temple of Avalokitesvara in Sumda Chhun yields important wooden statues and carvings. One of the best survived examples of carving is a pillar capital of front porch of the temple. The capital is adorned with a tiny figure of Maitreya, who is easily identified by his attribute, the water pot. Similar type of wooden objects from Tholing, Tsparang, Tabo and Alchi have been published by Dr. Francke. Tucci and later by Snellgrove and dated in the 10th-11th century. The scholars have indisputably accepted these wooden carvings and sculptures to have originated from the Kashmir School of tenth-eleventh century.

The most interesting item acquired from the temple is a three feet high figure of a Bodhisattava. The image is missing its both the arms and part of nimbus. The well-proportionate body of the deity is carefully modelled witth natural treatment. The figure is shown standing with suggestive flexion of body on a lotus pedestal. The anatomical details as modelling of chest and abdominal muscles and facial type relate this work to the mediaeval Kashmiri tradition perceptable in the Kashmiri bronzes of ninth to eleventh century (Pal 1977 : Pl 45, 52; Tucci 1973 : Pl 128).

The most imposing group of wooden statues was discovered by me in the debris of a ruined Buddhist temple in Sumda Chhe village of Zanskar valley. This group contains ten badly damaged wooden sculptures of Buddhist deities varying in size from one foot to nine feet in height. The figures are lying in open air and left to face hazard of severe climate of the trans Himalayas. The plastic quality, refinement in technique of chiselling and aesthetic merit of the sculptures provide an indisputable indication of their origin from the mediaeval Kashmiri style. It is important point to note that the wood is rare in the Western Tibetan terrain. While timber is found in Kashmir valley in abundance. Therefore, we canont ignore the possibility of wood being imported from Kashmir to Western Tibet in the time of Buddhist resurgency when Kashmiri craftsmen were already commissioned on work in Western Tibet. We know in the mediaeval times Kashmir was the bouncing centre of wood carving in the Western Himalayas (Goetz 1955 : 112).

The unportable size of statues fairly deny the possibility to have got imported from Kashmir. Most possibly the Kashmiri wood carvers with other craftsmen were commissioned to work in Sumda chhe. Local tradition informs that the temple of Sumda chhe was built by Rinchenzangpo prior to the construction of Alchi temples. Stylistically the wooden sculptures may be dated to tenth-eleventh century.

One of the example clipped up in the paper presents a figure about three and half feet in height, seated cross legged on the lotus throne supported by two lions (Pl 3). This figure can be identified as Varochana or Buddha.

The second startling example of the same height presents a figure of refined workmanship. The image is badly defaced ,yet it preserved some fine details. The identification of the image with Bodhisattava Maitreya is corroborated by a little stupa adorning his crown. All the four arms of the deity are missing or damaged. The facial type of the figure confirms its origin in the Kashmiri tradition. The plastic quality and refinement of carving reinforced by the craftsmen in the statues suggest as they were done in the stucco medium.

The same qualities are equally noticeable in hitherto unpublished wooden image of Bodhisattava Vajrapani (Pl 4), about two and half feet high, discovered by me in 1979 in the temple Rangrik Chhe of Charang village in Kinnaur near the Indo-China border. The figure adorns highly glazed lacquer polish which gives an impression of bronze figure. The figure presents a sturdy and sound built of bodily form with natural modelling of the chest and abdominal muscle. Stylistically, this figure belongs to the same Kashmiri traditional of tenth-eleventh century or it may be dated slightly earlier in the eight-ninth century on the basis of its close affinity with the Karkota idioms.

From the above discussion it can be concluded

that since the time of introduction of Buddhism in Western Tibet. Kashmir was the source of religion and its art. Later in the time of resurgency of Buddhism during tenth to twelfth century. Western Tibet was almost totally dependent on Kashmir. It was mediaeval Kashmir which provided teachers, artists, ritual-objects even material to fulfil the religious and cultural needs. It was most likey during somewhat later period the local artists learned and developed their own artistic sence of creation under the guidance of Kshmiri master artists and formed their own art tradition fundamentally based on Kashmir prototypes.

S.R.F., Bharat Kala Bhavan, B.H.U.

DR. A.K. SINGH

REFERENCES

Banerjee, P. 1963, Painted covers of two Gilgit manuscripts; *Oriental Art*, Vol. XIV, No. 1.

Cunningham, Sir, A. 1970, *Ladak-Physical, Statistical and Geographical* (reprint), New Delhi.

Francke, A.H. 1914, *Antiquities of Indian Tibet*, 2 parts; Calcutta.

Goetz, H. 1955, The Mediaeval Kashmiri Scultptures', *Marg*, Vol. VIII, No. 2.

——— 1965, *The Early Wooden Temple of Chamba*, Leiden.

Pal, P. 1975, Bronzes of Kashmiri; New Delhi.

Petech, L. 1939, *A Study of the Chronicles of Ladakh*; Calcutta.

Snellgrove, D.L. and Skoropski, T. 1977; *The Cultural Heritage of Ladakh*, New Delhi.

Tucci, G. 1949, *Tibetan Painted Scrolls;* 2 Vol., Rome; 1973, *TRANS HIMALAYA; Geneva*, 1973; Ghersi, E. 1935, *Secret of Tibet* London; Glaxogow,

Waddell, L.A. 1895 *Buddhism of Lamaism of Tibet* London.

Exploration—Reveals a Fresh Light on the History of Kisan Bilas, District Kota—Rajasthan

The hamlet of Kisan-Bilas, locally known as Vilas Garha or Krishna Vilas (25°5′ N and 76°45′ E) is situated on the right bank of the rivulet Bilas (Gahlet 1960) a tributary of the river Parvati, 19 kms. southeast of Baran Railway Station on the Bina-Kota line in the district of Kota, Rajasthan.

Earlier the site was mentioned by Gerrick as having some carved sculptures (Cunningham and Garrick 1883-84). Jha mentioned Charkhambha temple and traditional story of the site (Jha-1959), whereas Kumar mentioned only few rock shelters at Kanyadeh (Kumar 1981).

The exploration was conducted in the year 1981-82, under Western Circle, Vadodara, on both the banks of the rivulet Bilas and also on the slope of the hillock which stands on the right bank of the rivulet. According to geologist Kisan Bilas hilly tract is a part of Vindhyan range.

The rivulet Bilas has meandering course of about 15 kms, and flows east-west direction. Topographically the entire valley is trough-shaped,

The exploration by the Survey revealed continuous sequence of cultures which can be testified by the presence of pre-historic stone tools, rock-paintings, painted inscription on the rock shelters and early and late medieval stone sculptures, ruins of temples belonging to different sects, step-wells, remains of fort, roads, street, and a well planned settlement of the medieval times.

Stone Age Industries

The exploration on the banks of the Bilas has brought to light palaeolithic tools comprising Abevellion type pear-shaped handaxe with broken tip (heavily relled) round scraper, side scraper and upper palaeolithic tools with two ridges and burin in both ends. The material commonly used is quartzite. It also yielded large number of geometrical and non-geometrical microlithic tools belonging to mesolithic age. These are arrow head with broken tang (chalcadony in light yellow) triangle (chert), used blade flake (chert), side scraper (chalcadony with reddish cortex) trapez and lunet (chert). The finished tools and waste product of the process were spread all over the flat surface of the hill in the open air near the rock-shelters.

Rock-Paintings

During the course of exploration one hundred and twentyeight (128) rock-shelters were located and documented on the banks of the rivulet Bilas. Among them thirtysix (36) contain rock paintings, some of which could perhaps be pre-historic, while the others are of the historical times, on the analogy of the rock shelters elsewhere in India. White colour has been generally used for filling the gap and writing is of the Sankha-Lipi character of the Gupta period. Paintings represent boar, monkey, deer, rhinoceros, dog, ox, buffalo, bison, and running animals, bullock-carts driven by four unidentified animals, fish, peacock besides the Sun, Moon, Circle, concentric circle, human figurine in a group, man with bow and arrow, hunting scene, mythical figures, geometrical and floral designs. The superimposition of painting is also noticeable in several rock shelters.

The earliest group of rock-painting consists of vertical line drawing of deer, hunters, rhinoceros and bison are similar to Tarsang (Sonewane: 1980), Bhaldaria (Wakankar: 1975), Bhimbetka, Kharwai and Raisen ones belonging to Mesolithic age (Wakankar and Brooks: 1976). Painting of fish at Bilas is similar to Siganpur painting of fish (Ghosh: 32).

The next group of paintings belongs to Chalcolithic age. The paintings of humped bull are similar to that in Bhimbetka (Wakankar and Brooks : 1976). Painting of group dancing is similar to that over pottery of Navadatoli Period III (Sankalia, Subbarao and Deo 1952-53).

Noteworthy is a single line inscription painted in Brahmi characters on the ceiling of Rock-shelters (K.V.-110), which on the basis of Palaeography may be of *circa* second century B.C. The *Sankha-lipi* of Gupta characters, geometrical and floral motifs may be tentatitvely dated to *circa* fifth and sixth century A.D.

Medieval Remains

The exploration on the slope of the hillock (measuring 2000x750 metre) yielded the medieval ruins spread on an area of about 1½ Kms. These ruins are divided into three main groups according to religious faith of the people of that time.

(A) *Remains of Siva temple, Monastery, Sculptures and Fort.*

On the right bank of the Bilas within a fort remains of temple dedicated to Siva known as Chhipa-ki-Chandini and Saiva monastery (Pl. 1) are noticed. Only the *Mandapa* of the temple is existing. It is supported by four stone pillars which are highly decorated with bloomed lotus. The pillars bottom to top are square, octagonal, sixteen sided and circular in sequence. The circular portion is crowned with series of *Kirtimukhas* and upper portion of the pillars is decorated with lotus and diamond design. The capital is decorated with four *Bhutas* brackets.

Towards the south of the fort there is another *Panchayatana* temple dedicated to Siva known as *Charkhamba*. It is built *Pancharatha* on plan and belongs to *circa* eleventh century A.D. About 20 m. south of this temple is stepwell of the same period.

The sculptures of Siva, Parvati, Ganesa, Navagraha-panel belonging to *circa* 9th and 10th century A.D., are interecting.

Monastery: Inside the fort area towards the north of *Chipp-ki-chandini.* remains of a Saiva monastery can be noticed.

(B) *Remains of Vaisnavita temple, sculptures and door-jamb.*

On the western side of the fort near the entrance gate ruins of a Vaisnavite temple measuring about 16.10x10 m. can also be noticed. It is interesting to note that a figure of Varah, *Sesasayi-Visnu* and *Amrita-manthana* carved on red-stand stone are still lying there.

A door-jamb of early Gujara-Pratihara temple decorated with three *Shakhas* i.e. *Pushpa-Shakhas* (Lotus petals) *Mithuna-Shakhasa* and floral motifs was noticed. The lintel of the *dwar-Shakha* is decorated with flying Garuda in the centre of *Lalatabimba.* It is holding a *Kiritamukba* of Visnu flanked by flying *Vidyadhara* couple carrying a garland. At present it is fixed in the rock-shelter No. 127 on the left bank of the rivulet Bilas.

(C) *Remains of Jaina temples, sclupture*s, *monastery, roads, street and house blocks:*

In between the southern fort wall and Charkhambha temple there is anothere fortified Jaina settlement of *circa* eleven century A.D.

Inside the habitational area, there is a big Jain monastery and temples belonging to *circa* twelfth century A.D.

Monastery: The Jaina monastery measuring 25.10x13.80 m. is built on a rectangular platform. It consists of miniature shrines on three sides facing east, west and north. Each of the shrines measures 1.80x1.50 m.

All these medieval settlements are made of local sand stone in 'dry' masonry.

Acknowledgment: I am thankful to Shri B.M. Pande, who allowed me to publish this paper, Thanks are also due to Shri N. Vyas, Shri Hadpad, Shri Indora and Miss Moon for their various help.

Archaeological Survey of India

S.C. SARAN

REFERENCES

Gahlot, J. 1960, History of Rajaputana; Jodhpur; Hindi Sahitya Mandir, Part II; Kota Rajya-ki-Itihas, p. 27.

Garrick, H.M.W. & Cunningham 1983-84, A tour in Punjab and Rajputana, Vol. XXIII, p. 134.

Ghosh; R.S. Manoranjan, 1932, Siganpur Painting-Memors of Archaeological Survey of India No. 24, Plate XVIC, fig. 3.

Jha, L.K. 1959, Kishan Vilas Marg. Vol. XII; No. 2, p. 51.

Kumar Giriraj, 1981, Painted Rock-shelters from Rajasthan (Dr. Satya Prakash) Felicitation Volume, ed. by Srivastava V.S. pp: 277-85:)

Sankalia H.D.M, Subbarao, B., Deo; S.B., 1952-53, The excavations at Maheshwar and Navdatoli Period III. Fig. 42, Type 63-64.

Sonwane, V.H. 1980, Rock Paintings at Tarsang (Paper read in Archaeological Congress, Allahabad).

Wakankar V.S., 1975, Pre-historic Cave Paintings Marg Vol. XXVIII No. 4, See Fig. 17:

Wakankar, V.S. and Brookes Robert, R.R: 1973; Stone Age Paintings in India, Bombay. See deers and rhinoceros of style 3 and 5 page 96-97.

Archaeology and the Problem of Regional Identity

At the very outset it may be stated that archaeology is mostly taken simply as a source material providing agency for making possible the understanding of civilizational processes to a certain limited extent. The approach adopted here also accepts that changes in the socio-economic, religious and political outlooks of the people determine the natur of inquiry concerning that process as well as the nature of the efforts made in that direction. And, in accordance with these changes, researchers emphasize on this or that aspect of the human past from time to time.

Viewed in the said context, the political ideals of our country since the days of our struggle for freedom remained nationalistic without any doubt. The fervour which nationalism had before independence continued in the post -independence period in spite of the challenges thrown by forces divisive in nature. Accordingly, efforts of the students of Ancient Indian History and Archaeology have been mainly to portray the country as a great nation and having a glorious past. Whensoever the divisive elements were pointed out, efforts were made to explain them away otherwise and, wheresoever there was evidence for unifying factor it was enlarged to the highest limit.

In due course of time, however, the national earnestness started losing its relevance and regional feelings gained upper hand. As a result of this the whole approach became 'regional', at least at provincial levels, emphasising on the eulogy of a region, a people or a particular tract of land. In the beginning such attempts were quite constructive and aimed at presenting an elaborate and specialised account of a region along with contributions to the nation. Later, political and economic factors induced the element of extremism which generally tries to emphasise only on the role of a region or its people either superior to, or separate from, the other regions and peoples of the country. In response to such a growing sense of regionalism, regional centres of education had no alternative except promote a study of regional problems in maximum possible details in the garb of the micro-study. Such studies created on the one hand scope for the deep specialization and on the other an extreme love for a region—sometimes even at the cost of the interest of naion as a whole. Yet, accepting the said trend as the order of the day and keeping in purview the distinct values of life of each and every region, state universities are generalaly pursuing this with utmost vigour. And, setting apart the dangers on its extreme side, it is proving its worth in the form of excellent works on various regional problems.

In view of the above, the role of the archaeology also requires a change. The change i.e., micro-study of 'the regional' is already there in the state universities having facilities for the study of the subject and for excavations. But the peoples of regions without such luxury (due to this or that factor) require such assistance from the Central agencies and experts not as a concession but as a residue. And this is perhaps the most appropriate time for a change in the policy of the Central organisation in control of the subject and approach of scholars claiming expertise in the field.

These apart, a change in the very disposition of the interested in the subject is required otherwise also. For, things which are without much importance in their national context are often very important in their regional contexts. The reason, as stated earlier, is that every region wants to establish its separate identity and in such an effort whatsoever is in its possession is treated as most valuable. Thus the value-determining process should take care of the regional sentiments as well. The point would become more clear when the region of Jammu is taken into consideration for the sake of an example. Inspite of the fact that the region has Harappan' and other historical sites, archaeology to its people is not of much meaning as it does not answer the questions which are more important to them. They are completely in drak about their systematic pre- or proto-history telling them the peculiarities of artifacts etc., as well as the history of its early medieval phase. It is true that the coherent cultural or political account of these is perhaps not possible even if experts waste their time in this regard, yet at least material culture of the region can be discussed elaborately with the help of Archaeology with an amount of certainty. Similar is the problem created due to the clash of interests of lay—worshippers and priests. If to the experts historical phase is less significant in comparison with the earliest known phase of human culture, it is certainly much more relevant to the people who are trying to establish their separate identity.' Sometimes, therefore ,it is found that both—the experts and the people seeking the attention of experts towards things of sentimental values—condemn each other in absence of a mutual understanding of the situation.

Thus, in this context, it is suggested that if the problem of archaeology of such regions is further neglected by experts, such neglect will damage national cause as well. For, if this aspect is not taken into consideration by the experts it will be studied by quack antiquarians causing irreparable loss to the very subject. Contrary to this, if it is studies by the experts it will provide clues at least in the form of socio-and ideo-facts relevant for a region to determine is identity within the national framework by highlighting the interdependence of various regions and peoples on each other and their contribution to the total sum i.e. the nation.

University of Jammu, Jammu.

DR. Y.B. SINGH

REFERENCES

Examples can be had from the writings of Dr. R.K. Mookerji who against heavy odds succeeded in projecting India as a nation by eulogising the concept of 'unity in diversity'. cf Munshi, K.M. (ed.), *Indian Heritavee;* Vol: II; pp: 86 ff. See also Dr. R.K: Mookerji's books *Fundamental Unity of India* and *Glimpses of Ancient India.*

Regional variations, too, have been explained and countered by citing the 'all embracing' nature of *tirthas* dotted throughout the country cf. Dave, J.H. *Immortal India;* p: x:

Portryal of Lord Buddha by Sir S. Radhakrishnan as a person 'who was born, grew up, and died a Hindu' is an excellent example of this trend. cf. Bapat; P.V: (ed.), *2500 years of Buddhism,* p. ix.

Attempts have been made even to explain certain aspersions cast on the Madra Jana by citing the regional bias without any effort to analyse the problem scientifically. See Singh F., *History of the Punjab,* Vol. I; pp. 173-76 see also my papers *From glory to gloom: The Case of the Madra Jana* published in *Gulab Bhawan Research series,* Vol. II, No. 1; pp: 29 ff, and *Some Social strictures agains ancient Punjab* analysed published in the *Proceedings of Punjab History Conference 15th Session* pp. 40 ff.

As per oral information given by the A.S.I. Officers Places like Manda and Ambara have yielded considerable material belonging to the said phase of Indain culture

The present state of monuments and wall paintings of Jammu region belonging to late medieval and early modern periods can be cited as an example in this regard.

'Chandragupta-Kumaradevi' Commemorative Medals

Shorn of details the Chandragupta-Kumaradevi Type (Altekar, 1954, Plate I, Nos. 8-10) may be described as below:

> The obverse shows Chandragupta I, usually nimbate, standing to left, wearing trousers and coat, holding a standard in the left hand, and the right offering a present (identified variously as a *sinduradani,* a ring or a bangle) to Kumaradevi wearing *sari* and ornaments. Two legends, *Chandragupta* and *Sri Kumaradevi* (or *Kumaradevi Sri),* occur. The reverse shows goddess Durga riding a lion and has the legend *Lichchhavayah.*

The type is found almost exclusively in the eastern Uttar Pradesh. It has been discussed by several scholars, and there is considerable difference of opinion regarding the interpretation of its device, legend and authorship. While some scholars (e.g. Smith, 1889; Altekar, 1954 and 1957) ascribe the type to Chandragupta, others (e.g. Allan, 1914; Mookerjee, 1952; Pathak, 1957) take it as an issue of Samudragupta.

We may, before giving our view on the authorship of the coin and circumstances of issue, briefly mention our own approach and value—judgement on this problem. While not entirely disregarding the role of typology in establishing chronology, we are of the view that it should play a secondary role to a relatively more categorical evidence. We would make our stand clear on the issue as below:

(i) If the reverse had the name Samudragupta or his stock epithet *Lichchhavi dauhitra* or his typical *viruda* then we would have definitely ascribed this issue to that ruler.

(ii) If the legend *Lichchhavavah* would not have been there then we would not have ascribed it to the Lichchhavis; instead we would have considered it as issued by Ghatotkacha, commemorating the marriage of his son crown-prince Chandragupta with Kumaradevi.

(iii) If there would have been simply the name of Chandragupta and not the name of Kumaradevi or the legend *Lichchhaviyah* there, then it would remain an open issue as to whether the coin-type should be attributed to Chandragupta I or to Chandragupta II.

We would now put forth our own view on the authorship of this type as also to the possible circumstances for its issue. In the absence of any positive data we suggest certain hypothesis below for consideration. We are of the opinion that the type under discussion was issued by the Lichchhavis to commemorate the marriage of their princess Kumaradevi with Chandragupta. Pathak (1957) points out that in the device Kumaradevi is shown on the right of Chandragupta. Usually a wife should be on the left of her husband. But, as the evidence of ancient texts (and he refers to a number of them) and the *vaivahika* or *kalyanasundara murtis* show, during the marriage ceremony the bride should be at the right of the bridegroom. He, therefore, concludes that the device represents the scene of Chandragupta-Kumaradevi marriage. Notwithstanding the view of Dani (1958) who disagrees with Pathak's contention that the intention was to show Kumaradevi on the right of Chandragupta, or Pandey (1976) who takes it as an issue of Samudragupta and thinks it unnatural for a son to portray marriage scene of his parents, we feel Pathak is justified.

The Lichchhavi state seems to have been governed by a council of Lichchhavis presided over by their chief, designated as *raja* (Shamasastry, 1960). Raychaudhuri (1956) rightly considers the reference to 7707 Lichchhavi ruling families in the *Jatakas* as exaggeration, and the evidence of Jain *Kalpasutras* referring to nine *gana rajas* as more reasonable. The office of the head had by then, as in the monarchical form, seems to have become heriditary. As most of the scholars also believe, the then ruling Lichchhavi chief, father of Kumaradevi, had no male issue. Naturally, therefore, some prominent Lichchhavi chiefs would have been keen to marry the princess primarily with a view to attain the headship of the State. As pointed out by Singh (1979), the *Vinayapitaka* mentions that the Lichchhavi chiefs, desirous of getting married could ask the corporation of the Lichchhavis to get them proper brides. Some of the chiefs might have made such a request and indicated their choice for Kumaradevi. This would have created a delicate situation. Offering of Kumaradevi's hand to one chief would have created bickerings in the minds of others who would be ready to take arms for their own cause. The Lichchhavis were haughty and egoistic people. Earlier in the fifth century B.C., king Ajatasatru's ministers playing on these characteristics of the Lichchhavis created dissinsions among them, each chief declaring himself as the leader of the *gana*.

The horror of would be civil war would have loomed large and created great tension in the minds of the Lichchhavis. Some relatively sober ones amongst them were keen to find ways and means to avoid such a struggle and subsequent bloodshed. They realised that marrying Kumaradevi within the Lichchhavi clan was full of dangerous consequences. It was, therefore, agreed upon that in the interest of the *gana* she should be married outside the clan. After due consideration they resolved that she be married to the Gupta prince, Chandragupta I. The Lichchhavis, however, were keen to safeguard the interest of the clan. They reached an understanding with the Guptas that the son born of this union will inherit the amalgamated Gupta-Lichchhavi kingdom. The Lichchhavis hailed the decision which, on the one hand, averted the impending civil war and also envisaged that the son of their princess would be the ruler of the combined kingdom. They decided to commemorate this matrimonial alliance by issuing medals depicting the scene of marriage ceremony, placing Kumaradevi on the right of Chandragupta, the names of the bride and the bridegroom on the obverse, and the name of their own clan on the reverse, as commemorators.

To conclude, the type under discussion is a commemorative medal. It was issued neither by Samudragupta nor by Chandragupta I, but by the Lichchhavis. The device represents the marriage of Kumaradevi who was head of the Lichchhavis with Chandragupta who was Gupta crown-prince. The Lichchhavis issued the medals as they considered this marriage of extraordinary importance, as on the one hand it forged alliance with the ruling Guptas, and, on the other, averted civil war in the Lichchhavi clan. The medals were presented as souvenirs to the bridegroom's party, who carried these to their homes. This would explain why majority of these medals have been found within the original Gupta territory and only a few in the Lichchhavi territory.

KIRAN KUMAR THAPLYAL

REFERENCES

Allan, J., 1914. *Catalogue of the Coins of the Gupta Dynasties and of Sasanka King of Gauda.* Oxford.

Altekar, A.S., 1954. *Catalogue of the Gupta Gold Coins in the Bayana Hoard.* Bombay.

1957. *The Coinage of the Gupta Empire.* Banaras.

Dani A.H., 1953. Chandragupta I-Kumaradevi coin type. *JNSI*, XX, pp. 4-8.

Mookerjee, R.K., 1952. *The Gupta Empire;* 2nd ed: Bombay.

Pandey, V.C., 1976. Chandragupta-Kumaradevi Type of Coins and the Dual Character of Samudragupta's Royalty. *JNSI*, XXXVIII, pp. 58-64.

Pathak, V.S., 1957. Notes on the Gupta Coinage-I: *JNSI*; XIX, pp. 135-44.

Raychaudhuri, H.C., 1956. *Political History of Ancient India;* 6th ed. Calcutta.

Shaasastry, R.; 1960. *Kautilya's Archaeology;* 6th ed. Mysore.

Singh, B.B., 1979. *Chandragupta-Kumaradevi* Coin-type. A Reappraisal. *JNSI*, XLI, pp. 78-31.

Smith, V.S., 1989. The Coinage of the Early or Imperial Gupta Dynasty, Journal of the Royal Asiatic Society.

Identification of Soma

Attempts to identify *Soma* have, so far, been self-defeating. Failure of scholars was not due to paucity of material available on *Soma.* Clouded with the presupposed notion of Aryan immigration into India, scholars felt that the plant must be foreign to India, and failed to take note of the most outstanding and unambiguous characteristics of *Soma.*

Whether we know it or not, all of us have tasted and do taste *Soma* in innumerable forms. Even so, most of us may start in surprise to know that *Soma* is sugarcane and the word Soma was not used only for the plant, its juice but also for its preparations.

However, *Soma* is no other plant but sugarcane, which like a luminous object, lost its identity and became a myth, shrouded by unrestrained eulogy by the ancient poets—a process which was completed by the liturgical love for secret terms , and its identification with moon and celestial waters. Legends, built around *Soma* also played a substantial role in estrangement of the concept from the real plant. Even so, we have sufficient evidence to conclusively prove that *Soma* is cognate with sugarcane.

Soma, it may be pointed out, was not a wild plant. It was grown in cultivated fields. After digging or ploughing the field, channels for water were drawn and it was irrigated through these channels. Alluvial soil with sufficient moisture was more suited to cultivation of the plant. This fact exposes the flaw in conjectures in favour of *Sacrostemma Bravistigma* and other uncultivated plants.

It was natural for the plant to come to its maturity in a proper season. There are frequent references of drinking of Soma in the right season. But this emphasis on right season covertly suggests that the juice could also be extracted from the plant when it was still immature, and this practice was not uncommon.

Soma plant is *Varsavriddha* which may be interpreted in two ways, i.e. the plant took one year's time for its maturity or the plant flourished in rainy season. Which ever way we interpret, it goes well with sugarcane.

Soma is *Munjanejanna* , i.e. born in *Munja* family of plants. There is mention of kins of SOMA' and surrogates of SOMA which very clearly suggests that SOMA is sugarcane . (Monier Williams defining ***Iksu Kanda*** writes "name of two different species of sugarcane, *Saccharum Munja Roxb.* and *Saccharum Spontenium*). Once placed in its proper family, the plant becomes somewheat recognizable.

The area to which *Soma* was indigenous lies to the north or east north-east of the main Vedic Territory.' It refers precisely to north-eastern U.P. and north-western Bihar, which has to this day been the principal area for sugarcane cultivation.

The plant was erect and high in view of other crop-plants. It was *Suhastya*, easy to grip, that is neither thin nor thick enough to cause any problem in handling. This feature goes against all other suggestions and perfectly suits the sugarcane.

Stem of *Soma* is nodal. Nodes are called *Parvan* and, as such, it is itself *Parvat* and is described as standing on parvat—It is like a snake in its form. Often it has been referred to as *Vritra* whom Indra killed. The next step was to identify the moon, who shares all the synonyms of *Soma*, as *Vritra*. Some confusion has been caused by this transference of attributes in Vedic litrature itself. However, it helps us quite a lot in identifying the plant as sugarcane.

Sugarcane plant has eyes or ankh on each of its nodes. This feature of *Soma* makes it *Bhuricaksu*.

Stem of sugarcane is covered by the stems of its leaves. It is *Tami* and *Andhas*. Coverings and dress of *Soma* have been mentioned frequently. The leaves of sugarcane gradually shed-off as the plant matures and the stem comes naked and shining as if a snake has shed off its worn-out skin. This is exactly the case with *Soma*.

Soma plant has no branches except its long branching leaves. This feature has been emphasised by the *Terms Suparna, Supalasa, Parnasakha* and *Parnin* . *Soma* is also *Sahasraparna Sahasra valsa*. There can be no mistake in identifying sugarcane leaves here.

The upper end of *Soma* plant is pointed. It makes it Tigmasringa. Even the leaves are sharp edged and work as a weapon and as such it is *Tigmayudha*. When the sugarcane plant is over-mature, it develops a broomlike flowery crest which resembles the feather of a peacock—*Soma* for this feature has been called *Mayurshepya* and the colour of its flower is described as *Arjuna* or white. *Usnisa* of *Soma* find their mention in Brahmanas.

Soma is *Naicasakh*. It shoots or grows from the root. The sprouts of SOMA were called *Vana, Vakshana* or *Kispa*. This perfectly resembles sugarcane shoots and sprouts, which are as thick as a finger and pointed like an arrowhead.

The most outstanding feature of *Soma* is that its stalk, when pressed, yields abundant juice, which is the sweetest. Abundance of water and sugar contents is the one quality of SOMA which was, in absence of any other hint, crucial enough to identify the plant as sugar-cane. This is the only quality for which SOMA has, time and again, been adulated in no frugal terms. It need no further elaboration.

However, The term *Madistha* derived from the same source as *Madhura* means both the sweetest and intoxicating. In their search of *Soma* scholars placed absolute reliance on toxity of the plant, However, the plant and its fresh juice was free from toxity, can be seen from the term *Saumya*, derived from *Soma*. Vedic people, no doubt, were familiar with the device of fermenting *Soma* and brewing *Sura*. There is mention of people having lost their sobriety and become violent after drinking *Soma* — But on such occasions the term used for the intoxicated is not *Madas* but *Durmadas*.

Soma was taken fresh as well as after fermentation—Fermented *Soma* is called *Tivra* and *Tri-Ahna* . *Sura* was prepared form *Soma* after adding ingredients of *Sura* in to *Soma*—No plant with narcotic or toxic content needs fermentation. This in itself is a proof against conjectures regarding toxity of the plant. Its fermentation and brewing both prove the plant to be sugarcane. We must differentiate between *Suta Soma* and *Asuta Soma* to understand the contrasting effects of *Soma* draught.

There is no mention of fruits or seed of the plant—The stalk cuttings were planted as seed. The stalk was itself pressed for juice. Authors favourably exposed to grapes should not have missed this fact.

Colour of the stalk is stated to be green, brown, or red. The plants which can boast of these three tinges are rare, and sugarcane is one such plant. We must not forget that even before the modern breeds of sugarcane came into existence, there were numerous varities of the plant

Soma juice is also stated to be of three colours —green, brown and red. No comment is required about the first two, but red colour of juice calls for some explanation. It may be pointed out that when any wild animal snipes at the stalk of sugarcane or when some disease attacks the crop, the inner core of the plant grows red. When pressed it yields juice, red in colour. Vedic people who held the plant in so high an esteem could hardly ignore this colour of the plant which they also treated as blood of *Soma*.

Extraction of juice from the plant was easy but not too easy. *Soma* is, of course, *Sudugha*, but once we know that it was sugarcane, we can easily understand that the sugar content of the plant could not be extracted in one pressing by the crude devices adopted during the vedic times. As such we find three courses of *Soma* extraction, morning, midday and late hour. The fact that the three sessions of *Soma* extraction are three stages of the same process, is evident from the hint that before the second session water was sprinkled on the pressed stalk and before the third pressing the residue was almost soaked in water with the result that the juice in the third session was not so sweet. It was emptied of pure *Soma.*

Soma husk was called *Rijisa*. It resembled a rope or a snake, and while throwing it away, it was prayed that it may not come alive and harm anyone. The resemblance of sugarcane husk with that of *Soma* is unique and exceptional.

Soma juice was taken neat or mixed with *Sattu, Dhana, Milk* and *Curd*. The practice has come down to this day. *Pancamrita* offered to deities and later served to devotees is nothing but *Misra Soma.*

We have references of *Sarkara* in Brahmanas in the context *Soma*. But vedic people boiled and concentrated the juice is clear beyond doubt. Descriptions of *Soma* as yellow wealth, cooking of *Soma* ', evaporation of water from *Soma* by heating it, and mention of *Drona & Kvathanestaka* (cauldron) only confirm our hypothesis.

Patients of jaundice are recommended sugarcane juice by traditional physicians. *Soma* juice cured jaundice.

All these references are clear and unambiguous. No other plant except Sugarcane can fulfill all the prerequisites of *Soma*. Similarities are so striking that one wonders why these were not attended to earlier. One is tempted to conclude that a slight shift in emphasis and over-indulgence with singular features or events, interpreted arbitrarity, may malign whole chapters of historical analysis, and I fear this has been the case with the Vedic chapter of our history.

BHAGWAN SINGH

REFERENCES

See. Vedic Index "*SOMA*"; Eggling IS.B. Pt. I; Introduction; Hertzfied: Zoraster and his World; II; 544; 551;

R. Gordon Wasson; Indo Iranian Journal 1970, Vol. VII, 4 of 237 et, seq. and H.H. Ingalls; paper read before members of American Oriental Society in Baltimore, 15 April, 1970.

References of Secrecy; and secret words is common to both the Indian and the Iranian people. The same object or diety when addressed by one name keeps its vigour and strength intact, but addressed by a different name, it looses its vitality and becomes impotent. So the enemies prefer the other synonyms of the same object or deity. See MSB 4.1.2:1:

All the synonyms of moon have been employed to *SOMA* and liberal use of other attributes of moon has also been made to deity, *Soma*. Once adulated as the source of nectar and *SABARDUGHA*, it had naturally adopted an elusive character.

RV. V 62.7, X. 94-13 and IX 86-37.

See *RV* 1-15.

YV 1-16.

RV. 1.161.8

RV. 9.97.17

See. *KS*. 34.3, TB 9.5.3.7; J.B. 1.354.355; *SB*. IV. 5.10. 1-6 etc.

Mention of surrogate of *SOMA* made some of the scholars doubtful about the first hand knowledge of Vedic people about *SOMA*. They have laid much stress of this point. They overlooked that surrogates not only of *SOMA* but almost of all the essential of *YAJNA* have been prescribed, and the practice is common even to day.

SB. 1.7.1.13 *AB*. 1.12

RV IX. 97.18

RV. IX. 107.21

RV. 1. IX. 1.

SB. IV. 14.8

MSB. 1.5.3.13; 18

RV. IX. 26.5

RN. IX. 98.2 IX. 1:8.

RV. IX. 97.2; SB III. 3.2.3

RV. IX. 86.44

RV. IX. 86.1

RV. IX. 43.4

MSB. 1:5.4.1

RV. IX. 82.3; 135.1

RV. VIII. 77.7.

RV. III. 3. 11; VIII-33-9,; IX-5.10

RV. IX.97.9;
RV. IX. 90.3
RV. VIII. 1.25
RV. IX. 69.4
RV. III. 53.14
RV. IV. 24.9.; IX. 50.1
RV. VIII. 1. 17
RV: IX. 79.4
IX. MANDAL of *RV* devouted to *SOMA* starts with *SVADISTHAYA MADISTHAYA PAVASVA SOMA DHARYA* and the rhetoric of its sweetness and juicyness runs through out the *MANDAL*.
RV. VIII 2.12; IX. 64.21 etc.
RV. IX. 17.8; 65.15 etc.
RV. 1.47.1; SB. XII. 7.3.6
RV. I.104.7; II 1-14; VII 97-7; VII-1-26.
RV: IX: 2.62;
RV. IX. 187. 19
RV. IX. 45. 2
SUSRUTA mentions a dozen varieties of Sugarcane, as mentioned by Monier Williams.
RV IX 3.9, 7.6;
RV IX: 33.2; 63.4;
RV IX. 40.2; 45.3:
See the Vedic Index *SOMA* also.
SB. 1-6.4.9; IV. 4.5.1.
S:B: IV. 3.5.17. SB IV 4-5-3
See *Vedic Index*. Soma.
MSB. VI. 1:3.5; 3.6.6.
RV IX. 72.8.
MS II. 3.8; KS 37-18; *SOMA SYSVIBHAYAM PACYASVA, SB* X. 6.1.8.
RV IX. 109. 22.
RV IX: 67.14:
RV IX. 67.14. *BSS* 29.3; 6.6; 23.5:
SB 1.6.4.9.

The Antiquity of Gold—Glasses in India

Glass has become one of the most important material in the modern world. In India, earliest example of the glass is in the form of two pieces of bangles (bracelets) coming from Bhagvanpura, Haryana (Joshi 1978; 180; IAR, 1975-76:16). Glass has a long history in India and its technological development is a broader area to be dealt with. In the present attempt, a small but important aspect in the technological point of view has been selected for the study, i.e. antiquity of gold glasses.

A technique by which a thin layer of gold leaf is laminated between two layers of transparent or semitransparent glasses was known in old world and in ancient India from very early period. One of the earliest example imitated contemporary Magarian and faience bowls. These gold laminated pieces have been generally attributed to Alexandria (Kisa 1908). Boon has drawn attention to the fact that colourless glass and gold casing were employed as early as the XVIIIth dynasty of Egypt for decorative purposes in the Tomb of Tutankham (Boon 1977:193-207; Partington 1935:127). Classical fragmentary glass ornament with gold leaf (1600 B.C.-1200 B.C.) have been kept in the Metropolitan Museum, New York (Forbes 1966:145). One of the gold vessel decorated and mounted in gold which are described as having been used at a banquet and in a procession during the region of Ptolmy II Philadelphus (284 B.C.-246 B.C.) (Schuler 1966:48). Fragments of three gold glass vessel from Rhodes (3rd cen. B.C.) are also interesting (Weinberg 1982:35).

A gilt glass fragment from Dura—Europas (250 A.D.); in Kertch-South Russia (Harden 1967: 252), in Nahariya—Israel, in Palmyra, in Begram—Kapisa, in Britain (Roman Period) and in Cologne, are the places where we find significant examples of gold glasses. Another group, supposed to be Eastern in origin, includes among others, laminated gold glasses found in Trasilico, Olibia (U.S.S.R.), fragments of shallow gold glass from Moscow Museum (Auth 1982:1-2) and in Kaula Selinsing in North Perak in Malaya (Lamb 1965:36-38).

The gilt glasses found in Cologne differs from others in the sense that they have no second protective glass layer (Morey & Ferron 1959).

It has been supposed that this technique of sendwitching gold foil in to glasses was transplanted from Alexandria to Syria and Palestine and then to other places. The technique is said to have reached its zenith under Bishop Damasus towards the middle of fourth century A.D. (Neuberg 1949:18).

So far as occurrence of gold glasses in India is concerned, evidently it synchronizes with the adoptation of that technique in the fourth centuries B.C. in West Asia and Europe. Process of gilting has been mentioned in Kautilya's *Arthasastra* in Adhikarana-2. Adhyaya-14 and Sutra-45

as:-
Abhra—Patalam ashtakena Dvi—guna—vastuke Va rupe bodhyate tasyapihita—Kachasyodake nimajjata ekadesah sidati patalatare Va suchya bhidyame....

Dr. Shamsastri has translated this passage as follows; "In some pieces mica may be firmly laid inside with wax and covered over with a double leaf (of gold or silver); when such a piece of mica or glass inside is suspended in water one of its sides dips more than other, or when pierced by a pin, the pin goes very easily in the layers of mica in the interior"......(Dikshit 1965). Here, we find that process of "backing" glass jewels with the foil of gold or silver is intended. Often the ornaments in ancient India were decorated with gold-foil in this manner and the practise is allude to some *Ratna-Sastra* work (Dikshit 1965: 67).

The gold glasses have been reported from a number of sites all over India, mostly in the form of beads. We have only one fragment of gold-glass other than beads is from Sirkap mound of Taxila (Ist Cent. A.D.) (Marshall 1951 : 689, Pl. 209 i), where we find a bowl fragment of mosaic glass with gold foil in it.

Early centuries of Chirtian era was the most popular period for the use of gold-foil beads in India. According to Dikshit, stratigraphically oldest glass having gold-foil in India are from Kosam (Kausambi) attributed to C.300 B.C. to 200 A.D. (Dikshit 1969). At Nevasa two gold foil glass beads were found in Period IV dated 150 B.C.-50 B.C. and one in period V dated 50 B.C.-200 A.D. (Sankalia & Deo 1960:353). Marshall has reported two glass foil beads from Bhita perhaps of Kushana Period (A.S.I. 1911-12 : 94); gold-foil beads had been also reported from Brahmapuri (Kolhapur) from Satvahana Period (Sankalia 1952-98). At Nasik three gold foil beads were associated with Period III and IV, where, according to the excavators, the gold-foil beads share a long survived at the site (Sankalia & Deo 1953 : 289). From Kondapur in Medak district of Andhra Pradesh gold-foil glass bead was known in the form of few specimens, (Dikshit 1952a : 56) which according to excavator, was a result of foreign contact.

At Nagra gold-foil beads were associated with period IIIrd (00 B.C./A.D. 8th cent. A.D.) and Period IVth (14th cent. A.D.) (Mehta & Shah 1968: 144). They are attributed to Satvahana Period at Ter-(Dikshit 1967:43) and Karad (Dikshit 1952: 5-6). They are also reported from Arikamedu (Casal 1949), an Indo-Roman trading centre of early centuries of Christian era and from Chandravali (Beads in Mysore Museum). The gold-foil beads are treated seperately at Tripuri (Dikshit 1955: 80), and were invented in early third period of Maheshwar and Navadatoli. Such beads were also associated with Period II (100 A.D.-300 A.D.) a Kumrahar (Altaker & Mishra 1959:62). From Masaon Dih and Rajghat Beads in Bharat Kala Bhavan) gold-foil beads were reported from unstratified levels. They were also found from Paithan and Ahichchhatra (350 A.D.-750 A.D.) Dikshit 1952c: 60-62). Dikshit has collected gold glass beads from Kaundinyapur (Dikshit 1969). Besides gold-foil beads, which can be traced from a number of other sites, there are examples of silver foil beads also such as lug collared barrel shaped beads from Paunar in Period IV (10th cent. A.D. to 15-16th cent. A.D.) (Deo & Dhavalikar 1968 : 83). From a general perusal of gold-foil beads in India, it seems that their occurrence mostly confind to early centuries of Christian era and to Deccan and Peninsular India.

Since the glasses used for the purpose were mostly transparent, having no inclusions and air bubbles, so it suggests advancement in technology and perfection in the skill of manufacture. Because every sites have yielded very small numbers of specimens so, it was difficult to obtain a sample for the analysis. But from the examination it is evident that, the glasses used for the purpose are very pure having a hardness between 5 to 6 on Moh's scale. Sand devoid of iron-oxide may have been used for the purpose with some decolourizing agent such as manganese(Biek and Bayley 1979: 2-11; Brill 1968: 47:68; Singh 1982 : 30-31).

These beads are made with colourless transparent fibrous glass enclosd with gold-foil to give pale golden colour. As C.G. Boon (1977) says, 'the working procedure was evidently to draw out a tube of glass over wire core; metal foil (Silver or gold) was wrapped round this tube and quoted with thin protective layer of glass. The completed ensemble was then thread upon a narrower wire tube crimped at intervals the segments which could be broken apart for use as single or multiple units'. So, many beads are made from drawn canes.

The problem of origin of gold glasses is still an open question (Silverman 1952: 151; Schuler 1966 : 48-59; Guido 1978 : 94; and Auth 1979:59). Though, most accepted assumption is that, it was originated in Near-East or Egypt. Schuler has established Jewish Origin theory. His assumption is that, whatever, may be the place of origin, its Jewish craftsmen who were responsible for the manufacture. As he says, 'Even when we could not trace the creators themselves, ..., the gold glasses were used in areas where a fairly, well developed Jewish community existed ....', In India we find almost contemporary production of gold-glasses which was certainly an indigenous innovation.

The gold glass technique, combining the skill of a gold-smiths, a potter and a glassmaker needs a well developed insight of technology. Ancient Indians attained all these technological perfections to compete the old world.

Banaras Hindu University. **RAVINDRA N. SINGH**

REFERENCES

Altaker, A.S. and V. Mishra, 1959;*Report on Kumrahar Excavations* 1951-53, Patna.

A.S.I., Ann. Rep:; 1911-12:

Auth, Susan Handler; 1979; 'A fragmentry Christain gold glass at Newark Museum' *J. Glass studies*, XXI, Corning; New York.

Auth, Susan Handler, 1982; 'Luxury Glasses with Alexandrian Motifs 'Abs. Papers, *1982 Int. Glass Conf.*, Corning, New York.

Biek, Leo and Justine Bayley, 1979; 'Glass and other Vitreous Meterials', *World Archaeology*, 11; No; 1.

Boon, C.G. 1977, 'Gold in Glass beads from Ancient World', Britannia, VIII.

Brill, Robert, H. 1963; 'The Scientific Examination of Ancient Glass', *Proc. VIIIth Int. Cong. Glass*, Shaffield.

Casal, J.M. 1949, *Fouilles de Virampatanam-Arikamedu*. Paris; cited by Dikshit, 1969.

Deo, S.B. and M.K. Dhavalikar, 1968; *Paunar Excavations*, Nagpur.

Dikshit, M.G. 1952a *'Some beads from Kondapur*, Hyderabad Archaeological series, 16, Hyderabad.

Dikshit, M.G. 1952b *'Explorations at Karad* 1949, Poona.

Dikshit, M.G. 1952c 'Beads from Ahichchhatra' *Ancient India*,8.

Dikshit, M.G. 1955 *Tripuri-1952;* Nagpur.

Dikshit, M.G. 1965 'Studies in Ancient Indian Glassts-I: Glass as Mentioned in Kautilya's Arthsastra' *East and West*, New Series 15; Rome.

Dikshit; M.G. 1967, *Excavations at Ter;* Poona.

Dikshit, M.G. 1969, *History of Indian Glass*; Bombay.

Forbes, R.J. 1966, *Studies in Ancient Technology;* V; Leiden.

Guido, M. 1978, *Glass beads of the Prehistoric Period and Roman Priod in Britain and Ireland.* London.

Use of Orthographic Projection in Archaeological Drawing

ORTHOGRAPHIC PROJECTION:

Orthographic Projection System is (Saar, 1982) the most concise as yet developed for the graphic communication of complex ideas. The relationship of one view with the other in this system is most important for the readability of the drawing. The two specified methods of orthographic projection used to illustrate any object are briefly explained below:

METHOD—1:

In method—1 which is called first-angle projection method, the object is supposed to be between the observer and the plane of projection.

METHOD—2:

In method—2 which is called third-angle projection method, the plane of projection is supposed

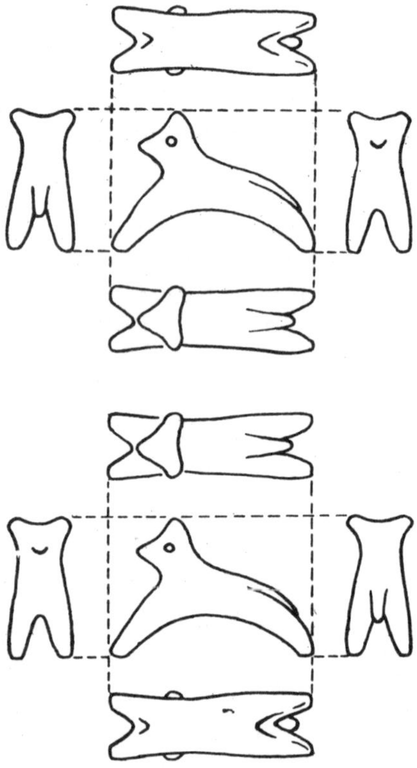

Fig. 1

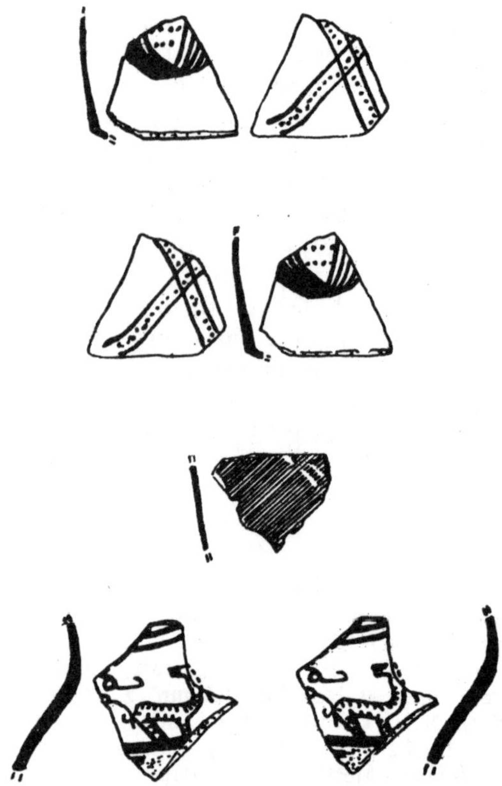

Fig. 2

to be between the observer and the object.

CODE:

In America and the continent or Europe the method of third-angle projection, explained in step 2, is used but in Britain the standard practice of first-angle projection method is followed. In India also the first angle-projection method was formerly in use. The Indian Standard Institution (I.S.I.), in their earlier versions of "Indian Standard code of Practice for General Engineering Drawing" published in 1955 and revised in 1960 had recommended the use of only the third-angle projection method. In subsequent revisions, however, in 1973 the committee had decided to leave the option on the user to adopt any one method. (Bhat, 1979). Besides we cannot but adopt only one out of the two methods to maintain symmetry in drawing, (Saar, 1982).

RECOMMENDATION:

In Engineering drawing, in general, preference is given to the third-angle projection method. While studying the following examples the writer proposes some improved methods of illustrating the object, based on the rules of drawing. The writer had an opportunity to discuss personally with Prof. B. B. Lal on this issue who agreed to the proposal in principle.

SHERD WITH A DESIGN:

In our presently employed method of illustration when we have to draw a pot sherd, keeping in view the importance of a painted, incised or applique design on its surface we are not sure whether to place the design to the right or to the left of its section. The drawing as in Fig. 3 is after Lal, 1954 & 55 (Fig. 10-76) where both internally and externally decorated views have been placed to the right of the section of the sherd. From this illustration we cannot distinguish the outer view from the inner one. According to recommended method, the inner view should be placed to the right and outer to the left of the section as in Fig. 4. Besides justifying the reorientation of internal and external views of the same sherd for clear understanding, this method has solved the problem of illustrating the sherds having singularly interior or exterior decorations as well. The illustrations as in Fig. 5 after Narain and Roy, 1968, (Fig. 15, 6c), is, however, correct as the inner view has been placed to the right of the section. The drawing as in Fig. 6, after Thapar, 1955, (Fig. 12, 1) has been made as per a procedure generally adopted in archaeological drawing. The externally decorated view here, has been placed to the right which according to recommended method should have been placed to the left as in Fig. 7.

ORIENTATION OF SECTION:

In these examples we are mainly concerned to highlight the designs on the sherd. Keeping in mind the shape of the pot and to which part of it the sherd belongs, we place it in such a way so that all the features of the design are fully revealed. The orientation of the section of the sherd helps us to locate it in the profile of the pot. A slightest departure in correct orientation of the section can bring the shoulder to the belly of the pot and vice versa. The section is, therefore, vital for pinpointing the sherd on the body of the pot.

S. S. SAAR

REFERENCES

Bhat, N.D. 1979, Engirneeing Drawing; Plane and solid geometry, fifteenth edition, 1979; (Anand).

Lal; B.B. 1954 & 55, Excavations at Hastinapura and other explorations in the upper Ganga and Sutlej Basins; 1950-55 (New Delhi); Fig. 10-76.

Narain, A.K. and Roy, T.N. 1963, The Excavations at Prahladpur, Banaras Hindu University, 1968 (Varanasi), Fig. 15, 6c.

Saar, S.S. 1982, Drawing in Archaeology; Puravid; 1982 (Patna).

Thapar, B.K. 1955, Chalcolithic Sites in the Tapti Valley, Ancient India No. 20 & 21, 1964 and 65, (New Delhi) Fig. 12, 1.

Parihati, a Mediaeval Smelting Site in Midnapur District, West Bengal

Parihati is an important village on one of the two Jhargram-Sildah routes (one goes via Binpur and the other via Parihati) in the northwestern part of Midnapur district, West Bengal. A copper hoard has already been reported from this area (Nag and Chakrabarti 1980), and in the lateritic tract adjacent to the village lower and middle palaeolithic tools and microliths have recently been found by the present authors (Chakrabarti and Chattopadhyay n.d.). It may alsa be noted that the report of the discovery of a copper hoard at Parihati is intriguing in the sense that there are at least two versions of the circumstances of this discovery current among the residents of the village. According to one version this board is not from Parihati bu from Jambani, a place about 9 km to the southeast of Parihati. According to another version the find was from the village area itself. Both the versions have "eye-witness" supporters.

The circumstances of the discovery of the Parihati copper hoard may be in doubt but the fact that Parihati was an important centre of copper metallurgy in an undefined period will be apparent even from a cursory inspection of the modern village. Pieces of slag, and what is more important, traces of hearths occur in plenty on the surface in various parts of the village. One of the areas where this can be studied easily is the village market-place which has some open space for the local weekly market.

In the course of their exploration in Midnapur

district in February, 1983, the present authors were impressed by these occurrences and realized that only a minor clearance work was needed in the first stage to understand their basic character. Consequently, a small area was cleared in the market-place.

In an area of roughly 3.5 m by 1.72 m and within a depth of about 25-30 cm the remains of 10 circular hearths were found. The diameter, (both internal and external), etc. of the individual hearts will be clear from the accompanying plan. The objects which have been found associated are (I) fragments of pottery, (2) fragments of tuyeres, (3) ore-pieces and slag, (4) heavy pieces of miscellaneous stone, presumably to break ore-pieces and (5) a large crucible. The soil is partly ashy and contains patches of burnt earth.

The results of analysis of slag and ore will be published in due course but the preliminary impression is that these hearths were used for copper-smelting. The fact which stands out is the following: if the small area cleared by us can show 10 hearths along with ore-pieces, slag, tuyeres, crucible, etc. the number of hearths in operation in the village at that (still undefined) point of time must have been singularly impressive. As we have already noted, the traces of hearths are found not merely in the present market-place but also in various parts of the village.

Regarding the probable chronological point we would like to emphasize the following points. First, as far as the associated pottery (to be published in due course) is concerned, the general range of shapes and fabric do not fit anywhere in the early historic or still earlier contexts of West Bengal. In fact, this ceramic assemblage does not even belong to the Gupta—post-Gupta bracket. This assemblage can only be mediaeval in an undefined way.

Secondly, the crucible found in this context is a large one, and we do not know of any early context in India, which has revealed crucibles of this type. This also can only be mediaeval.

Thirdly, the evidence of the pottery and the crucible fits in with whatever archaeological evidence we have of the antiquity of settlement in this village. Two pieces of sculpture deserve notice. The first is that of a goddess locally worshipped by the name of *Rankini mata* in a temple named after her in the central part of the village. The greyish stone stella is in the form of a miniature temple. It is an eight-handred female deity wearing a garland of human skulls and standing on a prostrate crown-headed male deity. There are attributes in all the eight hands. The left uppermost hand apparently holds an elephant. There is a mace in the next lower hand. The hand below this holds a conch. The attribute in the lowest hand is not clear. On the right side, there is an elephant in the uppermost hand but the attributes in the three lower hands on this side are not at all clear.

The temple is a very late one, but the fact that there was an earlier temple built of lateritic blocks on the same spot can be deduced from a reasonably large number of lateritic blocks lying in the immediate vicinity. One also notes a broken image of a *tirthankara* in the same area. Its upper part is missing but the bull on the pedestal identifies it is as an *Adinatha* image. *Adinatha* images of this type have been observed elsewhere in the western part of West Bengal and we would tentatively put it down to c. 13th century A.D. We would also claim that there was a Jaina temple with *Adinatha* around the 13th century A.D. at Parihati. One is fully aware that there can be no direct correlation between this fact and the extensive occurrence of smelting hearths in the village. At the same time there can be a piece of indirect argument.

Years ago, in the context of the old copper mines of Singhbhum (which, in fact, is the bordering district of Midnapur on this side) Valentine Ball (1869) drew attention to the tradition that the Seraks (whom Ball mistakenly thought to be a "race of Bengal Brahmins") or the Jaina lay-worshippers were responsible for mining and metal-working in that area. Ball, in fact, supported this tradition. That the Jainas were associated in a big way with mining and metal-working, at least in the m diaeval period, is true not merely in Singhbhum but also in Rajasthan. Nowhere is this more apparent than in the old Zawar mines south of Udaipur. Keeping this in mind we find no difficulty at all in associating the Parihati copper-smelting evidence with the period represented by the *Adinatha* image and the presumably associated temple-remains in the village. Thus we would date the copper-smelting evidence from Parihati in the 13th century A.D. or thereabouts.

Regarding the source of copper in this area two points may be noted. First, according to the Parihati villagers the Geological Survey of India prospected for copper in the vicinity of the village. This at least suggests that there is a strong possibility of the existence of copper-ore suitable for pre-industrial smelting (if not for modern exploitation) in this area. Secondly, we know for certain that there was ancient mining for copper at Chhedapathar which is about 30 km to the northwest. This mining area is now used for open-cast mining for wolfram but the area (about 1 km along east-west axis) is full of old shafts and chunks of malachite ore can still be picked up.

While concluding this brief note we may cite an interesting tradition cited by J. A. Dunn (1937) in the context of the neighbouring Singhbhum.

"From the Subarnarekha river east of Ghatsila to Tamluk on the Rupnarain river there is said to have been an old road used by the Chinese in Asoka's time. It has been suggested that the Chinese were the people who mined this copper. There is nothing to support this suggestion, however, although it is very likely that copper may have been traded to them. It is interesting to note that a skull found in one of the caves below the ruin at Roam has the measurements and characteristics of the Chinese" (Dunn 1937:58).

We would not have paid any attention to this apparently confused tradition but for the fact that Professor T. Sorensen of Scandinavian Institute of Asian Studies mentioned. in the course of a discussion, that some east Indian copper was possibly traded to the Chinese at some point of time. He said that there was a historical source to this effect.

Department of History, Delhi University Delhi-110007

DILIP K. CHAKRABARTI and R.K. CHATTOPADHYAY

REFERENCES

Ball, V. 1869. On the ancient copper miners of Singhbhum. *Proceedings of the Asiatic Society of Bengal* : 170-175.

Chakrabarti, Dilip K. and Chattopadhyay, R.K. n.d. Prehistoric stratigraphy in West Bengal: the evidence from Burdwan and Midnapur: *Man & Environment* VIII, (forthcoming).

Dunn, J.A. 1937. The mineral deposits of eastern Singhbhum and surrouding areas. *Memoirs of the Geological Survey of India* LXIX, Part 1.

Nag, A.K. and Chakrabarti, Dilip K. 1980: Cooper hoards from West Bengal. *Puratattva* 9:97-100.

Acknowledgement : Shri N.R. Lahiri of Sebabharati, Kapgari, looked after us during our work at Parihati. Shri Lahiri provided us with similar assistance during our work in Birbhum in March 1981. We are deeply indebted to him.

A Note on the National Museum, Bahrain

The present town of Bahrain is situated over the mound of Qalat-al-Bahrain. The antiquity of the Island dates back to middle palaeolithic times. There are also tanged flint arrow-heads of about 5000 B.C. in this region.

In 1879 a stone bearing a cuneiform inscription was found, now lost. This provided the first evidence that Bahrain was Dilmun for the god Inzak born on Dilmun as child of Enki and Ninhur sag. First written reference to Dilmun dating back to C. 2520 was found in Mesopotamia. Many tablets recording trading activities between Ur and Dilmun were noticed from 2000-1800 B.C. Ur-Nanshi inscription found at Telloh now in Louvre museum mentions that ships of Dilmun brought timber from foreign land as tribute.

The earliest city (Early Dilmun) dating back to C. 2675 B.C. belongs to Barbar culture. The city was destroyed by fire around 2300 B.C. by the army of Sargon of Akkad. The old city was unfortified and in its place a strong defended city was built. It revealed copper chisel, spear-head, disc, clay nude female of supplicant and animal figures and jars of steatite or soapstose. The stamp seals were also found from this level. The inhabitants worshipped their gods in the temple at Barbar.

Around 2000 B.C. the second city (Middle Dilmun) was founded and the temple of Barbar was rebuilt. The votive offerings, alabaster cups, copper hair-band, copper figurines of supplicant and copper bird perhaps peacock were found before the altar of temple III.

The round stamp seals of Dilmun were found in Mesopotamia and on Indus valley sites. The cuneiform tablets from Ur dating from the centuries around 2000 B.C. gives the following details of articles brought by a ship from Dilmun: Indus weights, Ingot of copper and stamped goblet decorated with gazelles.

The city III (Late Dilmun) was established around 1800 B.C. During this period magnificent buildings were erected. The Kassite pottery similar to contemporary Mesopotamian beaker, bowl, conical turnip-shaped cups, clay cuneiform tablets written in Babylonean language were also found. According to 14-C dates the city was destroyed around 1190 B.C.

From 1000 to 544 B.C. City IV was the place of Uperi kings of Dilmun. The remains include place area and objects of iron, copper and soapstone (a red ware cup with a short base in thin fabric having horizontal lines in black pigment reminds the contemporary Rangpur pottery noticed in Gujarat). In 544 B.C. there is a last reference to Dilmun in Mesopotamian records.

The city V (544 B.C. to 0 B.C.-A.D.) had Greek and Roman contacts. The Greek geographers described it as Tylos. A jar having Greek script in Aramic language, Mycenean pottery, terracotta animal and human figurines and Attic bowls are the important finds of this period.

Thereafter a long gap occurred in the history of Bahrain and when the curtain rises, the remains of Muslim period were seen. Masjid al Khamis is the standing structure of this period.

In 1510, Bahrain was conquered by Portugese. The burial mounds of A. Ali Sar and Janabiyyah are possibly the graves of the ancient kings of Dilmun and their subjects. These burial chambers are surrounded by stone-ring, then covered with sand and rubble. There are five types of burials of Sar based on the construction method and less on the shape and grave goods. The seals from al-Hajjar grave mounds also belong to Barbar period (C. 2400 B.C.).

The discovery of 50 seals made of shell and steatite (including cylindrical variety) from Qalat-al-Bahrain in the Barbar temples and in cities I and II (and more in levels of the same culture in Kuwait) together with the debris of seal-cutting workshop, shows that this seal type is native to Bahrain. The shell seal is made from the sawn off apex of a fossil shell. The stamp is consequently created from the natural convolutions of the shell. On the upper surface, generally two perforations to be used as a suspension, have been drilled on either side of the natural central rise. On some, there is a third hole which is due to the shape of the shell. These seals are the main evidence for Bahrain's trade connections found thousand years ago with the whole of the Middle East and the Indo-Pak sub-continent.

The Island of Bahrain was also explored in the last three years by Dr. Rafique Mughal who was the Archaeological Adviser to the State of Bahrain. His exploration and excavation work is under publication.

The National Museum, Bahrain is also having an ethnographical gallery showing the living traditions of the past.

The museum has many publications at its credit. "The Excavations of the Arab Expedition a Sar el-Jisr Bahrain" by Moawiyah Ibrahim of Yarmouk University and "Excavation of Qal' at Al-Bahrain" by Monik Kervran, Arlette Negre and Michele Pirazzoli t' Sertsevens were published in 1982. A few of the publications are in press also. The earlier work done by Danish Scholars is still in compilation stage. The Director of the museum is at present working on the stamp seals found in this region.

K.N. DIKSHIT

Mossbuaer studies of Black slipped and Northern Black Polished Wares

The black slipped ware (BSW) and Northern Black Polished Ware are the basic representative potteries of the Ganga Plains of India. In the Upper Ganga Plain, the black slipped ware was, for the first time, reported from the Painted Grey Ware horizon (datable from *circa* 1100 to 800 B.C.) of Hastinapura. In the Middle Ganga Plain, the ware was reported in a more precise datable context of *circa* 800 to 600 B.C. from the pre-NBP levels of Prahaladpur and Rajghat. What was significant in this context was that on sites of both these regions (the Upper and Middle Ganga Plains), the ware considerably precedes the earliest occurrence of the well known Northern Black Polished Ware (NBP). Although black slipped ware is quite different in fabric from the top-graded NBP (Fabric A) its occurrence in the immediately preceding strata led some archaeologists to believe that black slipped ware might be the forerunner of NBP (B.B. Lal 1954-55:11). Whether this supposed link between these two wares could be also established scientifically is the purpose of this paper?

So far we have not done any investigation on the actual mode of production of the black slipped ware. But the highly lustrous appearance of the NBP has raised several enquiries. The views of Sana Ullah in 1946, P.S. Rawson in 1953, B.B. Lal in 1955-56 and 1959-60, Miss Bimson in 1959, K.T.M. Hedge in 1962, 1966 and 1970, H.C. Bhardwaj in 1969 and T.N. Roy in 1983, who have scientifically examined NBP has been discussed in one of the author's article (T.N. Roy 1983:63-70) and hence need not be retraversed here. Suffice it to mention that the views expressed by all these investigators are at variance with each other. Keeping in view the conflicting result of these workers and minor work of Longworth and Tite on NBP slip (Longworth and Tite 1978), the present invesigation makes a fresh observation on the problem with the help of Mossbauer spectroscopy and X-ray diffraction.

SAMPLING AND METHOD:

Several sherds of black slipped ware and Northern Black Polished Ware recovered from Rajghat (Varanasi) archaeological excavations were chosen for this study. With utmost care the slip from both these wares was removed mechanically. The samples, after having been powdered were mixed in an organic glue and then painted on to a small area (2.0 sq. Cm.) on a piece of paper and allowed to dry. Mossbauer spectra were taken with a 5 mCi Co 57 Mossbauer source in Rhodium matrix in a constant acceleration mode. In both the samples, it took a very long time to acquire good spectra. This indicates that the amount of iron present in them is quite small. The spectra were analysed by least squares fitting them to a sum of Lorentzian functions. The velocities are referred to iron metal.

The spectrum of NBP slip was resolved into one singlet and one doublet, whereas that of black slipped ware into one doublet. The parameters are shown in Table-1. Isomer shifts are given w.r.t. alpha iron. The large widths observed can be attributed to amorphousness of the samples. Though a good enough fit could be obtained with the NBP sample, the black slipped ware sample did not provide a very good fit. We may arttibute this to a greater degree of disorder in the black slipped ware sample in the form of amorphousness and distribution of near neighbour configurations. Because of this uncertainty, no positive conclusion can be drawn about the black slipped ware sample. For the NBP sample the quadrupole splitting combined with isomer shift seem to suggest the presence of certain iron silicates, particularly orthopyroxene $(Mg, Fe, Mn)_2 Si_2O_6$ and actionlite $Ca_2 (Mg, Fe)_5 Si_8O_{22} (OH)_2$. The isomer shift of $\pm 1.0 + 0.1$ mm/s confirms that the oxidation state of iron atom is 2. The singlet is certainly a representative of the Fe^{***} state of iron, but it is difficult to identify it solely on the basis of isomer shift. The ratio of the areas of the subspectra of Fe^{**} and Fe^{***} comes out to be 4.5. We may, with a little loss in precision, assume that the recoilless fractions of the two are the same. Under this assumption, the ratio of Fe^{**} to Fe^{***} may be taken to be 4.5.

DISCUSSION AND CONCLUSION:

The Mossbauer spectrescopic findings suggest that the material used to produce the shining glossy coating on the NBP surface may either be acticolite or orthopyroxene or any other members belonging to this genera of silicate minerals. Although the X-ray diffraction lines indicate a large degree of crystallinity, the Mossbauer results, on the contrary point to a high degree of amorphousness. The only explanation for this apparent discrepancy is that the crystallinity is due to some non-ferrous compounds (may be fractions of body clay incorporated due to mechanical scrapping of the slip), which, of course, does not make any contribution to the Mossbauer spectra. The iron based part of the slip, however, is mostly amorphous, as evidenced by the Mossbauer spectra. With high degree of pertinence it may be asserted that amorphousness resulted due to vitrification of glazing material. Thus it may be erroneous to rule out in to the possibility of glass like character of the NBP slip. The ratio of Fe++to Fe+++ (4.5) components or iron constituents ascertains the propositions. of the British Museum, related to the method of its manufacturing. The findings of the British Museum do not subscribe to the view of burnishing and its present suggestion is that the unfired pots were dipped into a suspension of ferrugenous material (that may be the presently detected acticolite or orthopyroxene) and firing to a temperature of about 800°C, the kiln was sealed, so that the pots cooled in a reducing atmosphere. This device of firing would have resulted in oxidation and subsequently reduction of iron compounds. The remaining small portion of ferric state of iron constituent may be due to incomplete reduction. This view also may be corroborated with the fact that when NBP pottery is fired at 1000°C in an oxidizing atmosphere, it becomes red due to conversion of Fe to Fe_2O_3. The colours and shades of slips are generally dependent on reducing atmosphere, time and temperature of cooling, besides their constituents (Beek, 1974). Therefore, on the basis of the present state of our knowledge, we may attribute time temperature atmospheric conditions of cooling to develop various and varied shades and colours to NBP slip. But, at the same time, the limited role of carbon in enhancing black lustre may not be overlooked. Our investigations do not suggest any link between NBP slip and black slipped ware slip. Thus, it may be safe to conclude their independent origin compositionally.

ACKNOWLEDGEMENT:

The authors are grateful to Sri N. Rajan and Sri A.K. Nigam of Nuclear Research Laboratory, Department of Physics, Banaras Hindu University for their kind help and guidance.

TABLE—1
Mossbaur parameters of NBPW and BSW pottery slip

Sample	Components	Isomer shift (Fe) (mm/s)	Quadrupole splitting (mm/s)	F.W.H.M. (mm/s)
N.B.P.W.	Singlet	—0.16 ± 0.07	—	0.5 ± 0.1
	Doublet	+1.0 ± 0.1	1.98 ± 0.04	0.88 ± 0.09
B.S.W.	Doublet	+0.4 ± 0.3	1.2 ± 0.2	1.0 ± 0.4

Banaras Hindu University **S. RAI AND DR. T. N. ROY**

REFERENCES

Lal, B.B. 1954-55; Excavations at Hastinapura and other Explorations in the Upper Ganga and Sutlej Basins, *Ancient India;* Nos. 10 & 11; p. 11.

Longworth and Tite, 1978; *J. Physique;* C2-436.

Roy, T.N. 1983; A critical study of the technical Investigations made on NBP, *Rangavalli; Recent Research in Indology;* pp. 64-70.

Prehistoric Uttar Pradesh : A Rejoinder to the Review by D. P. Agrawal

The review of my book *Prehistoric Uttar Pradesh (A Study of Old Stone Age)* by D.P. Agrawal, published in the *Puratattva*, bulletin of the Indian Archaeological Society, No. 11, 1979-80, pp. 167-168, is sarcastic, prejudiced, and obviously based upon non-academic considerations. Had it not been the case, the reviewer would not have ignored to write even the full title of the book, which reads *Prehistoric Uttar Pradesh (A Study of Old Stone Age)*. The omission appears to be deliberate, otherwise the reviewer would not have been in a position to make such remarks, as "One looked for some richer and general interpretation when the title claimed to be dealing with total prehistory." This wilful omission becomes all the more glaring, when one finds that in a short review of about two columns the reviewer keeps on reminding his readers about the 'unfair use' of the title in the book. (To be exact, he comments on the title three times).

The reviewer D.P. Agrawal has raised certain points of criticism against my book. He thinks that the book deals "with a very narrow aspects of the problem which has little general relevance", and hence its utility "for the general reader" is considerably restricted. I am really surprised to read this comment. I have never claimed to have written the book for a 'general reader' or a layman, nor it was intended to be a text book. I find it quite embarrassing to remind a scholar of D.P. Agrawal's stature that most of the good researches in archaeology either tend to investigate very narrow aspects of problems in a wider perspective, or they deal with a group of problems in limited time and space. The monograph under discussion belongs to the second category, in which an attempt has been made to describe and discuss the various palaeolithic industries of Uttar Pradesh in their geo-chronological settings. (This fact has been brought out in no uncertain terms in the Preface, as well as the Chapter I.) These researches serve as reference literature, specially meant for those trained in the discipline. If they fail to cater to the needs of general readers, the fault hardly lies with the researches.

I had admitted in the Preface of the book that the rich palaeolithic collections made by the Allahabad University during the last two decades or so were not available to me for study. D.P. Agrawal in his review has made it a point for criticising the book. It may be pointed out, however, that I had some opportunities to see the Allahabad collections, although I was not permitted to make a detailed study. Their inclusion in the monograph would have certainly enriched the study, but the fact remains that their omission did not vitiate the conclusions in any way, since they were drawn on a very minute study of a sizeable number of collections of different palaeolithic phases. My observation of the Allahabad assemblages reveals that they are hardly different from the collections I have made from the Belan and its surroundings. As regards K.P. Nautiyal's discovery in Garhwal, it has been briefly commented upon in the Chapter I. I had an occasion to see the photographs of the collection at Allahabad during the seminar on Indian Prehistory, 1980. Frankly speaking, I had my reservations about their being genuine artifacts. Subsequently, my doubts were confirmed by some knowledgeable persons, who had an opportunity to examine the collection personally. (I am not permitted to reveal the identity of these knowledgeable persons for obvious reasons). Hence, Nautiyal's collection does not find a detailed treatment in the monograph.

D.P. Agrawal is particularly critical of my approach to the subject, and accuses me for making "a drab techno-typological description of the tools." To him it is an "outmoded approach", which is "technical and not synthetic", and it is hardly desirable "in the present stage of synthetic models and multivariant analysis". I do not fight shy in accepting that I am a bit conservative in my approach, "even if it means bearing the rather undeserving label 'reactionary'" *(Prehistoric Uttar Pradesh,* p. 12). Unhesitatingly I admit, I am not convinced by the studies which tend to interpret prehistoric cultures by ignoring tool-kits. In fact, I have said so in so many words in my book also *(Prehistoric Uttar Pradesh,* pp. 11-12). It should not be forgotten that the stone artifacts are the only material equipment left by palaeolithic man in India. Obviously, one cannot make a meaningful study of his culture by ignoring these very material remains. It has been observed that the critics of techno-typological studies are those, who either do not have basic training in the discipline of Prehistoric Archaeology, or are ignorant of the limitations of the field data available. The reviewer of my book D.P. Agrawal claims to have synthesized the Indian Archaeology, including the palaeolithic phase, in his recently published book *The Archaeology of India* (Copenhagen, 1982), but he does not seem to recognize even such basic tool-types as handaxe and point. (For example, in illustration number 20, page 38, except the top two no other specimen can be classified as handaxe. Similarly, in the next illustration number 21, there is not a single point, although the caption says 'Middle Palaeolithic scrapers and points, Belan Valley, U.P.'.) Under the circumstances, one should not be surprised that he conveniently writes off the scholarly tradition of Henry Abbe Breuil and Francois Bordes. It is, thus, not at all shocking to me that Agrawal finds the use of 'a number of German and French terms' confusing, although they are understood throughout the world by those, who are seriously engaged in palaeolithic researches. For those who are not conversant with the internationally recognized tool-classes, I have meticulously explained each and every German and French term in my book (pp. 12-16).

In the Chapter on Stratigraphy, I have criticised Dassarma and Biswas for their interpretation of the Belan section, particularly that portion of their hypothesis, in which they try to associate some of the deposits with glacial climate. For example, I do not agree that the basal boulder-pebble deposit was formed as a result of solifluction. Nor there is any evidence to suggest that the yellow silt overlying the gravel-sand unit is at least partly of loessic origin. Similarly, I have also asked a query whether any of the animal species found from any of the deposits of the Belan section can be classed under the typical glacial fauna. I write, "If Dassarma's suggestion regarding faunal evidence is to be accepted, the whole of the Peninsular India, as also Sri Lanka, where a similar group of fauna has been found in the Ratnapura stage, must have been in the grip of glacial climate for a long part of the Late Pleistocene. Such a proposition is hardly tenable in view of the available evidence" (p. 27). In fact the whole question has been discussed in some detail in my book. I may be "blissfully ignorant of the global implications of bringing down the glaciers upto Rajasthan and Madhya Pradesh", and, for that matter, I may be ignorant of many other thnigs, but the fact remains that we do not have any moraines in central India which can be unmistakably assigned to the Pleistocene, nor do we have huge peri-glacial loesses, frost-soils, as well as typical glacial fauna and flora. All these factors are obviously important for me in the context, since I have been concerned only with the terrestrial evidence in my book. D.P. Agrawal accuses me for ignoring "the significant palaeoenvironmental studies carried out in Rajasthan, Maharashtra and Kashmir by various multidisciplinary groups", with which he has been himself associated. (Is it the reason why he chooses to criticise my book so vehemently?). But, is it not a fact that these studies, howsoever significant they might have been, are hardly relevant for my region? Similarly, the Pleistocene pollen evidence from Kashmir can hardly help interpreting the Quaternary problems of Uttar Pradesh. I am thankful to Agrawal for pointing out the mistake of writing a humus rich deposit as nonacidic. I write—"The entire deposit looks like humus rich in organic matter, which is probably responsible for the dark colour of the earth. Preliminary laboratory test confirms this suggestion, *and* also indicates that the soil is not acidic" (p. 35). In fact I had written *but* in place of *and* in my original draft, but somehow in the process of publication the *but* got replaced by the *and*.

In his enthusiasm for criticising my book, Agrawal attributes some "very confusing" statements to me, which I believe I never made. He gives only one example—"He says that Ganga never meets the ocean directly." I am surprised, how does he get this impression? The relevant statement in my book runs as follows—"The changes in the sea levels would have hardly influenced the nature of river deposits in our region, since all the rivers of the region belong to the Yamuna or Ganga systems, and none of them joins the occean directly" (p. 17). I believe, the sentence does not convey the meaning that Agrawal tries to derive from it.

Agrawal does not seem to like the title of my book also. In fact he suggests towards the end of his review, "it would have been better to label it as Palaeolithic culture in the valleys of the south on tributaries of the Yamuna." I really doubt whether Agrawal seriously means it, and expects me to accept such a clumsy title.

The reviewer hardly finds anything good in my book. He criticises it for almost every thing, such as, for not including the figures in the main text, for giving "graphs and sections separately", for no information value of the plates, for graphs having hanging scales, etc. I think, the presentation of tool drawings, graphs, section drawings and plates is a matter of ones personal reasoning, and the reviewer is free to hold his opinion.

It is admitted on all hands that a good review should concentrate on the achievements which an author claims to have made in his book. They are mostly summarized in the Preface, as I have done in my book. I have written, "It is heartening to note that the industries of all the three phases exhibit some new tool traditions...the Lower Palaeolithic phase was found to have two sets of industries in Uttar Pradesh, *viz.*, the true pebble tool industries of the chopper-chopping tradition, and the Acheulian industries of the handaxe-cleaver tradition. The pebble tools tradition seem to have continued also in the Middle Palaeolithic phase in a limited measure, though most of the industries of this phase appear to belong to the 'Denticulate Mousterian' category. The Upper Palaeolithic of Uttar Pradesh shows a definite evidence for bladelets and microliths ....", etc. (p. x.). It is very surprising that Agrawal not only does not discuss any of these points in his review, but he wilfully refrains from even making a brief notice of them, particularly when many of the claims appear to be new in Indian Prehistory. Does the reviewer fail to understand the implications of these points, or has he yet to learn how to review research publications on Prehistory.

Banaras Hindu University

P. C. PANT

Studies in the Archaeology and Palaeoanthropology of South Asia

Edited by K.A.R. Kennedy and G.L. Possehl, pp. 144. Rs. 120/-; Oxford-IBH. New Delhi 1984, though published and released in 1983.

It is a collection of a dozen articles, generally short and problem-oriented, but covering as diverse subjects as Hominid origins, Harappan granaries and Buddhist establishments. The book, therefore, lacks personality. However, it succeeds in focussing our attention to a few very important issues facing South Asian archaeology and to that extent no one seriously interested in Indian archaeology can offord to miss it.

The first paper on Hominoid Adaptation and Hominid origins in South Asia by J.R. Lukacs has for the first time given a clear insight into the evolutionary framework for South Asian hominoids.

However, Lukacs has relied almost exclusively upon functional dental morphology of the known examples, which are not very many. Moreover, many areas and their palaeoecology are yet to be worked out for a convincing outline.

The second paper, 'The Soan in Central Asia? Problems in Early Palaeolithic Culture History' by R.S. Davis is virtually a review of a chapter of the reviewer's book *Archaeology of Soviet Central Asia and Indian Borderlands*, Vol I (1979). It, therefore, adds nothing new to our knowledge. The author has questioned my observation as follows:

"Gupta has taken a very straightforward approach to explain the origins of the Central Asian pebble industries. 'It is probable that the Soan Culture, originating in the Beas-Sutlej basin (Gupta 1979) moved westward in the Soan region, crossed the Himalayas and then reached the Pamir-Alai system of mountains at a very early stage, somewhere during the uppermost Middle Pleistocene period." Subsequently Gupta maintains, the Soan Culture eventually died out in the Soan Valley, but it was preserved and developed in central Asia. Some of it then changed through contacts with the Asiatic monsterian coming in from West Asia. According to Gupta, the Soan Valley area followed a different route of cultural historical development in the upper pleistocene because the West Asiatic Monsterian never penetrated into this area'.

His objections to these observations are:

First, that it is a historical cultural model which is a British legacy;

Secondly, that it is based on typological/technological similarities which in essence mean nothing, and he quotes the examples of Chou Kou Tien with Vertesszollos (Collins 1969) and Solutrean with Sandia of north America (Greenman 1963) to bring home his point.

Thirdly, that Afghanistan has not yielded any Soan assemblage, through which diffusion, if any, may have taken place.

Now let us examine these objections. The first is methodological. All American archaeologists come from the Anthropology Departments and, therefore, can they ever hope to appreciate historical cultural approach of Indian archaeologists who come from History Departments. Those who have a history of only 200 years obviously treat pre-White history of America as subjects of anthropology. For them stone tools are stones in environment, but for us they are petrified human beings, who eat, think and move in time and space.

The second concerns typological/technological similarities—what does this imply about the origins of this similarity? Tp Davis, 'In essence', not a thing. To us a lot if.

(a) the two areas are in close proximity, as (Tadzikistan and north-western India are closest);

(b) if the time brackets do not fall apart, (Tadzik and Indian contexts belong to upper Middle Pleistocene), and

(c) and if the total assembalges are not divergent (which they are not in Central Asia and north-western India):

The reviewer, therefore, feels that it is patently absurd and non-sensical to quote examples of China and Hungary and France and America to condemn the case of Tadzikistan and north-western India which form part of a single mountainous system and are not seperated by thousands of miles, as the above mentioned countries are.

Lastly, yes, Afghanistan has not yielded the Soan assemblage but then who has explored north-eastern mountains of Afghanistan for lower Palaeolithic sites. None. And for quite sometime no one will be able to do that. Why then use this as an argument against a theory? And funny enough, in the foreward to the Prehistoric Afghanistan—A Source Book by V.C. Srivastava, Davis himself observes, "There is no reason at all to expect that the material is not there".

The trouble is that while Davis, when he wrote it had absolutely no first hand knowledge of the Indian material, the reviewer and V.A. Ranov, the Soviet prehistorian, whose theory, Davis chooses to criticise, had the first hand knowledge of both the collections and this Davis admits on Pages 26-27. The difficulty with our American friend is that he knew nothing about the Soan tools, the Soan technology, the Soan territory while writing this paper—a lot of theory, a lot of flesh, but no bones.

The limitations of the Lower Palaeolithic cultures are well known; variability will be there when we are dealing with 1/2 a million years' bracket, when Davis writes that he 'predicts' (p. 30) that it will be there, one wonders if any scholar will ever use this term in archaeology.

The question is not of variability to be found in the pebble tool assemblages in South Asia, it has always been clear to me and Ranov both; the question is about the range of variability and the range of similarity. We maintain that whether we accept Moviou's generalization or not on a world-wide basis, the fact remains that the southern Pamir—north-western Himalayan zone presents a picture in which pebble chopper chopping industry predominates to the extent that to imagine two separate origins for them within just a few hundred miles is preposterous at the present stage of our knowledge. To say that De Terra's system of terraces and their dates need revision in the light of various recent works is correct, but we all know that till now, what to say of 1979 when my book was published, not a single work has appeared in print which has substantially revised the dating of the terraces on which Soan tools were found in India and Pakistan. As a matter of fact, no one has so far doubted the Middle to late Pleistocene date of the Soan and Banganga terraces and this is what is important irrespective of the fact that soon there may be more cold and dry phases than those proposed by De Terra *et al.*

Coming to Monsterian and its effect on the directional changes in the lower Palaeolithic Central Asia and India what I maintained then, I still maintain while Central Asia and northern Afghanistan witnessed the coming of the Monsterian and changing its course in a big way, India remained outside this phenomenon. My conclusions are based on my world-wide personal handling of Monsterian assemblages, and digging Monsterian sites in France and not on the study of line drawnigs alone. Indian Middle Palaeolithic or Series II is *not* Monsterian, I maintain.

The paper does not require any more commenst since there has not been any substantial addition of fresh data on South Asian Soan complexes since I published my book. That there is a great need for a variety of environmental studies, techno-typological studies, explorations in Afghanistan, re-dating of terraces, etc. is clear enough but to say that techno-typological studies of assemblages from contiguous areas and from resonably sure though large time brackets have absolutely no meaning and that the cultural historical model we are using in India and the Soviets in Central Asia has no validity may suit the American anthropologists turned archaeologists but not to us who have long and continuous history.

The next paper is on Palaeo-environmental and Prehistoric studies in Kashmir by D.P. Agrawal which is of fundamental nature since after De Terra's group this is the first study of this kind; the archaeological studies are however, only marginal in this paper.

For protohistorians the most provocative paper is by Jim Shaffer-Bronze Age Iron from Afghanistan. It has tried to collect bits of data on iron nodules and a few pieces of iron decorative pieces on bronze articles from Mundigak, Said Kala and Deh Morari. He then presents data from Ahar. At the end are the conclusions which are worth serious consideration: iron in some form or the other was in use in Indian subcontinent since 3000 B.C. through the second and first millennium B.C. it was not brought by some mythical 'Aryans' or any other group. But Jacolson in his comments has rightly observed 'that the collection and utilization of iron ore does not necessarily presage iron processing'. The most important point made by Shaffer is, therefore, of a different kind: iron technology in India has not to be attributed to diffusion, it has a long autochthonous history.

Louis Falm's article on the Palaeogeography and Prehistoric settlement patterns of the Sind is the result of the author's re-exploration after Majumdar's in 1931 of the Lake Manchhar area with emphasis on geographical setting. It is quite informative to that extent. But at the end (p. 82) when he talks of Kot Dijian Ceramics at Nippur and Jemdt Nasr pottery at Amri, and without illustrating, them, then we only start remembering Piggott, McCown and others who are now completely out-dated. G.L. Possehl's note on the Harappan patterns in the Punjab raises a few vital issues-since the pre-or Early Harappan cultures in the Potwar, Bannu and Gomal Valleys do not develop what is called 'Mature Harappan' while in the Ghaggar and the Lower Indus Valley we get both the Early and Mature Harappan, how far the term Early Harappan is justified? Marcia Fentress, on the other hand, feels in her paper The Indus Granaries' that structures called granaries' at Harappa and Mohenjodaro were not granaries, these were only market places. But one of the most valuable papers is by K.A.R. Kennedy who reviews and rejects the old theories of racial origins of the Indus people, including the Aryan invaders of the Harappan towns theory. He shows, on the other hand, how people of various categories lived, whose descendants the present day people of Punjab are.

Anna King's paper on Early Historical Cultures like Painted Grey Ware and N.B.P. Ware makes a plea that these culturs should not be viewed in terms of literary references, as episodes. Like Shaffer, she makes a case for autochthonous development of Indian cultures in a continuous sequence. James Heitzman's paper on Early Buddhism, Trade and Empire creates a kind of economic model for the growth of Buddhism. The paper by Nandini Lyton on ethnoarchaeology is just a term paper and does not call for special comments.

There are two very important 'Comments' also, one by Robert West and the other by Jacobson.

S.P.GUPTA

BOOK REVIEWS

Monik Kervran *et al, Excavation of Qal'at Al-Bahrain,* The Ministry of Information, Directorate of Archaeology and Museum, Government of Bharain; Bharain, 1982, pp. 119 (including plates).

The excavation report which has virtually provided all the relevant material necessary for the study of mediaeval Bahrain is published in French, English and Arabic. It has 9 plates including coloured ones. It is divided into five parts-Baharain in the first centuries of the Hijra, discription and function of the fort, theories on the date and origins of the fort, coins and Chinese ceramics. The stratigraphy confirmed that the fort was built between 10th to 11th century of the Christian era and was abandoned in the 13th. century. However, this place was in contact with the Far East as is evident from the Chinese coins and pottery found inside the fort. The Celadon ware in Bahrain is datable from 12th-16th century. The report is illustrated with the excellent drawings of the fort and the pottery. The plates are well reproduced. It is a wlcome addition to our knowledge

K.N. DIKSHIT

V.C. Srivastava, *The Pre-historic Afghanistan—A Source Book* Indological Publication, Allahabad 1982, pp. XXV 234, price Rs. 250/- 18 maps and 135 other illustrations.

This is indeed the first complete review work of the prehistoric cultures of Afghanistan. One finds not only references of all publications but also illustrations of practically all the published material.

The book has been divided into four chapters — The Environment, The Discovery, The Source and the Reconsruction, each further divided ino logical sub-sections. At the end one finds charts of Radiocarbon dates, prehistoric sites wih references, overall cultural sequence, etc.

The portions dealing with the Lower Palaeolithic of Dash-t-Nawur (Gazani) in which chopper-chopping tools have been found (thus claimed) along with handaxes and clevers, is, however, controversial as Srivastava has himself mentioned — it is doubtful if even one of these examples is a tool. Therefore, the deduction of Srivastava that this complex originated independent of India and Central Asia (p. 190) is questionable.

The second point which deserves notice is the Aceramic Neolithic placed in the 9th millennium B.C. at Aq Kupruk by Radiocarbon date (8566 B.C.). There is clear evidence of domestication of goats and sheep, but so far no evidence of the domestication of plants from the same level has been published and Srivastava has mentioned this fact. But then I wonder why does he feel that 'the domestication of animals and some sort of domestication of plants generally go together *as they are* interconnected (p. 115). How are they interconnected and that too at Aq Kupruk or anywhere else in Afghanistan That in West Asia, Levant particularly, domestication of plants may have begun in the Epipalaeolithic times is a different matter, we have solid evidence from that region to go by, but there also first 'domestication' of animals (in terms of 'selection for kill-off') is not associated with real domesticated plant remains, only some 'selection' has been suggested. We need more data on morphological changes in animals or plants.

These difficulties are, however, the difficulties of the present day research status in prehistory of Afghanistan over which none of us has any control. More work is needed for sound deductions, as Srivastava rightly observes.

S.P.GUPTA

Meawiyah Ibrahim, *Excavations of the Arab Expedition at Sar el-Jisr, Bahrain,* Ministry of Information, State of Bahrain, Bahrain, 1982, pp. 224 (including plates), report of the Excavations of the burial mounds at Sar.

It is an excavation report of a rescue operation of the burial mounds at Sar ranging in date from the 3rd millennium B.C. It was sponsored by the State of Bahrain in cooperation with other Arab Departments of Antiquities and Institutions. It is published both in English and Arabic. It contains text dealing with the different types of burial complexes ranging in construction from single burial above surface to a complex variety provided wtih shaft entrance, pot-forms and minor antiquities such as steatite vessel, bituman coated baskets, beads, bronze finds and jewellery. The chapter on seals showing a development in the workmanship is one of the major contributions. The seals were manufactured in Bahrain itself. A preliminary report on the human remains helped in reconstructing the demographic profile of the people responsible for the erection of these burials. The tables—burial mound data-from type I toV have made the report very valuable. The architectural details of the burials, plates and figures are also well made and produced. A comperative study of the material in relation to other adjoining areas would have made it more useful. However, it is of lasting value, as it has added a lot of new information to our knowledge.

K.N. DIKSHIT

Byung-mo Kim, *MEGALITHIC CULTURES IN ASIA*, Hanyang University, Seoul, 133 Korea, 1982, pp, 204.

The proceedings of the International Symposium on the comparative study of megalithic cultures in Asia organised under the joint auspices of the Hanyang University and the Korean National Commission for UNESCO are published in the form of this monograph. There are eight papers including one by Byung-mo Kim on 'Problem and Sources' for comparing the nature, function and the date of the megalithic monuments in Asia. The concept of megalithic monuments in this symposium was confined to menhirs, statues, burials, coffins, altars and holy places made of stone. These monuments belong to Bronze-Iron age starting from 700-600 B.C. onward.

Masayuki Komoto's paper on 'Megalithic monuments in Ancient Japan' outlined three types of construction; Cap-stones, covering pit graves, stone-cists, urns and pit-graves with boulder brim; dolmens having three of four supporting stones under the capstone and the last type of dolmen has no supporting stones but small irregularly arranged boulders over the pit-graves. These dolmens are quite alike those in Korea in shape. Next paper on 'The General aspect of megalithic cultutre of Korea' by Yong-hoon Whang is about 'The Morphological Classification of Korean Megalith.' It deals with the distribution of dolmen and menhirs and their chronology. Dolmens in Korea are subdivided as table-tlpe, go-table type and unsupported capstone type. 'The Megalithic remains in Chinese continent and Taiwan' including Tibet again by Byung-mo Kim is another interesting survey of dolmens and stone-cists. R.P. Soejono's 'On the Megaliths in Indonesia' deals with the function of megaliths. In next paper. 'Megalithic Culture in Malaysia' by Chandran Jeshurun has given a survey of megaliths and associated finds in Peninsular Malaysia, Sarawak and Sabah. H. Sarkar's paper on 'Megalithic culture of India' deals wtih distribution, typology, dating and modes of disposal of the dead and study of human remains of these burials. In the last paper by Byung-mo Kim 'A New Interpreataion of Megalithic monuments in Korea', the distribution of menhir, stone cist and dolmen in Asia along with their builders have been discussed. This proceeding has contributed something new to world archaeology and will be of great help to those who aer interested in early Asiatic peoples.

K.N. DIKSHIT

Jorge Armand; *Archaeological Excavations in Durkadi Nala-An Early Palaeolithic Pebble-Tool Workshop in Central India*, pp. 198 plates 48 New Delhi, Price Rs. 150.00

The book, which is divided into five parts, relates to the excavations of a site Durkadi Nala on the ancient banks of Narbada river. Part I deals with the theoretical frame work, the theories of other excavations who have already worked in this region, and suggestion regarding the need for new aims and methods in Indian Prehistory. Part II is about the methods and techniques used in the excavation of this site, whereas in Part III concentration is on the system used for the classification of stone artefacts from this site. A code of attributes for the analysis of the palaeolithic stone artefacts including a glossary of common terms has also been suggested. In Part IV a complete analysis of comparative study of the Durkadian industry is given. In conclusion the author has advanced a hypothesis that the handaxe-cleaver culture of India was a result of the evolution of the Indian Chopper stage.

The book is a well documented work supported by plates, line drawing and sections. Prof. Sankalia has rightly remarked that this book would serve as a model for similar works where there is a scope and need for horizontal excavation.

K.N. DIKSHIT

Erwin Neumayer, *Prehistoric Indian Rock paintings*. Oxford Press, Delhi, 1983 pp. IV+159. 6 maps 210 line drawings and 15 photographs. Price Rs. 280/-

It is a new edition of a beautifully produced book on Indian rock paintings; earlier to it an excellent work on the same theme but with shorter scope and long introduction by V.S. Wakankar, was published in Germany. The 44 paged text composed in two columns in a large format includes chapters on Research and Recording Methods, Locations, Paintings of the Mesolithic, Chalcolithic and Historic periods. Bruisings in India and Sri Lanka. The presentation is neat and crisp and everyone interested in the subject will greatly benefit from it. As the author has acknowledged much of the discussion is based on the well known ideas, schemes and methodology evolved by Wakankar and Mathapal. The author has largely summarized and systematized their thoughts on the principle of overlap of drawings correlation with painted designs on chalcolithic pottery. Asokan Brahmi inscriptions over-riding paintings, typology of historic weapons of war. Chronological fixation of these paintings on these grounds is not contested but certainly doubted in the case of Mesolithic attribution, whatever its date. The only good example of Mesolithic paniting comes from Gupteshwar in Madhya Pradesh excavated by B.B. Lal since two rock chips, bearing parts of red ochre paintings, were found buried in the layers bearing microlithic tools, but this is not mentioned. On page 13 the author observes that although the Mesolithic people were hunters and gatherers, yet they wore loin cloth of some soft woven material, which is only a refinement of basket weaving'. How can one digest such views unless the Mesolithic, in effect was contemporary to the Early Chalcolithic cultures. But the reconstruction of the environment and every day life of he Mesolithic people on th basis of 'mesolithic' representations is laudable. The paintings of the later periods are well known from the earlier publications also, but here the author draws upon entnographic beliefs and customs also, though one wonders how far the present can be imposed on the past. The chapter on historic paintings is common place. But the chapter dealing with rock bruisings and paintings in South India and Sri Lanka is of special interest to all of us since not much was known about the Kerala and Sri Lanka examples.

Unfortunately, the book has no Indiex which makes it less academei a publication than what is was meant to be.

S.P.GUPTA

Ekrem Akurgal, *Ancient Civilizations and Ruins of Turkey*, Turkish Historical Society, Ankara, 1983.

This book is written for those interested in the archaeology of Anatolia, the birth place of some of the earliest civilizations in the world. It deals from prehistoric times until the end of the Roman Empire. Originally the book appeared in 1969 as the archaeological guide to the ruins of Turkey but was subsequently revised and enlarged for the specialist.

The Hittites created a new order in Anatolia as is examplified in the excavations at Alacahuyuk, the open sanctuary of Yazilikaya and the great temples of Hattusa at Bogazkoy. The roles of Phrygians, Lycians, Carnians and Lycians who moulded the Greek life and culture were duly dealt. All these periods are well illustrated.

The inclusion of latest prehistoric research in south-eastern Anatolia and the publication of the rescue works in the Lowor Euphrtes basin by the Middle . East Technical University would have made the book more uptodate.

This book revealed importance of Anatolian archaeology including the remarakable contribution made to contemporary archaeology by the excavations at Catal Huyuk, Hacilar, Bycesultan, Troy, Bogazkoy, Gordion, Ephesus etc. The information on the part played by Anatolia in the genisis and development of the earliest art of Greece is another contribution of this book.

K.N. DIKSHIT

V.P. Arora, *Motifs in Indian Mythology, Their Greek and other Parallels,* Indika Publishing House, New Delhi 1981, pp XXIV+248 Price Rs 98/-

Mythology is neither history nor novel nor story. It is the collective perception of a people about their past. So mythology is peculiar to a particular group of people, Hindu mythology to the Hindus, Greek mythology to the Greeks and so on. All of them show striking parallels. Comparative mythology deals with these parallels and tries to probe the generic relation between them. In the past the tendency was to see generic relations which was often absurd. Dr Arora presents his data in an unbiased fashion and this is the most commendable aspect of this book. The book is neatly printed and moderately priced.

S.P.GUPTA

T.N. Roy, *The Ganges Civilization,* New Delhi, Ramanand Vidya Bhawan, 1983. Price Rs. 300/-, 307 pp., 12 plates, 3 figures, 7 tables.

This is the first book of its kind and deserves careful consideration. The basic argument of the author in the introduction (chapter 1) is that R.L. Singh's division of the Gangetic valley into upper and middle sections along the modern Allahabad—Faizabad railway line is valid on the archaeological grounds as well because this more or less coincides with the easternmost extension of the OCP and the easternmost point of the primary distribution area of the PGW. On the other hand, the tradition of the painted BRW tradition of the middle Gangetic valley dies out along this line.

The present reviewer is rather unhappy that the author decided to include the Vindhyan and the Chhotanagpur material in his discussion of the archaeological assemblages of the valley itself. This unhappiness also extends to the author's neat distinction between Early Iron Age (c.800—400/300 B.C.) and Late Iron Age (c.400/300 B.C.—c.100 B.C. or the beginning of the Christian era) in the context of the Gangetic valley data. No useful classificatory purpose is served by treating our early historic material as belonging to the Iron Age simply because no archaeological nomenclature is needed to describe historic material. The term Iron Age should be reserved for our relevant protohistoric contexts.

Chapter 2 lists and documents the various excavated sites in the upper, middle and lower Gangetic plains and tries to isolate levels according to their position in the author's scheme of the early and late Iron Ages. The distinction between "the Lower Ganga Plain North" and "the Lower Ganga Plain South" is not clear to the present reviewer. Moreover, the author ignores the fact that sites such as Tulsipur are in the Chhotanagpur fringe of the lower valley and not in the valley itself. Chapter 3 deals with chronology and discusses all categories of evidence related to this issue. The next three chapters (4,5,6) are devoted to the documentation of the material traits of the PGW and NBP levels. The final chapter is "conclusion" where the author rightfully emphasizes the need of understanding the pre-iron base of the Gangetic vally civilization more fully.

One may disagree with the author on various points but the fact remains that it is a painstaking work of considerable value.

DILIP K. CHAKRABARTI

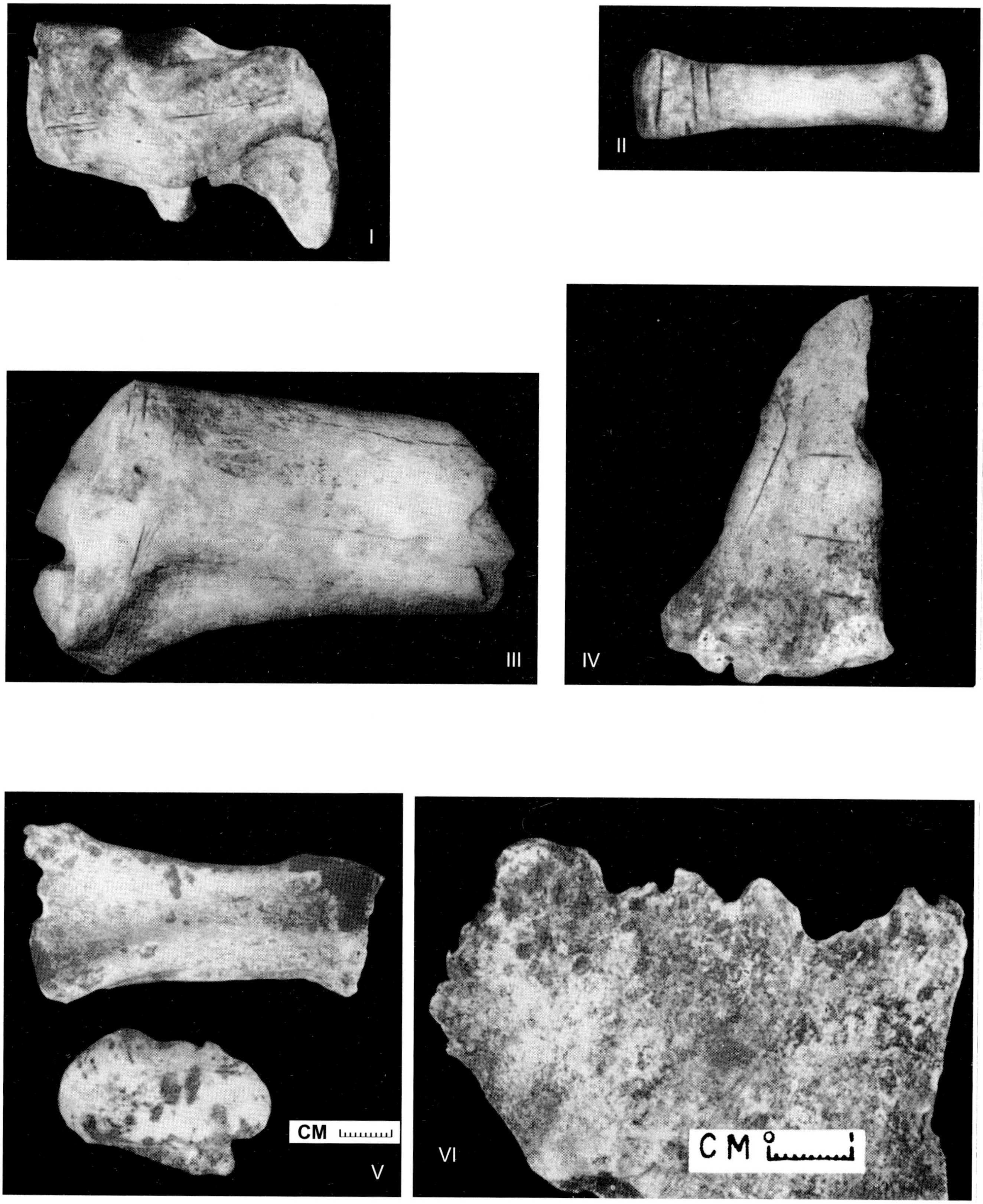

A.K. Sharma, Gufkral, Animal bones.

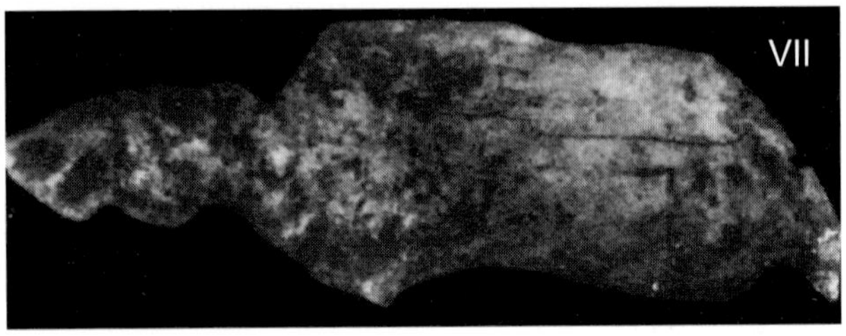

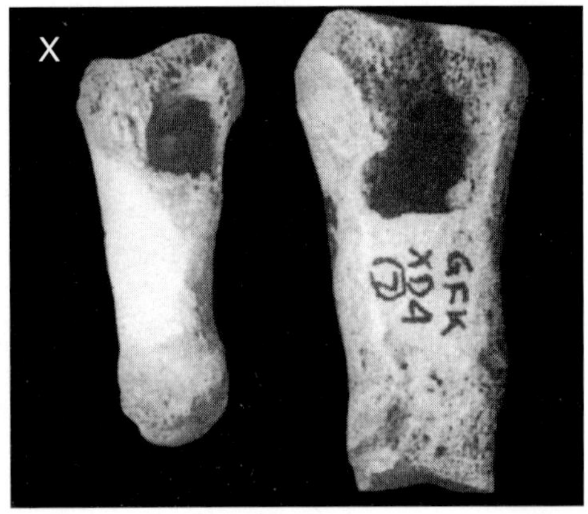

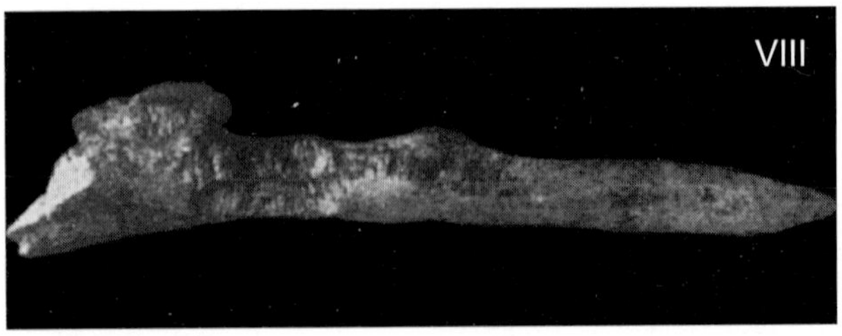

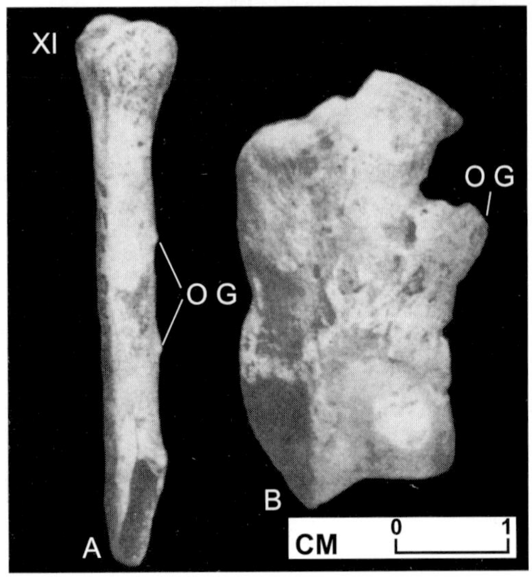

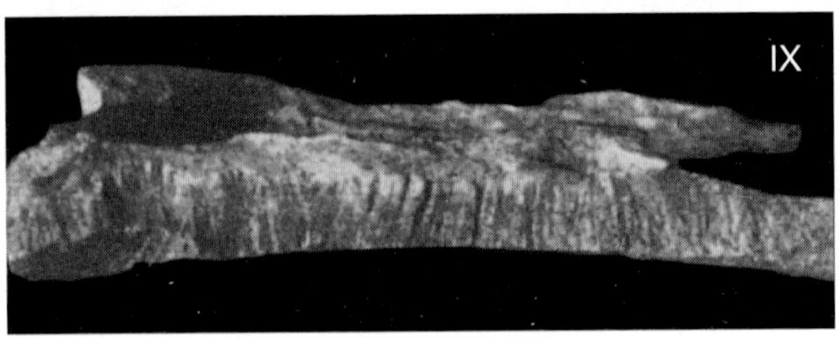

A.K. Sharma, Gufkral, Animal bones.

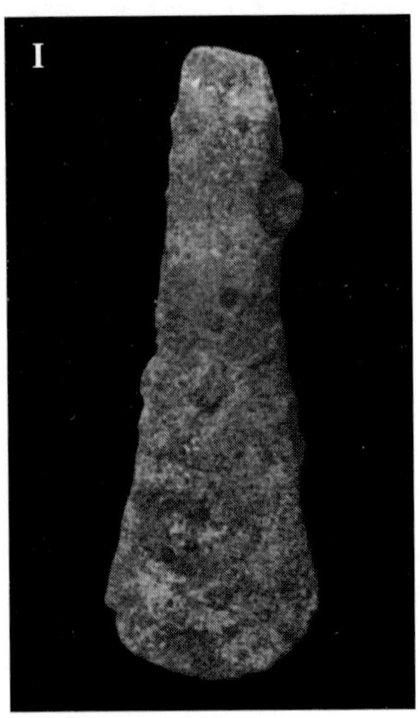

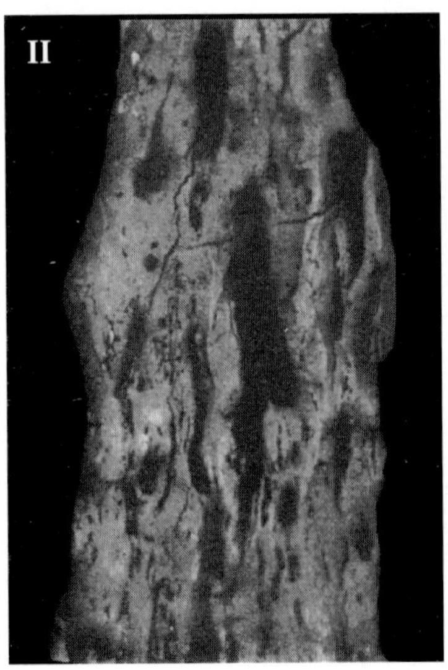

O. P. Agarwal, Tadakanahali, Iron Implements.

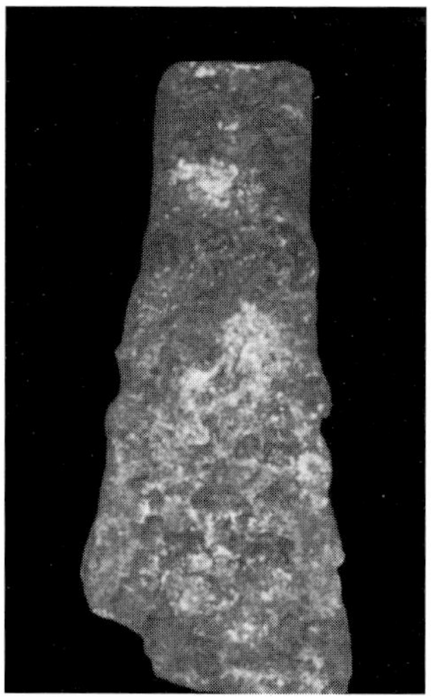

IV

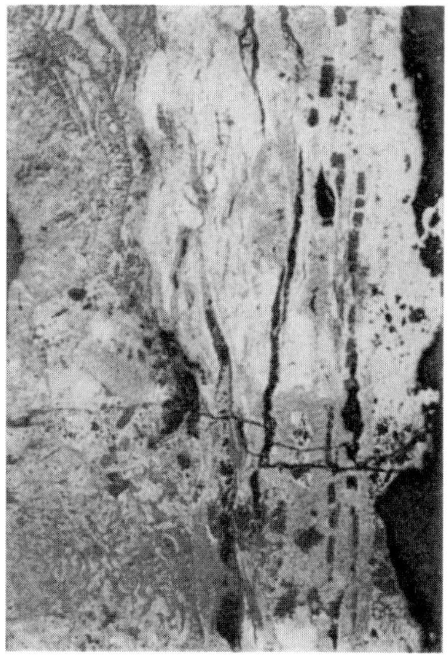

V

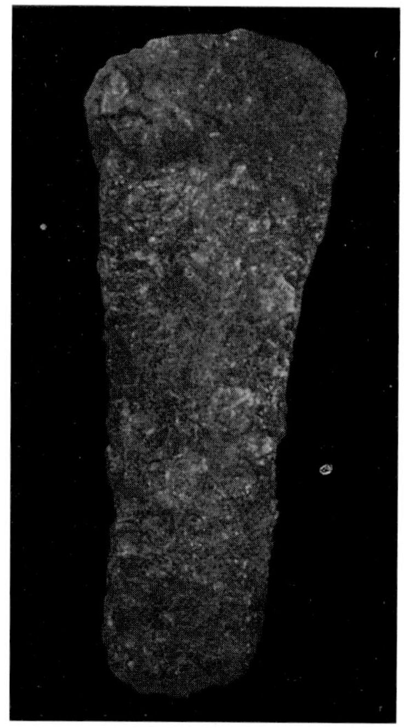

O. P. Agarwal, Tadakanahali, Iron Implements. VI

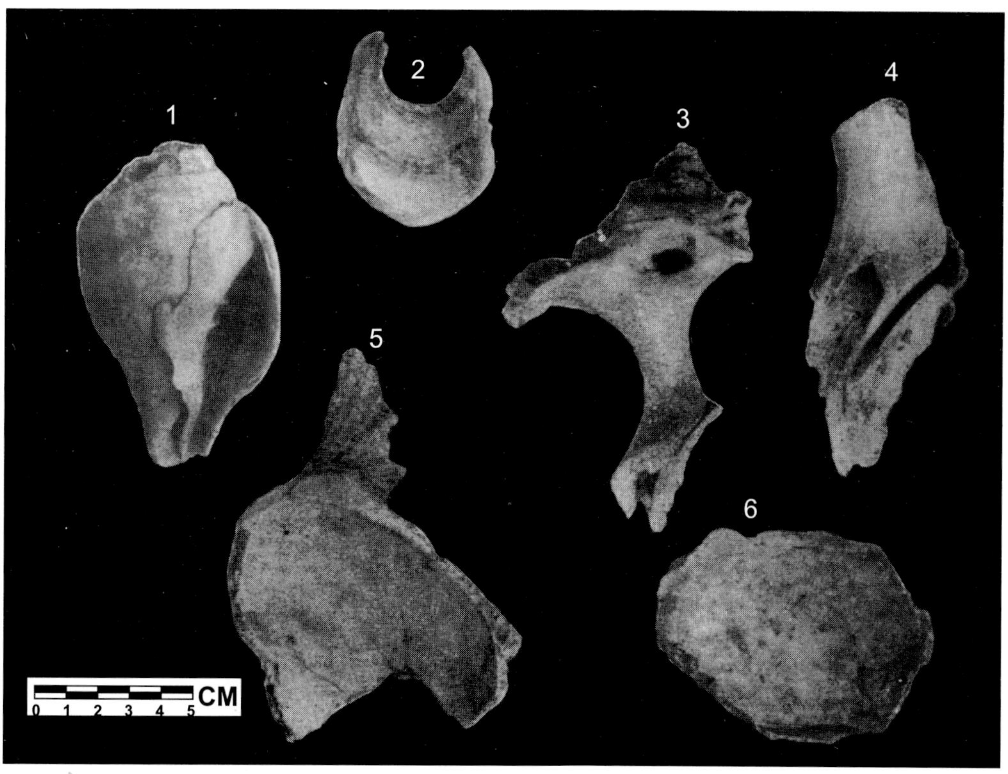

Kuldeep K. Bhan and J. M. Kenoyer, Nageshwar, Ladle manufacturing waste.

I. Mud brick wall.

II. Terracotta sealing.

III. Chert blades.

IV. Well.

G. B. Sharma, Rohira, Harappan period.

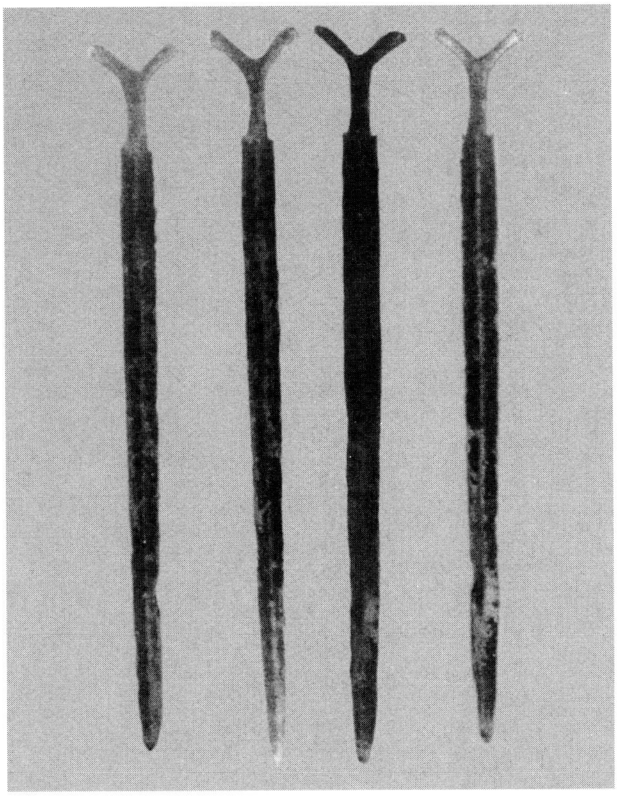

N. Devashayam, Shavinipatti, Antennae swords.

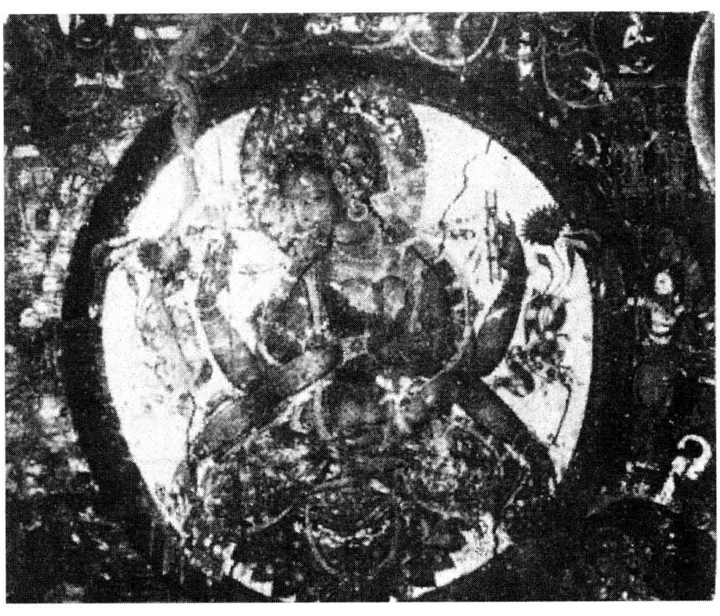

I. A. K. Singh, Wall painting of Prajnaparmita.

II. A. K. Singh, Wall painting of Bodhisattva Padmapani.

III. A. K. Singh, Decayed wooden sculpture of Gautam.

IV. A. K. Singh, Wooden statue of Vajrapani.

S. C. Saran, Kishan Bilas, Saiva monastery.

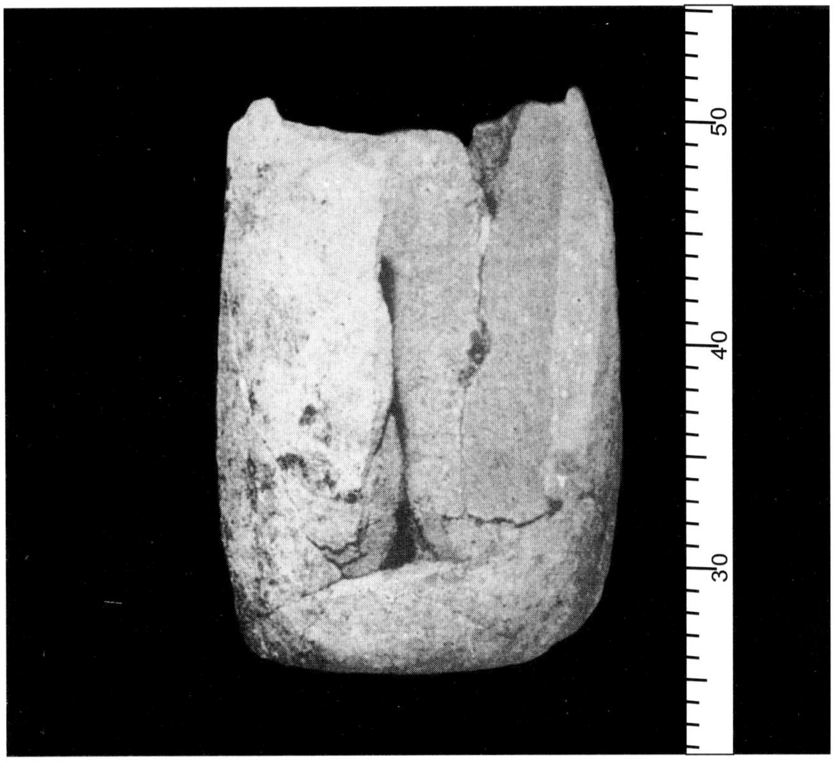

I. D. K. Chakroborty, Parihati, Crucible.

II. D. K. Chakroborty, Parihati, Hearth.

I. K. N. Dikshit, Allahapur Section.

III. K. N. Dikshit, Allahapur PGW sherds.

II. K. N. Dikshit, Allahapur Burnt-bricks. (IB)

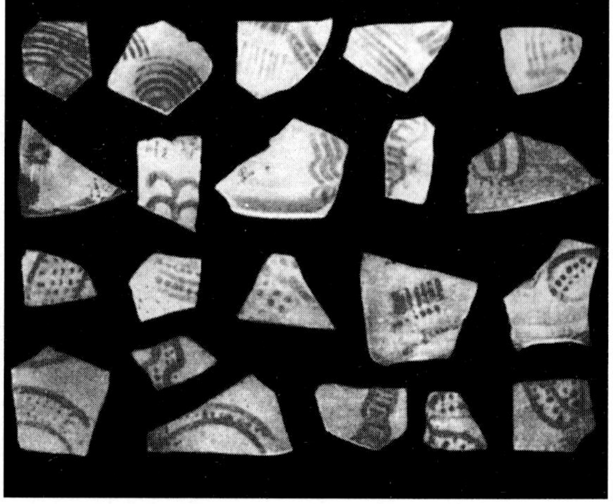

IV. K. N. Dikshit, Allahapur PGW sherds.